Kamala Nehru

Kamala Nehru

Ideology of Swaraj

Dr. Shiv Gajrani

Dr. S. Ram

Commonwealth

Kamala Nehru

First Published : 2012

ISBN 978-81-311-0364-7

Published by :
COMMONWEALTH PUBLISHERS PVT. LTD.
4831/24, Prahlad Street,
Ansari Road, Darya Ganj,
New Delhi - 110002
Ph. : 23272541, 23257835
Fax : 91- 011- 23257835
e-mail : commonwealthbooks@gmail.com

Laser Typesetting by :
Dimple Computers
Delhi

Printed at :
Roshan Offset Printers
Delhi

Preface

Kamala Kaul Nehru (1899–1936) was the wife of Jawaharlal Nehru, leader of the Indian National Congress and first Prime Minister of India. Kamala married Nehru on 8 February 1916. Their marriage was arranged by his parents.

Brought up in a traditional Hindu Brahmin family, she felt alienated amongst the more Westernized Nehrus. It was only with the involvement of the Nehrus in the national movement, that she emerged into the forefront. In the Non-cooperation movement of 1921, she organized groups of women in Allahabad and picketed shops selling foreign cloth and liquor. When her husband was arrested to prevent him delivering a "seditious" public speech, she went in his place to read it out. She was twice arrested by British authorities. Described as pretty, slim, and tender, Kamala was quiet, unobtrusive, and is thought to have had little impact on her husband. In 1917, she gave birth to a daughter, Indira Priyadarshini, who later succeeded her father as prime minister and head of the Congress party. Kamala died from tuberculosis in Switzerland while her husband was in prison.

She spent some time at Gandhi's ashram with Kasturba Gandhi where she built a close friendship with Prabhavati Devi wife of Jayaprakash Narayan.

Authors

Contents

1

Contemporary Political Developments

The most significant proof of Mr. Gandhi's growing influence was that, having reached these conclusions for himself, he was able to impose the policy of Non-Co-operation upon millions of his countrymen, and upon the National Congress. It was a fateful decision, and it was not reached without determined opposition from men who believed that the adoption of Non-Co-operation was a false step, which would not advance the cause of India's freedom. But Mr. Gandhi triumphed over all opposition. If he lost the confidence of some of India's wisest men he carried with him the bulk of the literate classes, and established a personal ascendancy over the masses which is unexampled in Indian history.

In preparation for the Special Congress in September, 1920, he delivered great speeches about Non-Co-operation in various parts of the country, and week by week articles appeared in *Young India,* explaining it and answering objections. At the Congress itself, in Calcutta, his success was complete. In the Subjects Committee he carried his resolution by a small majority against the opposition of such men as Mr. C.R. Das and Mr. B.C. Pal, of Mrs. Besant, Pandit Malaviya, Mr. Jinnah, and on some points even of the President, Mr. Lajpat Rai. At the Congress itself his motion was carried by a majority of 1,855 to 873. Over, 2,000 delegates did not present themselves, and 64 of those present did not vote.

After reference to the Khilafat question and the Punjab disorders, the resolution ran as follows :

'This Congress is of opinion that there can be no contentment in India without the redress of the two aforementioned wrongs, and the only effectual means to vindicate national honour and to prevent a repetition of similar wrongs in future is the establishment of *swarajya.* This Congress is further of opinion that there is no course open to India but to approve of and adopt the policy of progressive non-violent Non-Co-operation until the said wrongs are righted and swarajya is established. And inasmuch as a beginning should be made by the classes who have hitherto moulded and represented opinion, and inasmuch as Government consolidates its power through titles and honours bestowed on the people, through schools, controlled by it, its law courts and its legislative councils, and inasmuch as it is desirable in the prosecution of the movement to take the minimum risk and to call for the least sacrifice compatible with the attainment of the desired object, the Congress earnestly advises :

(a) Surrender of titles and honorary offices, and resignation from nominated seats in local bodies;

(b) Refusal to attend Government levees, durbars, and other official and semi-official functions held by Government officials or in their honour;

(c) Gradual withdrawal of children from schools and colleges owned, aided or controlled by Government, and, in place of such schools and colleges, establishment of national schools and colleges in the various provinces;

(d) Gradual boycott of British courts by lawyers and litigants, and establishment of private arbitration courts by their aid for the settlement of private disputes;

(e) Refusal on the part of the military, clerical and labouring classes to offer themselves as recruits for service in Mesopotamia;

(f) Withdrawal by candidates of their candidature of the reformed Councils, and refusal on the part of voters to vote for any candidate who may, despite the Congress advice, offer himself for election;

(g) The boycott of foreign goods.

'And inasmuch as Non-Co-operation has been conceived as a measure of discipline and self-sacrifice, without which no nation can make real progress, and inasmuch as an opportunity should be given in the very first stage of Non-Co-operation to every man, woman and child, for such discipline and self-sacrifice, this Congress advises adoption of swadeshi in piece-goods on a vast scale; and inasmuch as the existing mills of India, with indigenous capital and control, do not manufacture sufficient yarn and sufficient cloth for the requirements of the nation, and are not likely to do so for a long time to come, this Congress advises immediately stimulation to further manufacture on a large scale, by means of reviving hand-spinning in every home and hand-weaving on the part of the millions of weavers who have abandoned their ancient and honourable calling for what of encouragement.'

In moving the adoption of this scheme, Mr. Gandhi made the assertion, so often to be repeated, that if a sufficient response were made to it swarajya would be gained in the course of one year. It is noteworthy that the only reference to the Reforms in his speech was this :

'I now come to the burning topic, namely, the boycott of the Councils. Sharpest difference of opinion existed regarding this, and if the house has to divide on it is must divide on one issue, namely, whether swarajya has to be gained through the Councils, or without the Councils. If we utterly distrust the British Government - and we know that they are utterly unrepentant - how can you believe that the Councils will lead to swarajya, and not tighten the British hold on India?'

The Congress was indeed at the parting of the ways. Britain had offered the Reforms as the first step on the road to responsible government. Thousands of Indians were prepared to accept them, and the officials were pledged to work them honestly to their designed end. It is not difficult to see why Mr. Gandhi would have nothing to do with them. There was much to justify his distrust. Nevertheless, it was a very serious decision to make and at least some of its results have been disastrous. When all is said, as things are, swaraj can only come to India by the conversion of Britain to the belief that it is in the interest of the people of India that it should come. It is conceivable that by general and consistent non-violent non-co-operation Britain might have been converted; for it would have been an impressive protest against the blunders and moral deficiencies of British rule. But it is doubtful whether the kind and degree of non-co-operation which did result convinced anyone that India was ready for self-government. And in the meantime everything was done to discredit those Reforms, which, however, inadequate they might prove to be, were an honest attempt to meet India's need, and to prepare the way for independence within the British Commonwealth, while obloquy was thrown, though not by Mr. Gandhi, upon those who found in membership of the Council a road to the service of their country.

But Mr. Gandhi and his followers had no misgivings. The victory at Calcutta was followed by one more overwhelming still at the regular Congress at Nagpur in December. The creed of the Congress itself was changed into 'the attainment of swaraj by the people of India by peaceful and legitimate means', without any reference to the permanence of the British connection. Mr. Gandhi had won over to his view many of those who had at first been opposed to it, and with the added prestige which his victory gave him, and with a prophetic fervour all his own, he went about preaching everywhere the gospel of Non-Co-operation. He was wholly unsparing of himself, accepting the homage which everywhere met and embarrassed him, not as a tribute to his person, but as a growing recognition by the people that the way he showed them was the road to peace and freedom.

Only the briefest resume can be given of the events of the next fifteen months. They were such as might have been foreseen. The propaganda to which Mr. Gandhi devoted himself, with untiring energy and with a clearness of conviction unclouded by any doubt, resulted necessarily in rousing the people to increasing hostility to Government. All his great qualities, his disinterestedness, his personal simplicity of life, his care for all who suffered from oppression, gave him and his words enormous influence. When he told unthinking multitudes that the Government was satanic, they believed him. The spirit of lawlessness spread through the land. Though he preached non-violence, not without lasting results, yet again and again violence broke out, to Mr. Gandhi's intense grief. To most people it seemed inevitable that it should. But that it was inevitable he would never acknowledge. A Government charged with the duty of preserving order was patient with all agitation which did not actually lead to a breach of the public peace. But disorder and violence had to be put down with a strong hand. In the end, rightly or wrongly, Government saw no alternative but interfering with the liberty of the leader himself, who had brought into being forces of unruliness which he was not able to control.

Through all these months Mr. Gandhi worked in close co-operation with the Khilafat organisations, and in particular with the Muslim leaders, Mohamed Ali and Saukat Ali. He had made the Khilafat cause his own, and now that he had captured the whole machinery of the Congress he was able to unite its forces with those of the Khilafat committees. He convinced himself that, though they did not share his views on non-violence, they were as pure-minded and religious as himself. They toured the country together, and no doubt Mr. Gandhi did something to restrain his friends from violent speech. He was of immense value to them; for his high reputation gave the Muslim cause a respectability and strength which it might not otherwise have possessed and screened it at times from interference by the authorities; and, on the other hand, the strength of Muhammadan religious sentiment gave to the Non-Co-operation movement an intensity and fire which it might have lacked. How far the alliance was holy and natural in another question. It imported into the agitation more racial hatred than there would have been, and it increased the danger that agitation might cross the boundary which divided it from open revolt.

When Lord Reading arrived, the famous interview took place between the new Viceroy and Mr. Gandhi. One of the results of that interview was that the Ali brothers were induced to express their regret for certain speeches which, in the opinion of many, had a 'tendency to incite to violence,' and induced also to undertake not to advocate violence so long as they were associated with the movement of non-violence. The Viceroy, on his part, promised that so long as this undertaking was kept there would be no prosecution. But later in the year the extreme section of the Khilafat Non-Co-operators began to throw prudence to the winds. The Muhammadans in the country were disturbed by the Greek offensive against Angora, and by the strained relations between the Turkish Nationalists and the British Government.

At the Khilafat Conference at Karachi, in July, the Ali brothers spoke with extreme violence, proposing that, if no settlement of the Khilafat question were reached by Christmas, the National Congress at Ahmedabad should proceed to declare an Indian republic. They also called upon Muhammadan soldiers to desert. Though this action added to Mr. Gandhi's difficulties and weakened the cause of Hindu-Muhammadan unity, yet he remained loyal to his friends, and when the brothers were tried and condemned, he asserted his belief that the Ali brothers did not really intend to give up the principle of non-violence, and that there was nothing inconsistent with the Congress creed in the advocacy of independence.

He was himself entirely faithful to the principle of non-violence, and was personally strongly opposed to the idea of severing the British connection. He lost no opportunity of impressing upon his countrymen that there must be a moral preparation for swaraj, and that until they learned to exercise self-discipline, and to practise brotherhood among themselves, and to give up all mill-made clothing, they could not attain their end. Much which he included in his programme was most truly in the interest of progress. The development of cottage industries, by which cultivators could fill up spare hours and add to their income, could do nothing but good. Homespun cloth is a good substitute for the cheaper kinds of imported cloth. Temperance reform was needed. Yet the attempts made to hinder the use of liquor shops, and to boycott those who dealt in or used foreign cloth, led in many place to intolerable intimidation and to disturbance of the peace. Mr. Gandhi shocked and alienated numbers of people by the bonfires which he incited people to make of imported garments. It seemed a wicked waste at a time when many poor people were naked. But Mr. Gandhi is severely logical. Convinced that India can do without foreign cloth, and that its importation has impoverished her people, he had no hesitation in urging that the unclean thing should be destroyed, certain as it seemed to others that the result would be to provoke lawlessness and to inflame hate.

As the months passed it became more and more evident that Mr. Gandhi was awaking forces of disorder far beyond his power to control. Though he did not wish it, his propaganda led to the inflaming of racial hatred. The distinction which he was able to make between a system, and the persons who have to administer it, was beyond the wit of the average man, and constant abuse of Government naturally led to open disorder. During the year there were as many as sixty outbreaks in different parts of India, due in large measure to the unrest caused by the Non-co-operation campaign. There was agrarian riots, and strikes leading to riots. The most common cause of disorder was the violence following upon the arrest of 'national volunteers' for breach of the law. At Giridih (Bihar) a mob of 10,000 people looted the police station and burned the records. At Malegaon a peculiarly brutal outrage followed upon the trial of some Khilafat workers for intolerable terrorism, and resulted in the murder of a sub-inspector and four constables. In Assam thousands of labourers were persuaded to break their contracts and try to make their way home to the villages, often far away, from which they had originally come. There were labour troubles in Madras, and riots arising out of aggressive picketing of liquor shops in Dharwar and Karachi.

But much the most dreadful outbreak was that among the Moplahs on the Malabar Coast. The Moplahs are fanatical Muhammadans of mixed Arab and Indian descent, and always have been subject to waves of religious mania. On this account the country has for many years been administered under a special law. Government tried to exclude the Khilafat preachers from the Moplah district. But excitement was stirred and spread. Arms were secretly collected, and preparations were made to bring in the kingdom of Islam. In August rebellion broke out through the whole district. The administration was paralysed. The few Europeans who did not escape were murdered. But the chief sufferers were the helpless Hindu inhabitants, who, until authority was re-established, suffered unspeakable barbarities. 'Massacre, forcible conversion, desecration of temples, foul outrages upon women, pillage, arson, destruction, were freely perpetrated.' There is no doubt that it was largely an agrarian outbreak, a revolt of landless men against their Hindu landlords. All the worst justices due to social inequality and to an even unusually rigid system of case exclusiveness were rife among them. Trouble was never very far away. The conditions of a peaceful community life did not prevail. It was the sense of past wrongs which, when the pot did boil over, led to such monstrous savagery. But there can be as little doubt that the explosion of angry discontent, which might have come sooner or later in any case, was precipitated and spread more widely by the general Khilafat and Non-co-operation agitation. Certain Khilafat leaders tried to make out that it was a fight conducted by the Moplahs for their religion. Even Mr. Gandhi, accepting information only through certain channels, spoke of 'the brave, God-fearing Moplahs,' who were fighting for what they considered as their religion, and in a manner which they considered religious. He treated the whole terrible business as irrelevant to his campaign, and, refusing to open his eyes, went on his way. There is nothing in his whole career more difficult to understand and to vindicate.

In November, 1921, the Prince of Wales arrived in India. In spite of the Viceroy's declaration that the Government had never intended to use the visit for any political purpose, Mr. Gandhi appealed to his countrymen not to join in demonstrations of loyalty. He was careful to make it plain that they had no ill will to the Prince as man, and appealed to everyone to take precautions to shield his person from harm. But he believed that the visit would be exploited to add prestige to a satanic Government, and to exalt the bureaucracy. It seemed to him unpatriotic and false to join in the festivities.

Mr. Gandhi's motives were clear, and they were not dishonourable. He had a right to say that he harboured no ill will. No less rancorous spirit ever was. But strategically it was a fatal mistake. Already the boycott of the Duke of Connaught at the beginning of the year had alienated the friends of order. And what could only seem in England a gross discourtesy to a beloved prince irritated the British public, and materially lessened sympathy with Indian aspirations. It conveyed, too, a false impression. The completeness of the welcome was undoubtedly broken. In a few places the Non-cooperators succeeded in restraining the people from any friendly demonstrations. In many places hartals were proclaimed and held. In Bombay there was a blood riot. But the Prince won from nearly all sections of the people enthusiastic goodwill. When he left Bombay he received a send-off such as had been rarely given to him anywhere. On the whole, and throughout India, the dissentients were in a small minority, and but for terrorism they would have been fewer still.

No one more than Mr. Gandhi deplored the violence which broken the peace of Bombay on the morning of the Prince's arrival, and ended in the death of over fifty people and in serious damage to four hundred more. He made personal appeals to stop the disturbance, and as a penance for the ghastly tragedy he pledged himself to fast until peace was restored. He admitted his responsibility. 'I am more instrumental than any other in bringing into being a spirit of revolt. I find myself not fully capable of controlling and disciplining that spirit'. Yet he did not materially change his policy, or retire from public life, as he is said to have offered to do. But he did suspend his intention of starting civil disobedience at Bardoli, and did his best to explain the conditions on which alone civil disobedience could be permitted.

Meanwhile, the last struggle with Government began. Government had been very slow to interfere with the Non-co-operation movement, lest worse harm should come. But the outbreak in Bombay, followed by similar if less serious disorders in Calcutta and in the north, convinced them that stronger measures must be taken to prevent the growth of a dangerous spirit of anarchy. They determined to apply certain Acts conferring extraordinary powers upon the executive. The volunteer associations were declared to be illegal, and the provincial administrations were called upon to deal promptly with all violence. Many hundreds of volunteers, including many men of high character and repute, were arrested and imprisoned, sometimes for interfering with peaceable citizens and causing riot, in most cases for no other crime than that of being admittedly members of an organisation declared to be illegal. The situation was uncomfortable in the extreme. An attempt was made by such men as Pandit Madan Mohan Malaviya and Sir P.C. Ray to bring about a reconciliation between Government and the Non-cooperators. But, as Mr. Gandhi demanded as a preliminary to any conference the withdrawal of the recent proscription of the volunteer associations, and the release of all prisoners not actually convicted of violence, including the Ali brothers, and as, on the other hand, the Viceroy insisted that before even the idea of a conference could be discussed the unlawful activities of the Non-cooperators party must be suspended, the project came to nothing.

Meanwhile, the annual meeting of the Congress was held at Ahmedabad. Mr. Gandhi, though his influence in the country had begun to wane, had still unabated power with his followers. He became virtual dictator. He was appointed 'sole executive authority of the Congress,' and invested with full power to convene a special meeting of the Congress, and also with the power to appoint a successor in emergency. It is noteworthy that, while adamant to any suggestion that the campaign against Government should be stayed, Mr. Gandhi fought stoutly against the notion, urged by Maulana Hazrat Mohani, of complete severance from Britain. Neither then, nor at any other time, did he cease to desire that the British connection should be maintained if it could be held to with honour.

In January, 1922, further attempts were made to mediate between Government and the Non-co-operation party. A conference was held in Bombay, presided over at first by Sir Sankaran Nair. But it failed because a point had been reached at which neither the Government nor Mr. Gandhi would yield. While the negotiations with the Viceroy were still going on, Mr. Gandhi addressed to Lord Reading what was practically an ultimatum. He declared that civil disobedience had been forced upon the Non-Co-operation party to secure the elementary rights of free speech, free association and a free Press. He accused the Government of lawless repression, which had made immediate adoption of civil disobedience an imperative duty. But he announced himself willing to postpone that extreme action if the Government would agree to set free all prisoners convicted or under trial for non-violent activities in the country. To this Government replied by a statement repudiating Mr. Gandhi's allegations, and explaining why the measures complained of against the volunteers had been adopted, and giving plain warning that the adoption of civil disobedience must lead to measures of 'sternness and severity'. Mr. Gandhi wrote again a letter of strong protest, accusing Government of lawlessness and barbarism, and reiterating his demands. It is difficult to read these communications without feeling that the situation had become hopeless. It is possible to hold different views of the wisdom of the policy Government followed in dealing with the volunteer associations. But to Mr. Gandhi's ultimatum no Government which had not abdicated its responsibility for maintaining order could yield. The choice was, according to Government, between 'lawlessness with all its disastrous consequences on the one hand, and on the other the maintenance of those principles which lie at the root of all civilized Governments'. According to Mr. Gandhi the choice before the people was 'mass civil disobedience with all its undoubted dangers, and lawless repression of the lawful activities of the people'. He took high ground. He believed that he had behind him the mass of the people in an indignant protest against unjustifiable repression. He claimed to have presented his case with 'extreme reasonableness and moderation'. But an increasing number of his countrymen, though they still believed that he was sincere, could see neither reasonableness nor moderation in his demands, and felt that the inevitable end was drawing near.

CHAURI-CHAURA

Mahatma Gandhi proceeded to carry out his threat, and went to Bardoli to superintend the beginning of civil disobedience there. At that moment there came the news of a shocking outbreak at Chauri-Chaura, in the United Provinces, on February 4. An infuriated mob of volunteers and peasants attacked the police station, beat to death twenty-one policemen and watchmen, and burnt down the building. The brutality of the crime horrified the country, and convinced Mr. Gandhi that the plan of civil disobedience must be given up. He took it as a third warning from God that there was not yet in India 'that truthful and non-violent atmosphere which can alone justify mass disobedience,' the first warning having been the disturbances which followed the passing of the Rowlatt Act in 1919, and the second the Bombay riots in November, 1921. Why, precisely then, his conviction became final, many both of his followers and of his opponents could not understand. He was freely accused of having brought humiliation upon the national cause. But, as always, he had the courage of his convictions. He wrote :

'Let the opponent glory in our humiliation or so-called defeat. It is better to be charged with cowardice and weakness than to be guilty of our oath and sin against God. It is a million times better to *appear* untrue before the world than to be untrue ourselves.'

For personal cleaning he imposed upon himself a five days' fast.

At a meeting of the working committee, held at Bardoli on the 11th, he had his will. It was resolved to suspend civil disobedience and all other offensive activities, including processions, picketing and public meetings. The country was to confine itself to positive measures towards reform, to enlisting a crore of members for the India National Congress, to the production of hand-woven cloth, to the organizing of National schools, to the salvation of the depressed classes, and lastly to the organisation of village and town arbitration committees for the private settlement of disputes. It was a complete *volte face,* which dismayed and estranged the more extreme of his colleagues and followers. But he held firm. When the Bardoli resolutions were considered by the Congress Committee at Delhi, he had indeed to submit to certain modifications. But in his own mind, and ultimately in the general mind, the Bardoli programme became the fixed policy of the Congress. Nevertheless, it was becoming clear that his influence was declining. Many of his friends, Hindu and Muhammadan, had little sympathy with his uncompromising preaching of non-violence. Others were perplexed and made uncomfortable by the constant change of programme. The people were disappointed because the swaraj he had promised was no nearer, forgetting that they had not fulfilled the conditions without which he had always told them it could not come. The upper classes saw the danger of Non-co-operation, and were afraid to grave, widely-spreading disorder. Without ceasing to reverence the character of the man, an increasing number came to doubt the wisdom of his policy.

There can, we think, be little doubt that this decline of Mr. Gandhi's personal influence was one reason why the news of his arrest, on the 10th March, was received throughout the country with such quietness. The other reason was of a completely opposite kind. It was that Mr. Gandhi had succeeded in winning the minds of many of his countrymen to a sincere belief in non-violence. The tragedy of Chauri-Chaura had helped towards that end. Ever since then the mind of India has began turning away from violence as a remedy for wrongs. When their master told them to remain quiet, whatever happened to him, they obeyed. 'I would regard the observance of perfect peace on my arrest as a mark of high honour paid to me by my countrymen.' That honour they gave him, bitterly as many of them resented the fact of his imprisonment. To himself there can be little doubt that it brought a welcome rest. His indomitable sprint was housed in a very frail body, and the incessant labours and excitements of the last months had been a strain which few stronger men could have endured.

There have not been many more remarkable trials in the history of mankind. Perhaps there have been only two. It was conducted with the most perfect dignity and courtesy, with the utmost consideration of the character of the accused. He pleaded guilty. He read a statement explaining why he had become a Non-cooperator. It ended with these words :

' . . . .I have no personal ill-will against any single administrator, much less can I have any disaffection towards the King's person. But I hold it to be a virtue to be disaffected towards a Government which, in its totality, has done more harm to India than any previous system. India is less manly under the British rule than she ever was before. Holding such a brief, I consider it to be a sin to have affection for the system. And it has been a precious privilege for me to be able to write what I have in the various articles tendered in evidence against me.

'In fact, I believe that I have rendered a service to India and England, by showing in Non-Co-operation the way out of the unnatural state in which both are living. In my humble opinion, non-co-operation with evil is as much as duty as is co-operation with good. But in the past, non-co-operation has been deliberately expressed in violence to the evil-doer. I am endeavouring to show to my countrymen that violent non-co-operation only multiplies evil, and that, as evil can only be sustained by violence, withdrawal of support of evil requires complete abstention from violence. Non-violence implies voluntary submission to the penalty for non-co-operation with evil. I am here, therefore, to invite and submit cheerfully to the highest penalty that can be inflicted upon me for what in law is deliberate crime and what appears to me to be the highest duty of a citizen. The only course open to you, the judge and the assessors, is either to resign your posts and thus dissociate yourself from evil, if you feel that the law you are called upon to administer is an evil and that in reality

I am innocent, or to inflict on me the severest penalty, if you believe that the system and the law you are assisting to administer are good for the people of this country, and that my activity is therefore injurious to the public weal.'

The judge, Mr. C.N. Broomsfield, I.C.S., then pronounced the following sentence :

'Mr. Gandhi, you have made my task easy in one way by pleading guilty to the charge. Nevertheless, what remains, namely the determination of a just sentence, is perhaps as difficult a proposition as a judge in this country could have to face. The law is no respecter of persons. Nevertheless, it would be impossible to ignore the fact that you are in a different category from any person I have ever tried or am likely ever to try.

'It would be impossible to ignore the fact that in the eyes of millions of your countrymen you are a great patriot and a great leader; even all those who differ from you in politics look up to you as a man of high ideal and of noble and even saintly life. I have to deal with you in one character only. It is not my duty, and I do not presume, to judge or criticize you in any other character. It is my duty to judge you as a man subject to the law, who has by his own admission broken the law and committed what to any ordinary man must appear to be a grave offence against such law. I do not forget that you have consistently preached against violence or that you have on many occasions, as I am willing to believe, done much to prevent violence.

'But having regard to the nature of your political teaching and the nature of many of those to whom it was addressed, how you can have continued to believe that violence and anarchy would not be the inevitable consequence it passes my capacity to understand. There are probably few people in India who do not sincerely regret that you should have made it impossible for any Government to leave you at liberty. But it is so. I am trying to balance what is due to you against what appears to me to be necessary in the interests of the public, and I purpose in passing sentence to follow the precedent of the case, in many respects similar to this case, that was decided some twelve years ago, the case of Mr. Bal Gangadhar Tilak, under the same section. The sentence that was passed upon him as if finally stood was a sentence of simple imprisonment for six years. You will not consider it unreasonable, I think, that you should be classed with Mr. Tilak, and that is the sentence—two years' simple imprisonment on each count of the charge, six years in all—which I feel it my duty to pass upon you.

'I should like to say in doing it that, if the course of events in India should make it possible for Government to reduce the period and release you, nobody would be better pleased than I.'

THE UNITY CONFERENCE

Delhi, September 26th—October 2nd, 1924

During Mr. Gandhi's incarceration the relations between the Hindu and Muhammadan communities were becoming increasingly strained. Communal quarrels had become very frequent in three provinces, and in several places had resulted in riots. The serious Lucknow riot of September 1924, led Mahatma Gandhi to take to penance and prayer, according to his own conviction and practice under all untoward and extraordinary circumstances. In his statement, which he issued to the Press on September 18th, he indicated the reasons as well as the scope and duration of his fast. He said : 'The recent events have proved unbearable for me. My 'helplessness' [wrongly transmitted as 'hopelessness' in the telegraphed version] 'is still more unbearable. My religion teaches me that, whenever one is very distressed (distress, which one cannot remove) one must fast and pray. Nothing evidently that I can say or write can bring the two communities, Hindus and Mussulmans, together. I am therefore imposing on myself a fast of twenty-one days, commencing from today and ending on the 8th October. It is both a penance and a prayer. As a penance I need not have taken the public into my confidence, but publish the fast as (let me hope) an effective prayer both to the Hindus and the Mussulmans, who have hitherto worked in union, not to commit suicide. I respectfully invite the heads of all communities, including Englishmen, to meet and end the quarrel, which is a disgrace to religion and humanity. It seems as if God has been dethroned. Let us reinstate Him in our hearts.'

Again Mr. Gandhi's mind is clearly revealed and understood when his later statement, of September 25, *i.e.* on the very eve of the Unity Conference, is taken into account and read with the above. In his own paper he gave the following history of his mental suffering. 'I was violently shaken by Amethi, Sambhal and Gulbarga. I have read the reports about Amethi and Sambhal prepared by Hindu and Mussulman friends. I had learnt the joint finding of Hindu and Mussulman friends who went to Gulbarga. I was writing in deep pain and yet I had no remedy. The news of Kohat set the smouldering mass aflame. Something had got to be done . . . . My longing is to be able to cement the two (the Hindu and Mussulman) with my blood.'

The Mahatma entered upon his fast in the house of the Muhammadan leader, Muhammad Ali, at Delhi, were he had gone from Bombay, and the conference was called at Delhi to suit the convenience of the members of the Legislative Assembly and of the Council of State. Invitations were sent to and accepted by the leaders of all parties, including Dr. Besant, Messers Jinnah and Chintamani, Dewan Bahadur Rangachariar, the Hon. Mr. Lalubhai Samaldas, and Dr. S.K. Datta. The most Rev. Dr. F. Westcott, Metropolitan in India, was present by special invitation. The original date, September 23, had to be changed to the 26th, and Pandit Motilal Nehru was elected president. The Mahatma was urged to break his fast, and was reminded by the Metropolitan that a fast in itself does not provide a basis of unity, however great may be the sympathies excited by it. Mr. Gandhi holding on his own way, the conference proceeded with this terrible background of the voluntary suffering of the best loved and most revered man in India. There was a Subjects Committee of eight, which did the real work of the conference. A series of resolutions was put forward, but it was found that the solution was not along those lines. A new committee of eleven then recast the resolutions, which are given below. It is not yet time to pronounce an opinion on their merits or their effects.

Messages of sympathy were published in *The Statesman* of Calcutta, October 8 and 9, from Lord Olivier (Secretary of State), H.E. the Voceroy, Sir A. Muddiman (Home Member), Rt. Hon. V.S.S. Sastri, Sir T.B. Sapru, H.E. the Government of Bengal, H.E. the Governor of the U.P., H.E., the Governor of Assam, H.E. the Governor of Bihar and Orissa, the Bishop of Bombay, Mrs. Sarojini Naidu.

RESOLUTIONS PASSED AT THE UNITY CONFERENCE, DELHI

September 26th - October 2nd, 1924

Resolution No. 1

This conference places on record its deep grief and concern at the fast which Mahatma Gandhi has undertaken. This conference is emphatically of opinion that the utmost freedom of conscience and religion is essential, and condemns any desecration of places of worship, to whatsoever faith they may belong, and any persecution or punishment of any person for adopting or reverting to any faith, and further condemns any attempt by compulsion to convert people to one's faith or to enforce one's own religious observances at the cost of the rights of others.

The members of the conference assure Mahatma Gandhi and pledge themselves to use their utmost endeavours to enforce these principles and to condemn any deviation from them even under provocation. This conference further authorizes the President to convey personally to Mahatma Gandhi the united wish of this conference that he should immediately break his fast in order to permit this conference to have the benefit of his co-operation, advice and guidance in deciding upon the speediest means of effectively checking the evil which is fast spreading over the country.

Resolution No. 2

This conference deplores the dissensions and quarrels that are now going on between Hindus and Muslims in several places in India, resulting in loss of life, burning and plunder of property, and desecration of temples. The conference regards them as barbarous and contrary to religion. This conference tenders its warm sympathy to the sufferers. This conference is of opinion that it is unlawful and irreligious for any person to take the law into his own hands by way of retaliation or punishment. The conference is of opinion that all differences, no matter of what nature soever, should be referred to arbitration, and if that be impossible even to a court of law.

Resolution No. 3

There shall be a Central National Panchayat of not more than 15 persons, with power to organize and appoint local panchayats in consultation with the local representatives of the different communities, to enquire into and settle all disputes and differences, including recent occurrences, where necessary and desirable. The said National Panchayat shall have power to frame rules and regulations for carrying out this resolution.

The conference appoints the following to act as the Central National Panchayat, with power to add to their number up to 15 and co-opt local representatives as additional members : Mahatma Gandhi (chairman and convener), Hakim Ajmal Khan, Lala Lajpat Rai, Mr. G.K. Nariman, Dr. S.K. Datta, Master Sunder Singh of Lyallpur.

Resolution No. 4

With a view to give the effect to the general principles promoting better relations between the various communities of India laid down in Resolution No. 1, and to secure full toleration of all faiths, beliefs and religious practices, this conference records its opinion :

(a) That every individual or group shall have full liberty to hold and give expression to his or their beliefs and follow any religious practice, with due regard to the feelings of others and without interfering with their rights. In no case may such individual or group revile the founders, holy persons or tenets of any other faith.

(b) That all places of worship, of whatever faith or religion, shall be considered sacred and inviolable, and shall on no account be attacked or desecrated, whether as the result of provocation or by way of retaliation for sacrilege of the same nature. It shall be the duty of every citizen, of whatever faith or religion, to prevent such attack or desecration as far as possible, and where such attack or desecration has taken place it shall always be promptly condemned.

(c) *(i)* That Hindus must not expect that the exercise of right of cow-slaughter by Muslims can or will be stopped by the use of force, resolution of a local body, act of legislature, or order of court, but only by mutual consent, and must trust to the good sense of Muslims and the establishment of better relations

between the two communities to create deeper respect for their feelings.

(ii) Nothing stated in the above clause shall unsettle or affect any local customs or agreement between the two communities already in existence, nor will it authorize cow-slaughter in a place where it has not taken place before. Any dispute on facts should be settled by the National Panchayat formed under Resolution No. 3.

(iii) Cow-slaughter shall not take place in a way offensive to the religious sentiments of the Hindus.

(iv) The Muslim members of the conference hereby call upon their co-religionists to do everything in their power to reduce cow-slaughter.

(d) *(i)* That Muslims must not expect to stop Hindu music near or in front of mosques by force, resolution of a local body, act of legislature, or order or court, expect by mutual consent, but must rely upon the good sense of Hindus to respect their feelings.

(ii) Nothing stated in the above clause shall unsettle or affect any local custom or agreement between the two communities already in existence; nor shall in authorize the playing of music in front of mosques where it has not been played before. Any dispute with regard to the latter shall be referred to settlement to the National Panchayat formed under Resolution No. 3.

(iii) The Hindu Members of this conference call upon their co-religionists to avoid playing music before mosques in such a manner as to disturb congregational prayers.

(e) *(i)* That Muslims must not expect to stop by force, resolution of a local body, act of legislature, or order of court, except by mutual consent, the performance of *arti* or the playing of music, including blowing of *shankhs* by Hindus during worship and on other occasions, in their house or temple or public places, at any time, even if the house or temple or public

place in question is situated in close proximity to a mosque; but they should trust to the good sense of the Hindus to accommodate them.

(ii) Nothing stated in the above clause shall unsettle or affect any local custom or agreement between the two communities already in existence. Any dispute or facts should be settled by the National Panchayat formed under Resolution No. 3.

(f) That Muslims are at liberty to chant *Azan* or offer prayer in their own houses or in any mosque or public place not set apart for the religious observance of any other community.

(g) (i) Where the slaughter of an animal or sale of meat is permissible on other grounds, no objection shall be taken to the method of slaughter, whether by *jhatka, bali,* or *zibah*.

(ii) Wherever there is any dispute regarding the sale of any kind of meat in a particular locality or quarter it shall be referred for settlement to the local panchayat.

(h) That every individual is at liberty to follow any faith and to change it whenever he so wills, and shall not by reason of such change of faith render himself liable to any punishment or persecution at the hands of the followers of the faith renounced by him.

(i) That every individual or group is at liberty to convert or reconvert another by argument or persuasion, by must not attempt to do so, or prevent its being done, by force, fraud or other unfair means such as the offering of material inducement. Persons under sixteen years of age should not be converted unless it be along with their parents or guardians. If any person under sixteen years of age is found stranded without his parents or guardians by a person of another faith, he should be promptly handed over to persons of his own faith. There must be no secrecy about any conversion or re-conversion.

(i) That no community should attempt to stop by force the construction of a new place of worship by a member of another community on his own land, but such new place of worship should be built at a reasonable distance from an existing place of worship of any other community.

Resolution No. 5

This conference is of opinion that a section of the Press, specially in the North, is responsible for increasing the tension between different communities by publishing wild exaggerations, reviling each other's religion, and by every means fomenting prejudice, and condemns such writings and appeals to the public to stop patronage of such newspapers and pamphlets, and advises central and local panchayats to supervise such writings, and from time to time to publish correct versions.

Resolution No. 6

It having been represented to this conference that in certain places acts of impropriety have been committed in relation to mosques, the Hindu members of this conference condemn such acts wherever committed.

Resolution No. 7

The Hindu and Muslim members of this conference call upon their co-religionists to extend full tolerance to the minor communities of India, and to deal with them in all questions of communal intercourse with justice and generosity.

Resolution No. 8

This conference is of opinion that attempts, on behalf of members of one community, to boycott members of any other community and to stop social or commercial relations with them, made in certain parts of the country, are reprehensible and are an effective bar to the promotion of good relations between the vairous communities in India. The conference therefore appeals to all communities to avoid any such boycotts and exhibitions of ill-will.

Resolution No. 9

This conference calls upon men and women of all communities throughout the country to offer daily prayers during the last critical week of Mahatmaji's fast, and to organize mass meetings on the 8th of October in every town and village, to express the nation's thankfulness to the Almighty, and to pray that the spirit of goodwill and brotherliness may pervade and unite all the communities of India, and that the principle of full religious toleration and mutual goodwill declared in this conference may be adopted and given effect to by members of all communities in India.

Shuaib Qureshi
Jawaharlal Nehru
Secretaries of the Conference

Delhi,
2nd October, 1924.

MESSAGE TO THE NATION

Dandi
April 9, 1930

At last the long expected hour seems to have come.

In the dead of night my colleagues and companions have roused me from deep slumber and requested me to give them a message. I am, therefore, dictating this message, although I have not the slightest inclination to give any.

Messages I have given enough already. Of what avail would this message be if none of the previous messages evoked a proper response? But information received until this midnight leads me to the belief that my message did not fall flat, but was taken up by the people in right earnest. The people of Gujarat seem to have risen in a body as it were. I have seen with my own eyes thousands of men and women at Aat and Bhimrad fearlessly breaking the Salt Act. Not a sign of mischief, not a sign of violence have I seen, despite the presence of people in such large numbers. They have remained perfectly peaceful and non-violent, although Government officers have transgressed all bounds.

Here in Gujarat well-tried and popular public servants have been arrested one after another, and yet the people have been perfectly non-violent. They have refused to give way to panic, and have celebrated the arrests by offering civil disobedience in ever increasing numbers. This is just as it should be.

If the struggle so auspiciously begun is continued in the same spirit of non-violence to the end, not only shall we see Purna

Swaraj established in our country before long, but we shall have given to the world an object-lesson worthy of India and her glorious past.

Swaraj won without sacrifice cannot last long. I would, therefore, like our people to get ready to make the highest sacrifice that they are capable of. In true sacrifices all the suffering is on one side - one is required to master the art of getting killed without killing, of gaining life by losing it. May India live up to this *mantra*.

At present India's self-respect, in fact her all, is symbolized as it were in a handful of salt in the satyagrahi's hand. Let the first holding it, therefore, be broken, but let there be no voluntary surrender of the salt.

Let the Government, if it claims to be a civilized Government, jail those who help themselves to contraband salt. After their arrest the civil resisters will gladly surrender the salt, as they will their bodies into the custody of their jailors.

But by main force to snatch the salt from the poor, harmless satyagrahis' hands is barbarism pure and simple and an insult to India. Such insult can be answered only by allowing our hand to be fractured without loosening the grasp. Even then the actual sufferer or his comrades may not harbour in their hearts anger against the wrong-doer. In civility should be answered not by incivility but by a dignified and claim endurance of all suffering in the name of God.

Let not my companions or the people at large be perturbed over my arrest, for it is not I but God who is guiding this movement. He ever dwells in the hearts of all and he will vouchsafe to us the right guidance if only we have faith in Him. Our path has already been chalked out for us. Let every village fetch or manufacture contraband salt. Sisters should picket liquor shops, opium dens and foreign cloth dealers' shops. Young and old in every home should ply the *takli* and spin, and get woven, heaps of yarn every day. Foreign cloth should be burnt. Hindus should eschew untouchability. Hindus, Mussalmans, Sikhs, Parsis and Christians should all achieve heart unity. Let the majority rest content with what remains after the minorities have been satisfied. Let students leave Government schools and colleges, and Government servants resign their service and devote themselves to service of the people and we shall find that Purna swaraj will come knocking at our door.

Young India, 8-5-1930

Letter to Mahadev Desai

April 9, 1930

Chi Mahadev,

I am halting in Surat for a few hours on my way to Bhimrad. The car took the wrong road, with the result that I missed the train and came here by car. At present my very thoughts have grown wings and they seem to have effect even when not expressed in speech or action. That is a fact. Thoughts which are part of *tapascharya* are single-pointed, and hence their power is greater than that of electricity or of still subtler either. Your suggestion, therefore, was acted upon immediately yesterday. All the men in my batch will have to be dispersed and posted wherever they may be needed. Surajbhan has already left, and so has Jayantiprasad, each for his own district. Vamanrao Pataki also has gone to his district. I did not have to suggest to any of the three that he should go. They themselves felt that they should go. Surendra is waiting at Navsari to proceed to Bhimrad. Puratan and Haridas Gandhi are at Navsari waiting to leave for Olpad. I have sent Abbas Saheb to Nadiad, where I will send other men whom he may ask for, provided I am not arrest by then. However, if I am not free and you are, it will be for you to send them; and if even you are not free, those who are left behind will make the necessary arrangements. Fortunately, Dayalji at least will stay behind, and he will issue orders through the children. If none else, there will always be Lord Krishna whose orders are bound to be felt by all in their hearts and the work will go on somehow. I am certainly ready to send Chhaganlal to Wadhwan, but Kevalram can go there as well. I think you know that he has offered to do so. However, that may be, you may, if you are free, communicate to me any other suggestions which may occur to you. I have sent word to the Broach Sevashram people that they may ask me if they need any men. As for you, I think you will not be free man for long.

I also have written to Saraladevi, but that was only about the drink evil. Yesterday I sent a letter addressed to Kaka on this subject. I think you must have read it. You will have seen from it that I, at any rate, wish to start the movement against the drink evil and foreign cloth along with the salt agitation on the 13th. Even if that should not be possible, I should like the fight against the drink evil to start from Monday if you, Kaka and other men and the Ashram women and other women visitors feel the necessary self-confidence. I wrote to Saraladevi suggesting that she might throw herself into this very work. If, however, my plan itself does to appeal to all of you, you may leave it. I do not at all believe that the salt tax will go in seven days. But I think it very necessary to utilize this golden opportunity and combine these three aims of our movement. Personally, I am convinced that if we should succeed in these three things, swaraj would soon be an accomplished fact, the women would realize their power in no time and, without any effort on our part, the whole world would see for itself how ours was indeed a holy war. Many women can contribute their share in this movement even while attending to their domestic duties. We have the land revenue tax as a last resort. That is why, though I have discussed the subject in my article. "The Immoral Foundation." I do not wish to touch the tax just now. Nor is it necessary to do so. At present, my eyes are fixed on the 91 crore rupees and considering the prevailing atmosphere in the country I think we shall easily succeed in our aim.

Blessings from
BAPU

[PS]

I have talked at length on these matters with Mithubehn. She has made up her mind. The Anavil Ashram will be handed over to her for the use of women workers. Those women who are willing to give all time to the work will be admitted to it. Of course, there will be other conditions for admission. The present idea is to make an intensive effort in the Surat district where some work of this kind has been done, and to extend the area of activity as the women's self-confidence increases. Such of the Ashram women as are ready for this, like Mithubehn, should start coming here. Mithubehn herself has already had experience of this work and, therefore, the women who come here will have the benefit of that experience. As the women coming from the Ashram are trained in discipline, Mithubehn will find it easier to take work from them. I have already discussed the matter with Shardabehn. She and Dr. Sumant liked the idea very much. Shardabehn said that she would certainly go there.

SPEECH AT BHIMRAD

April 9, 1930

Brothers and Sisters,

This is the camp of civil resisters. Some of you have been arrested but instead of being sorry for it I find you all more cheerful. We prepared for a thing and asked for it. After receiving it we must not be afraid of it, otherwise we would be considered ungrateful to the Almighty God. We pray to God for imprisonment, hanging or independence. We do not want slaver and dependence. God has said that without sacrifice you will get nothing. We must qualify ourselves to go to jail. It will be useless to go to jail for thefts or for being drunk. We only congratulate those who go to jail for pure actions. From our point of view those who go to jail for good deeds do not deserve imprisonment but freedom. In a Satanic Government innocent persons must suffer. Under this rule, if we are good, we will get hand-cuffs, kicks, daggers and gallows. Women will have to make greater sacrifices. I have brought material for sacrifice. We consider it a picnic and I hope it will continue as such till the end. This is just a beginning. Sardar Vallabhbhai ought to have been sent to jail for 30 years. The Government is trying us. At Bhimrad you will not be killed. Salt will be snatched away from you but if you have courage you should not part with salt in your possession until you are unable to withstand the force used for snatching it away from you. I understand that by keeping salt in our possession we (shall) have kept with us 6 crores of rupees and in it lies the independence of India. We want boys who are 16 years old for the present struggle. If a fist containing salt be clenched, none dare to open it. They may open fire upon you. Men may come with bayonets and sticks and use them on you, but salt should not be taken out of your hands. If none of you then cry over it, I would consider it a picnic. Bodies may be lying dead, hands may have been cut off but still you keep to your promise. I will then understand that swaraj is approaching. The Government is testing us because this Government is of bold persons. Do not consider that we are fighting against impotent persons. They would not suffer defeat quietly and we cannot defeat them soon. If 30 crores unite in the struggle, the Government would yield to it. If you remain true, I am sure I shall see the light of success. I have come here to request you to stick to the present struggle until we have won. You are all doing good work. Do not doubt about the salt tax. When Ukabhai received an injury I considered it a sign that the salt tax would go. Do not consider that you will be happy after the repeal of the salt tax. Rs. 6 crores are nothing for a nation of 30 crores. I asked Tyabji and he left willingly (for Kaira district). Picketing of liquor shops should be done by women and not by men. If men go there, it will be presumed that they were there to assault others. Government would not like it because they would lose Rs. 25 crores income from the sale of liquor. I, therefore, advise all of you sisters to act according to the instructions of Mithubehn. Foreign cloth is as bad as liquor. Those who have put on foreign clothes should burn them. If you use khaddar 60 crores of rupees will remain in India. You should spin cotton. You sisters should do three things, *viz.*, assist the temperance movement, use Khaddar and do spinning. I have sent my son Manilal for the work, and he will do it. Do not fight in the jail for food but for your self-respect. Patels who have resigned have not yet been relieved by the Government. There is some trick in it. They should hand over the records to the Government or lock the office and hand over the key to the Mamlatdar.

Bombay Secret Abstract, 1930.

TO THE WOMEN OF INDIA

The impatience of some sisters to join the good fight is to me a healthy sign. It has led to the discovery that, however, attractive the campaign against the salt tax may be, for them to confine themselves to it would be to change a pound for a penny. They will be lost in the crowd, there will be in it no suffering for which they are thirsting.

In this non-violent warfare, their contribution should be much greater than men's. To call woman the weaker sex is a libel; it is man's injustice to woman. If by strength is meant brute strength, then indeed is woman less brute than man. If by strength is meant moral power, then woman is immeasurably man's superior. Has she not greater intuition, is she not more self-sacrificing, has she not greater powers of endurance, has she not greater courage? Without her man could not be. If non-violence is the law of our being, the future is with woman.

I have nursed this thought now for years. When the women of the Ashram insisted on being taken along with men something within me told me that they are destined to do greater work in this struggle than merely breaking salt laws.

I feel that I have now found that work. The picketing of liquor shops and foreign cloth shops by men, though it succeeded beyond expectations up to a point for a time in 1921, failed because violence crept in. If a real impression is to be created, picketing must be resumed. If it remains peaceful to the end, it will be the quickest way of educating the people concerned. It must never be a matter of coercion but conversion, moral suasion. Who can make a more effective appeal to the heart than woman?

Prohibition of intoxicating liquors and drugs and boycott of foreign cloth have ultimately to be by law. But the law will not come till pressure from below is felt in no uncertain manner.

That both are vitally necessary for the nation, nobody will dispute. Drink and drugs sap the moral well-being of those who are given to the habit. Foreign cloth undermines the economic foundations of the nation and throws millions out of employment. The distress in each case is felt in the home and, therefore, by the women. Only those women who have drunkards as their husbands know what havoc the drink devil works in homes that once were orderly and peace-giving. Millions of women in our hamlets know what unemployment means. Today the Charkha Sangh covers over one hundred thousand women against less than 10,000 men.

Let the women of India take up those two activities, specialise in them; they would contribute more than man to national freedom. They would have an access of power and self-confidence to which they have hitherto been strangers.

Their appeal to the merchants and buyers of foreign cloth and to the liquor dealers and addicts to the habit cannot but melt their hearts. At any rate the women can never be suspected of doing or intending violence to these four classes. Nor can Government long remain supine to an agitation so peaceful and so resistless.

The charm will lie in the agitation being initiated and controlled exclusively by women. They may take and should get as much assistance as they need from men, but the men should be in strict subordination to them.

In this agitation thousands of women, literate and illiterate, can take part.

Highly educated women have in this appeal of mine an opportunity of actively identifying themselves with the masses and helping them both morally and materially.

They will find when they study the subject of foreign-cloth boycott that it is impossible save through khadi. Mill-owners will themselves admit that mills cannot manufacture in the near future enough cloth for Indian requirements. Given a proper atmosphere, khadi can be manufactured in our villages, in our countless homes. Let it be the privilege of the women of India to produce this atmosphere by devoting every available minute to the spinning of yarn. The question of production of khadi is surely a question of spinning enough yarn. During the past ten days of the march under pressure of circumstances I have discovered the potency of the *takli* which I had not realized before. It is truly a wonder worker. In mere playfulness my companions have without interrupting any other activity spun enough yarn to weave four square yards per day of khadi of 12 counts. Khadi as a war measure is not to be beaten. The moral results of the two reforms are obviously great. The political result will be no less great. Prohibition of intoxicating drinks and drugs means the loss of twenty-five crore of revenue. Boycott of foreign cloth means the saving by India's million of at least sixty crores. Both these achievements would monetarily be superior to the repeal of the salt tax. It is impossible to evaluate the moral results of the two reforms.

'But there is no excitement and no adventure in the liquor and foreign-cloth picketing', some sisters may resort. Well, if they will put their whole heart into this agitation they will find more than enough excitement and adventure. Before they have done with the agitation, they might even find themselves in prison. It is not improbable that they may be insulted and even injured bodily. To suffer such insult and injury would be their pride. Such suffering if it comes to them will hasten the end.

If the women of India will listen and respond to my appeal, they must act quickly. If the all-India work cannot be undertaken at once, let those provinces which can organize themselves do so. Their example will be quickly followed by the other provinces.

Young India, 10-4-1930.

THE IMMORAL FOUNDATION

This Indian Empire was conceived in immorality, for it was to perpetuate the exploitation of India's resources that it was founded. The pages of history written by Englishmen amply prove the assertion that no fraud was considered too much, no force too frightful by Englishmen, to gain the end. There is perhaps not an inch of ground lawfully acquired by or for the British crown in India.

The rule of nurtured by immoral means. English statesmen assure us that it is the British bayonet that keeps the Empire free from attack both from without and within.

SPEECH AT GUJARATI WOMEN'S CONFERENCE, DANDI

April 13, 1930

There are certain activities which are meant only for women. Prohibition and boycott of foreign cloth are such activities; which if you do not take up, will never be accomplishment. In 1921 I compelled men to take up these tasks and they did so out of fear, but how long could it last? In the end I had to accept defeat and suspend the activities. I would not have had to do so had I entrusted the work to women. But when I was utterly confused and had been defeated on all sides, God, like in that *bhajan* of the tortoise couple, made me entrust the work to women. It is no doubt very difficult to picket shops but women had been taking great risks in the past. It is for that reason that the world is still going on. Moreover both these activities required persuasion and change of heart. Women alone can enter the hearts of men and transform them. Moreover those women who have come here must be aware of the plight of the families where husbands drink. It is your duty to help your sister's families from breaking up. Foreign cloth has taken away from fifteen crores of your sisters the noble profession of plying the spinning-wheel and have rendered crores of villagers unemployed. Khadi activity of ten insignificant years have brought ten lakhs of rupees to the women's homes. I want you to expand the activity so that crores of rupees are brought in. Once you take up this work, you have to discard foreign clothes - you should burn them. You may say you will wear out whatever you have or that you will preserve them. Even a drunkard might say that he would consume whatever liquor he had or kept it. How can we keep a thing which we consider to be a poison even for a day? We should throw it away lest our children by mistake take the poison. You may think that you have thrown that much money into water. A woman picketer of Vejalore had asked what the women should do if they were attacked while they were picketing. Gandhiji replied : There is no danger of such attack. However, if that happens or if the police try to disperse you with the help of horses then put up with it quietly. A woman has a remarkable capacity for suffering. Take it from me that the liquor shops will be closed down the day there is such an attack on women. You may be certain he will give up drinking for ever from that day.

Prajabandhu, 20-4-1930

SPEECH AT DANDI

April 13, 1930

I am happy that you have on your own come here in such large numbers on this the last day of the self-purification week, but you will not be happy if I do not say something to you on this occasion.

I have just concluded the women's conference. You will like to know your place in what I have told the women to do. The women have resolved to picket shops selling foreign cloth as also those who use it, and those who sell liquor as also those who drink it. We men may not interfere in this work. Let us treat this as the special field of women.

The success of this work depends entirely on the self-control of men. The assumption behind this is that men cannot easily control their anger, cannot easily practise non-violence, while women can do so. Renunciation and non-violence come naturally to women. Having been inspired by this idea I have tried to explain it to women. If my assumption is false, my conclusion will also be false to the same degree.

It is the duty of men to make the atmosphere congenial or women to do their work. We men should go to the dealers in liquor and foreign cloth and try to convince them that now that the women of India have come out they should give up trade in these two things. Confronted by the large groups of women even liquor-booth owners and owners of shops selling foreign cloth will be startled and give up their trade. I know it is not easy to give up one's trade. But, at a time when the atmosphere is filled with national pride and patriotism, the people's capacity for renunciation automatically increases. During this week alone this capacity has increased a hundred-fold, but it should increase a thousand-fold.

Dealers in foreign cloth still seem to be calculating whether to give up their trade. They take a vow for three months or a year. Behind this act there is a lurking belief that they will be able to buy foreign cloth after a year. They do not make the effort that is needed to secure swaraj. This is because they lack the faith. But as this movement makes progress - trading in liquor and foreign cloth cannot but come to an end. When hundreds of thousands of our countrymen have sacrificed their all, even these sceptical traders are bound to develop the strength to make sacrifices.

If women lack funds to continue the work after once starting it, I shall stretch out my hand to you, though at present, by the today, about a thousand rupees were collected at the women's meeting and a lady belonging to the Galiara family of Kathor gave four gold bangles without even being asked.

If we men are not indifferent and begin the work on our own, if, for instance, for want of enough khadi it becomes necessary to wear only a loin-cloth and we start doing so, to that extent we shall have lightened the burden of our womenfolk.

Miss Mayo has accused us saying that many of our men have no consideration for women, that we make them work as drudges, as if they were born to be slaves. The world will be convinced that what Miss Mayo said was not true when women wake up and accomplish the tasks of boycotting foreign cloth and of prohibition.

The stocks of khadi in the country are dwindling and I am, therefore asking everyone to spin and wear khadi and I am demonstrating this before you every day by spinning on the *takli*. Just as we grind and cook cereals which are available in every home we ought to spin the large quantities of cotton which grows in India into some kind of yarn, make cloth from it and then wear that cloth. When spinning becomes a universal activity in the country, you can rest assured that the trade in foreign cloth will come to an end.

Mills can never entirely meet the cloth needs of India and as most mills in India are either wholly or partly foreign, cloth made by only a few of them can be used if the need arises.

Women from good families have come out to take up these activities. Divan Shri Manubhai's daughter Shrimati Hansa Mehta and some other ladies have only recently issued a circular and begun the work of prohibition in Bombay. If Gujarati women continue to work in this spirit and if the men lend them support this activity will become widespread in India. All these three things are easy. When we have accomplished these three things we shall have saved six crores from the salt-tax, twenty-five crores from prohibition and sixty crores from the boycott of foreign cloth—ninety-one crores in all. We shall have become purer and added to our strength, and then it will not take long for us to secure swaraj.

Finally, we should take care that we do not lose what we have gained during these seven days.

I have just received news that some youths in Calcutta, who were reading out passages from prescribed books at meetings, were dispersed. On seeing the police committting such atrocities, Shri Sen Gupta, the Mayor of Calcutta, also started reading out paragraphs from those banned books and was immediately arrested.

Dr. Suresh Chandra Banerjee, the able khadi worker of Abhoy Ashram, who at one time received a salary of Rs. 600 a month from the Government has been sentenced to a term of two and a half years' rigorous imprisonment for violating the salt law.

Notwithstanding such atrocities, just as we in Gujarat have not become frightened and given in, there too, they are not only not frightened but have become more resolute. Whatever the atrocities perpetrated on us, we do not want to use force on anyone or to insult anyone. A certain gentleman has informed me that in Bombay when they were making bonfires of foreign cloth, caps from other people's heads were forcibly removed and burnt. I do not know how far this is true. But if it is true, rest assured that this struggle cannot go on. If force is used, people will not tolerate it; they will start fighting amongst themselves and the Government will take advantage of this situation.

If people do not want swaraj through the boycott of foreign cloth, we cannot make them do good under compulsion. In order to melt their hearts, we must make greater sacrifices and even practise satyagraha against them if it becomes necessary to do so.

What should I do if I was convinced that people were deceiving me, that having decided to boycott foreign cloth through khadi alone they pledged themselves to do so and then broke their pledge?

If I was convinced that I had become purified and wholly compassionate, I should, when the occasion arose, offer satyagraha and go on a fast. What should I do if you should raise your hands every day, say that if there is not enough khadi you will wear *lungotis* and then it should turn out that not a single sister spins? I might perhaps even at this advanced age have to say the same thing I said when I saw that the labourers of Ahmedabad had broken their pledge, and do what I did at the time of the riots in Bombay. I would do so unwillingly if I felt that we were deceiving God daily. I have faith that the people of Gujarat will never deceive me.

We want to live in peace and win swaraj peacefully. I do not wish to live to see disturbances in the country.

You just come on this day of my fast and I have said simply what I wanted to. You must prevent any use of force whether in Bombay or elsewhere. Whenever I hear of one of our men having abused someone, having been discourteous to someone or having used force against someone I feel deeply hurt and truly my heart beings to thump violently. If a doctor were to examine me at the time he would hear the sound. Despite this, I am able to survive, for at such times I close my eyes for a couple of seconds and repeat Ramanama. If I did not do so, my heart would stop beating there and then. You all may well call me Mahatma, but my task is that of a weak person. Do not, therefore, deceive me, at any time in this struggle. It will be all rights if you sit at home, but once you join the campaign work sincerely.

Navajivan, 20-4-1930

MILL-OWNERS AND KHADI

Shri Ranchhodlal Amritlal, who is himself a mill-owner, write to say :

It is a distressing tale. I am convinced, however, that as people's sacrifices increase, the hearts, of the mill-owners will melt. I know that the khadi activity has benefited Indian mills. If, however, the latter instead of enjoying the sweet fruit of the tree attempt to eat up its roots, they will find they cannot do so and will even lose the fruit. Let me cite a brief example. Let us suppose that boycott of foreign cloth is successful; let us suppose that spurious khadi is passed off as genuine; and let us suppose that genuine khadi is unable to lift its head. In that case one of two results could follow. Spurious khadi and other cloth made in mills would not be adequate. As people are not used to khadi they would clamour for foreign cloth and we would be worse off than we previously were. Indian mills would be swept away in the storm, the chain of non-violence would be broken and the enraged public would take to boycotting Indian mills. Or, supposing the goods from Lancashire were totally rejected, since the shield of khadi would not be there, the capitalists from Lancashire might start their mills in this country and Indian mills would suffer as a result of foreign capital and foreign talent establishing themselves here and thereafter swadeshi mills would regard it their duty to join the foreign mills in exploiting the people. Though one cannot yet claim that the sentiment for khadi has taken root in villages, nevertheless it has established itself to the extent that many well-educated persons are prepared to dedicated themselves to the cause of khadi. They will not allow khadi to die so long as they are themselves alive. If, therefore, mill-owners do not stop producing and selling mill-made cloth as khadi, there is every possibility of a fierce movement being launched against them. It will become our duty to start such a movement.

They ought to save themselves from such a movement. It is in their hands to do so Here are the terms :

(1) Indian mills must not produce cloth which resembles khadi.

(2) That which has been already produced should be exported.

(3) They should altogether stop using the khadi stamp.

(4) They should give up making cloth which could compete with khadi.

(5) They should consult with the Charkha Sangh and produce only such cloth as is beyond the scope of khadi.

(6) In consultation with the khadi committee, they should fix reasonable prices for mill-made cloth.

(7) No foreign yarn should be used in mills even for making borders.

(8) Mill-owners and others should totally give up using foreign cloth and wear only khadi as far as possible.

(9) They should stock khadi as far as possible.

During this period of self-purification it is highly essential for the mills to observe the above rules. If they do so the boycott of foreign cloth can ne accomplished soon.

Navajivan, 13-4-1930

TO THE WOMEN

Last week, writing about prohibition, I had mentioned that there was another activity also which women could and ought to take up. This activity is the boycott of foreign cloth through khadi. This is, or should be, the special field of women. For foreign cloth has ruined millions of homes and taken away from millions of women an employment which sustained them. Foreign cloth has ruined seven lakh villages in India. While on the one hand, women have lost employment, on the other they have to pay for cloth which they could have produced in their own villages. People have developed a great liking for foreign cloth and they will not give it up without great effort and great penance. It is the women who embody that penance. Man can never make an impression upon people such as women can.

Besides, amongst those who wear foreign cloth the number of women exceeds that of men. And, in the final analysis, women will create a greater impact upon other women.

Hence it is for women to start picketing in front of shops selling foreign cloth. Men have failed in this task. But there is no reason why women should fail. Moreover, in 1920-21 we did not have the same climate that there is now. It is women alone who can take advantage of this climate.

But there is also another aspect of this work. Supposing everyone was to burn their foreign clothes today, what then would they wear? Indian mills would not be able to produce all the cloth within a short period and perhaps even if they did we would not achieve the purpose that we wish to.

That purpose would be served through khadi alone. Khadi implies the *takli* or the spinning-wheel. In the latter lies the prosperity of India. It is *Annapurna*. If people in every home work on the spinning-wheel, we can produce today as much khadi as we want. Producing khadi means spinning yarn. Men may well spin, but for generations the profession of spinning has been practised by women and men's hands do not possess the same skill in this what women's do. Women alone can bring about this solidarity among their own sex. I would, therefore, advise women to make this their special field of work.

In this Non-violent campaign, although our weapons are small they are very powerful since they have in them the power of God.

Therefore, all those sisters who have faith in the spinning-wheel and the *takli* and who wish to devote themselves to saving sixty crores of rupees every year, should take up this work of boycott and the task of propagating spinning.

It should be remembered that those sisters who wish to take up this work have to be prepared to go to the villages.

Sisters who have faith not in both but in only one of these activities should take up only that. I have suggested the two activities through which millions of women can develop themselves and contribute their full share in the *yajna* of swaraj.

Navajivan, 13-4-1930

SPEECH AT UMBER

April 15, 1930

Mr. Gandhi asked the village women gathered there if they knew Pandit Jawaharlal Nehru.

They said, 'How can we know?' Gandhiji remarked :

It is not your fault but of us men who have hitherto been satisfied with your being and remaining as house-keepers, cooks, scavengers and drawers of water but now you will no longer remain in that position. If this movement is to succeed, yours will have to be as big share as men's, if not much bigger.

Referring to Pandit Jawaharlal Nehru, Gandhiji said :

He was to all India what Sardar Vallabhabhai, was to us in Gujarat. He was wearing himself out in the nation's service and has been punished because he was the greatest among us all.

Hitherto I have asked, you to resist snatching of salt by the police from your closed fists and suffer mutely and meekly whatever injuries the police might inflict upon you. If you have got strength, and faith in your mission I want to go many steps further.

I would like you henceforth to regard yourselves as trustees or guardians not merely of the precious national wealth locked up in your fists but of the whole treasure now being prepared in salt pans. Defend that treasure with your life if that be the price you have to pay for it. When the police come and raid these pans, surround them and do not let the police touch them till they have overpowered you by sheer brute force.

Even if you are beaten you must not lose your temper. I hope that Gujarat has now become courageous to that extent. I am getting my strength from the strength of Gujarat. You must be prepared to endure suffering and keep the peace at any cost. Let them destroy pans but only after they have either arrested you or beaten you. This is altogether a new experiment and I leave it to you to make more pans wherever possible.

From your sufferings will rise into being not only Purna Swaraj but a non-violent army for its defence. Women ought not to take part alongside of men in defence of salt pans. I still give to the credit to the Government that it will not make war upon our women. It will be wrong on our part to provoke them into so doing. This is men's fight to long as the Government will confine their attention to men. There will be time enough for women to court assaults when the Government has crossed the limit. Let it not be said of us that men sought shelter behind women, well knowing they would be safe if they took women with them in what may be called, for want of a better name, aggressive non-violence. Women have in the programme I ventured and risk they may be capable of undertaking. The Labour Association of Ahmedabad has undertaken to picket liquor shops. Selling of contraband salt which was going on in Ahmedabad is now stopped. It will be done in villages by sending batches of volunteers.

He said that they must either make their own arrangements for food or must take whatever is cooked for them. They could not maintain kitchen for different tastes. This was a fight for self-purification and, therefore, they must leave off all bad habits. They must have perfect discipline and strength to suffer hardships. He asked all those who cannot submit themselves to do discipline to resign in the beginning. But let them not cheat the community and nation. Even if there were only a few true volunteers the fight would go on. The fight has been well begun, and Gujarat has earned credit for it. Let it not be said that Gujarat lost the fight because of mistakes and lapses.

The Hindu, 16-4-1930

INTERVIEW TO FREE PRESS OF INDIA

Jalalpur,

April 17, 1930

It is too early for me to speak with certainty anything about the so-called riots in Calcutta and Karachi. Having become used to grossly exaggerated accounts and distorted versions of things happening before my eyes, I am inclined largely to discount the stories of violence alleged to have done by people. But be it ever so little, I have no manner of doubt that it harms the struggle, and the same time the struggle has to go on unchecked. If non-violence has to fight people's violence in addition to that of Government, it must still perform its arduous task at any cost. I see no escape from it.

At the very outset of the campaign I had declared that there was every possibility of some violence breaking out on the part of the people. It seems now to have broken out; and it hurts me, only because it hurts the cause I hold as dear as life itself. But I must say that Government have provoked it in dispersing the meeting where no violence had been done : to prohibit public meetings and processions altogether is a thing calculated to precipitate violence. Government have with utmost deliberation picked up the leaders of the people who were known to be partial to non-violence and to possess controlling influence on the people. It would have been miraculous if this gross interference with popular liberty had not evoked reprisals from easily inflammable people, who were to be found in every community and in all parts of the world. Take Gujarat itself, and in the out-of-the-way Dholera and near Viramgam unnamable and indecent atrocities are said to have been committed upon defenceless national workers. Their only crime was that they would not easily yield up the salt in their possession.

In the first place, I do not know that outside India under any civilized Government, authority has been given to the police forcibly to take away from people anything unless it is of a dangerous character. I know that Salt Acts do give such powers. That merely illustrates my view. A barbarous act does not become less so by having the authority of law, and the practice of indecent torture is utterly intolerable and calculated to exhaust the patience of any people. The obvious fact is that Government (do not) want peace. I observe that Mr. Jairamdas Daulatram has come in for a bullet wound in the thigh. I am delighted it is Mr. Jairamdas Daulatram rather than some unknown person to have been thus injured. Mr. Jairamdas is one of the greatest persons to be found in all India. If he was in the crowd, he was there not to incite people to violence but to prevent it.

Spilling of such innocent blood will hasten the end, but such casualties will only result in the manifestation of greater response from people. Let me, however, warm those whom my message may reach that if they cannot restrain themselves, they must not interfere with the struggle. If they do, they will only retard the country's progress towards its goal.

I know, however, that soon my word will cease to reach the people. All instruments I possess will have been snatched away from me, but they cannot snatch away one thing from me and that is my unshakable faith in my cause. A mass movement like that one we see in front of us is regulated not by men but by the God. Manifestation has been spontaneous. It has required but little guidance.

If what I have seen happening in Gujarat is an index to what has happened in order provinces of India, the movement has been largely self-directed. I have, therefore, still every hope that at the end of the struggle it would be possible to say of it that even though regrettable violence now and then broke out, it remained predominantly and overwhelmingly non-violent. Not what happens in cities but what happens in villages will decide the fate of India.

The Bombay Chronicle, 18-4-1930

A SURVEY

The mass manifestation in Gujarat has exceeded all expectations. Bombay and its suburbs have done no less. And the reports slowly coming to me at this out-of-the-way place from all over India are fully encouraging. It is a matter of the keenest joy to me to see Maharashtra united once more and Sjt. N.C. Kelkar and his friends joining the struggle. Sjt. Kelkar's and Sjt. Aney's resignations are events of great importance in the struggle. Bengal is the most tempestuous province in all India. It is pulsating with life. Its very factions are symptomatic of its great awakening. If Bengal responds in the right style it is likely to overshadow every other province. I do not know that any province, even Maharashtra, can claim the credit that Bengal can for voluntary sacrifice. If its emotional side is its weakness, it is also its greatest strength. It has the capacity for reckless abandon to non-violence, if such use of language is permissible. Sjt. Sen Gupta's action in response to the wanton assault on the students' meeting has evoked the sentiment above expressed. The sentence of Dr. Suresh Banerji and others pales into insignificance before the possibilities of the move on the part of Bengal students and the savage counter-move on the part of the police. I know what the Calcutta Commissioner of Police will say if he sees these lines. I hear him saying, 'But you do not know my Bengal.' Well, I know his Bengal more than he ever will. His Bengal is the creation of the Government. If the Government will cease to molest Bengal and not keep India from hear cherished goal, Bengal will be as gentle as the greatest province of India. If Bengal is seething with the violent spirit, it is because of her sufferings.

But I expect Bengal's imagination to come to her assistance and to realize that non-violence is the trump-card. All the suffering must be dedicated to the goddess of ahimsa.

Soon after the Jallianwala massacre, I used to express and reiterate the hope that next time in no part of India must people run away on bullets being discharged against them, and that they must receive them in their chests with arms folded and with courageous resignation. That testing time seems to be coming faster than I had expected. And if we are to train ourselves to receive the bullet wounds or bayonet charges in our bare chests, we must accustom ourselves to standing unmoved in the face of cavalry or baton charges. I know that it is easier said than done. Nevertheless, I must say it if we are ever to complete our training in mass non-violence. That mass non-violence is a perfect possibility has been sufficiently demonstrated during the past eight days. Mahadev Desai has given a realistic account of the brutal treatment of volunteers in the Dholera salt bed and the volunteers suffering the brutality with meek heroism. What thousands in Bombay did when the police acted with rashness and harshness if also with comparative considerateness can be studied from a condensed translation published elsewhere of a graphic description sent to me by Pandit Mukund Malaviya. His report is in the main corroborated by Dahyabhai, Sardar Vallabhbhai's son, who was also an eye witness.

Perinbai and her companions as also Kamaladevi acted with rare courage and calmness. But they would allow me to say that they would have done better to remain outside the venue of the men's fight. For women to be in the midst of such danger as they put themselves it was against the rule of chivalry. Anyway that time is not yet. Let them by all means manufacture salt in their thousands. But they may not remain deliberately in crowds which they know are likely to be charged. I have in all humility suggested to them an exclusive field in which they are at liberty and are expected to show their best qualities. There is in that field enough scope for adventure and heroism.

To revert, if then we are to stand the final heat of the battle, we must learn to stand our ground in the face of cavalry or baton charges and allow ourselves to be trampled under horses' hoofs or bruised with baton charges. An armed crowd would stand firm and retaliate if there were such charges. We, if we would learn the lesson of non-violence, should show greater courage by standing our ground without anger, without retaliation. Then a reincarnation of Dyer will find us ready for receiving bullets in the bare breast.

People have already begun to defend their salt pans. If we have evolved that sufficient amount of courage, it must be done methodically and regularly. As soon as the police come to charge us and break through the living wall, women should, if the police give the opportunity, stand aside and let their men be wounded. They do so all the world over the armed conflict, let them do so in a conflict in which one party deliberately chooses to remain unarmed.

When there are no men left to fight the battle of free salt, if (they) have courage let them take up the work deserted by men. But I have no doubt that men will give a good account of themselves in this struggle.

I have already examined elsewhere the argument that the police must use force if people will not surrender the contraband salt in their possession. Here I would only remind these critics that even from confirmed thieves they do not take stolen property by force except after they are brought under arrest and then too never if they are not to be brought to trial . . . . That the salt regulations make the policeman the arresting officer, prosecutor and judge all rolled into one is no answer to my charge of barbarity in respect of the procedure adopted by the authorities.

Young India, 17-4-1930

SPECIAL TASK BEFORE WOMEN

The conference of women on Sunday last at Delhi became a Congress as I had wanted it to be. Thanks to the Government prohibition against the Baroda territory cars plying between Navsari and Dandi, many had walked the full 12 miles to Dandi. The following resolutions were unanimously adopted.

Resolution 1

This conference of the women of Gujarat assembled at Dandi on 13th April, 1930 having heard Gandhiji, resolves that the women assembled will picket liquor and toddy shops of Gujarat and appeal to the shop-keepers and the shop-goers (to desist) from plying their trade or drinking intoxicating liquors as the case may be, and will similarly picket foreign-cloth shops and appeal to the dealers and the buyers to desist from the practice of dealing in or buying foreign cloth as the case may be.

Resolution 2

This conference is of opinion that boycott of foreign cloth is possible only through khadi and, therefore, the women assembled resolve henceforth to use khadi only and will so far as possible spin regularly and will learn all the previous processes and preach the message of khadi among their neighbours, teach them the processes up to spinning and encourage them to spin regularly.

Resolution 3

This conference appoints the following Executive Committee with power to draw up a constitution and to amend it from time to time and add to their number :

1. Mrs. Tyabji (President)
2. Shrimati Mithubehn Petit (Secretary)

Members

3. Shrimati Manibehn Patel
4. Shrimati Rohini Desai
5. Shrimati Chandubehn

This conference hopes that Gujarati women will welcome this activity and participate in it.

This conference hopes that women all over Gujarat and the other provinces will take up the movement initiated at this conference.

The same resolutions were passed also in Vejalpur; only the first resolution was divided into sections. Two distinct sections dealt with prohibition and the boycott of foreign cloth through khadi, so that women who believed in only one of these cause could vote for that one alone. At the second conference three more name were added :

Shrimati Shardabehn Sumant Mehta

Shrimati Savitabehn Trivedi

Shrimati Surajbehn Manilal

This vote need not be considered as having much value. It is valuable to the extent that not a single resolution was opposed at the meeting, for it shows that even if the women present may not be prepared to put the resolution into practice, nevertheless they approved of its substance. At both these conferences women from villages were present in greater numbers. The struggle this time is of the villages especially. The awakening in the villages is astonishing which is a good sign. Salt, the boycott of foreign cloth and prohibition - all these three are specially meant for villages and the women would benefit especially.

Even if a few women are ready to lay down their lives for the sake of this resolution, they will come forward. If this does not happen the conferences will not be deemed to have completed its work. If the number of women present at the conference is any indication, the women would seem to be prepared for work.

The soul of any organisation is its executive committee. Hence the success of the work depends upon the enthusiasm, the *tapascharya* and the skill of the ladies who have given their names for the committee.

Mithubehn Petit has started the work with great alacrity. According to her accounts habitual drunkards are enthusiastically breaking earthen jars containing toddy. Thousands of persons in Surat who are given to drinking have started having resolutions passed by their castes prohibition drinking.

Once women become self-confident and gain faith, they will find from experience that the fear which they entertain has no basis. Rama and Ravana dwell in every human being. If women would act through the Rama who is in them; the Ravana who dwells in man would be powerless. Rama awakens less readily in men than in women. Who can harm one who is protected by Rama? Who can protect one with whom Rama is displeased?

In the work of prohibition, once the initial fear is shed, things become easy. For all it involves is picketing. These self-interest is not involved in drinking. Once they are convinced, they will give up liquor. The liquor-booth owners do have their self-interest involved but they realize that this is an immoral trade.

I regard this extension of the swaraj movement as of the highest importance. I need not reiterate the argument already advanced in these pages. Mithubehn has already commenced operations. She is not the women to let the grass grow under her feet. The idea is for twenty to twenty-five women to go in one batch and plant themselves near each liquor shop and come in personal contact with every visitor to the liquor or toddy shops and wean him from the habit. They will also appeal to the shopkeepers to give up the immoral traffic and earn their livelihood through better means.

Foreign-cloth shops are to be treated in the same way as liquor shops as soon as there are enough trained women volunteers. Though the same committee will carry on the two boycotts it will necessarily have two branches. It will be open to any woman to offer her services for only one branch of work, nor is it necessary that every worker should belong to the Congress. Only this must be clearly understood, that the work is part of the Congress programme and has tremendous political results if it has also equally great moral and economic consequences.

Those who will belong to the foreign-cloth boycott branch should realise that without the constructive work of khadi production the mere boycott will be a mischievous activity. Its very success without the production of khadi will prove the ruin of the national movement of independence. For the millions will take it up in simple faith. But they will curse us if they discover that they have no cloth to wear or the cloth they can get is too dear for their purse. The formula, therefore, is : discard foreign cloth and make your own khadi and wear it. Already there is a dearth of khadi.

The boycott of foreign cloth is, however, a difficult matter. It has two aspects; boycott and khadi production. The boycott does not require much effort. Only a few women would suffice for the work. For the production of khadi thousands and even hundreds of thousands would have to be regularly active. Hence it would require organisation and planning. However, it is a work needing patience, as it requires intelligence and faith. In the course of it you have to come in contact - directly or indirectly - with crores of women. It requires a pure co-ordination between towns and villages. And, through it all the khadi India needs can be produced in a short time. We have before us all the means to produce it. We have the necessary skill too. All that we lack is workers. It is the sisters who must create these workers. They can do so only when they themselves learn to card and spin and disseminate the art among others. Most of the khadi workers are in the salt campaign. Therefore, the production has suffered a temporary check.

But there need never be any dearth of cloth the moment the country gets disabused of the superstition that it must buy cloth to cover its nakedness. It would be on a par with someone saying that we must starve if we cannot get Manchester or Delhi biscuits. Even as we cook our food and eat it so can we, if we but will it, make our own cloth and wear it. We did it only a hundred years ago and we can relearn the trick now. All the vital process are almost too simple to learn. At this supreme crises, this turning-point in the nation's history, we must not hesitate and nurse idleness. I do not need to restate the argument about our mills. Even if every mill were genuinely swadeshi and even if all became patriotic, they could not supply all our wants. Whichever way we look at it, whether we like it or not, we cannot escape khadi if we are to active independence through non-violent means and if we are to achieve the boycott of foreign cloth on which we began concentration in 1920.

Of men's part in the boycott I have said enough in my speech which I unexpectedly delivered to the men who had come to Dandi. Relevant parts of this speech are reproduced elsewhere. Suffice it here to say that men will damage the movement if they will meddle with women's picketing wherever it is undertaken by them.

By passing the above two resolutions Gujarati women have taken up the responsibility and Begum Amina Tyabji and their committee have shouldered the responsibility on their behalf.

May God grant them strength!

Young India, 17-4-1930

Letter to Satyagraha Committee, Bombay

(Before May 5, 1930)

Friends from Bombay have been to me asking me to lead a raiding party from there instead of from Karadi, assuming of course that a raid is to be decided upon. I should be proud and consider it a privilege to lead it provided that certain preliminary conditions are fulfilled. I observe that there is a great deal of misunderstanding about this contemplated raid. It has been arisen because of the use of the world "raid". Now all my speeches in Gujarat are invariably delivered in Gujarati. The word "raid", therefore, is not the one I had used. I admit, however, that it is a legitimate translation of the original. But my audience know the original word "dhad" used to alliterate with "dhar" in "Dharasana", was used playfully. Fortunately or unfortunately even for a non-violent war military expressions have got to be used. But even as nobody is deceived by the use of such military expressions, no one need be perturbed over the use of the word "raid" when it is to be civil, non-violent or satyagrahi. The use of that potent adjective alters the whole colour of the transaction. But, however, innocent the raid, if it even comes being, may be, it will be fraught with the consequences perhaps far more serious than those flowing from a violent raid. Those, therefore, who would join the contemplated raid have to satisfy some test, and since the battle is meant not merely for the removal of the salt tax but for establishing Purna Swaraj, the conditions have to be in keeping with the objective. They are three : *(a)* Observance of complete discipline. *(b)* Complete abstention from drink under a permanent pledge. *(c)* Wearing of hand-spun khaddar also under a permanent pledge and actual spinning on the *takli* for one hour per day except when spinning is made impossible through want of time or capacity. If Bombay produces a hundred thousand such men I should lead them without the slightest hesitation. I know that the citizens of Bombay will not laugh at my conditions nor will they consider them impossible to fulfilment. The only difficulty they might feel will be about the *takli*. Surely if a hundred thousand men in Bombay have the will *takli* spinning is child's play. Sustained work from day to day may be a task for easy-going citizens of Bombay but Freedom's battle has never been won by easy-going people. No one need be irritated against me for maintaining these conditions because they are not in any sense obligatory; they are meant to be a consideration in a voluntary contract. It is open to the citizens of Bombay to reject my terms and do as they please. Rejection then of terms will not make them less Congressmen than they are today.

The Bombay Chronicle, 5-5-1930

Arrest at Midnight

Karadi
May 5, 1930

The Magistrate proceeded to Gandhiji's hut and woke him up, "I have warrant for your arrest, Mr. Gandhi," said the Magistrate. Gandhiji asked politely :

I am not surprised, but will you read out the warrant to me?

The Magistrate complied with this request and read the following which was signed by Sir Frederick Sykes, Governor of Bombay.

"Whereas the Government view with alarm the activities of Mr. M.K. Gandhi, they direct that he should be placed under restraint under Regulation 25 of 1827 and suffer imprisonment during the pleasure of the Government and be immediately removed to the Yeravada Central Jail."

Gandhiji was smiling when the warrant was being read. He said :

I am prepared to accompany you, but will you allow me to have a wash and clean my teeth?

"With pleasure," said the Magistrate.

In the meantime the whole Ashram was up, and everyone was anxious to have a parting 'darshan' of Gandhiji. Having finished his wash, Gandhiji came out of the cottage to say his prayers. The whole Ashram knelt down to recite the prayers while the police officers watched. Gandhiji himself led the chorus. He then collected his papers and gave them in charge of a volunteer whom he had chosen as Captain during his incarceration.

The Bombay Chronicle, 6-5-1930

Letter to Viceroy

Yeravada Central Prison
May 18, 1930

H.E. The Viceroy of India

Dear Friend,

The authorities having permitted the use of newspapers. I am able somewhat to follow the course of events in the country. I should fail in my duty if I did not express my opinion on your latest statement.

You seem to ignore the simple fact that disobedience ceases to be such immediately masses of people resort to it. Do you not see that hundreds of men who have been known for their peaceful nature, who have an unbroken record of service to their credit and whose integrity is beyond suspicion are imprisoned? They are no law-breakers; they are no haters of the English. And what of the most peaceful demonstration of thousands of simple villagers who are by instinct the most law-abiding? To describe the movement of such men and women as lawlessness is, in my opinion, doing violence to the language. The very motive which is the essence of crime is lacking. It is the noblest of motives which takes away men like the hoary-headed Abbas Tyabji from their soft ease to court the hardships of a jail life.

You protest your affection for India. I believe in your profession. But I deny the correctness of your diagnosis of India's disease. The best constitution that can be devised will fail to bring real contentment and peace unless the grievances on which public attention is concentrated are immediately removed. The salt tax cannot remain. The liquor revenue must go. The foreign cloth importation which has produced a partial paralysis of the village life must be stopped. Have you not noted the strength of popular feeling in these matters? Or are the hundreds of thousands of men and women who are taking part in the movement wicked-minded or misled or fools and the English officials the best judges of what is good for India?

If I am not mistaken, you will find the spirit of the people to be proof against repression, no matter how severe it may be. You will not coerce millions of people into subjection for all time. India must not live for England. She must live for herself, so as to enable her to make her contribution to the world's progress. As a slave nation she is a mere burden on earth because it is a false life. No Round Table Conference can, therefore, be of any avail, unless you see things from our standpoint and, leaving coercion, rely simply on carrying conviction. Even those who you think are with you are with the Congressmen so far as wants are concerned.

I remain,
Your sincerely friend,
M.K. Gandhi

Note to Nehrus

Yeravada Central Prison
July 23, 1930

CONSTITUTIONAL ISSUE

1. So far as this question is concerned, my personal position is that if the Round Table Conference is restricted to a discussion of safeguards that may be necessary in connection with full Self-Government during the period of transition. I should have no objection, it being understood that the question of independence should not be ruled out if anybody raises it. I should be satisfied before I could endorse the idea of the Congress attending the Conference about its whole composition.

CIVIL DISOBEDIENCE AND ITS CALLING OFF

2. If the Congress is satisfied as to the Round Table Conference, naturally civil disobedience would be called off, that is to say, disobedience of certain laws for the sake of disobedience, but peaceful picketing of foreign cloth and liquor will be continued unless the Government themselves can enforce prohibition of liquor and foreign cloth. But manufacture of salt by the populace will have to be continued and the penal clause of the Salt Act should not be enforced. There will be no raids on Government Salt made a clause in these terms, but is accepted as an ideal in writing.

3. *(a)* Simultaneously with the calling off of the civil disobedience, all satyagrahi prisoners and other political prisoners convicted or under-trial, who have not been guilty of violence or incitement to violence should be ordered to be released.

   (b) Properties confiscated under the Salt Act and Press Act and Revenue Act and the like should be restored.

   (c) Fines and securities taken from convicted satyagrahis - or under the Press Act should be refunded.

   (d) All officers including village officers who have resigned or who may have been dismissed during the

civil disobedience movement and who may desire to rejoin Government service should be restored.

N.B. The foregoing should refer also to the Non-Cooperation period.

(e) Viceregal ordinances should be repealed.

This opinion of mine is purely provisional, because I consider that a prisoner has no right to pronounce any opinion upon political activities of which he cannot possibly have a full grasp while he is shut out of personal contact. I, therefore, feel that my opinion is not entitled to the weight I should claim for it if I was in touch with the movement.

Mr. Jayakar and Dr. Sapru may show this to Pandit Motilal Nehru, Pandit Jawaharlal Nehru, Mr. Vallabhabhai Patel and those who are incharge of the movement. Nothing to appear in the Press.

This is not to be shown to the Viceroy at this stage.

Even if the foregoing terms are accepted I should not care to attend the Conference unless, in the event of going out of the prison, I gained self-confidence which I have not at present and unless among those Indians who would be invited there was a preliminary conversation and an agreement as to the minimum by which they should stand under all circumstances.

I reserve to myself the liberty, when the occasion arises, of testing every swaraj scheme by its ability to satisfy the object underlying the eleven points in my letter to the Viceroy.

M.K. Gandhi

2

Early Career

In the political struggle for swaraj under the leadership of no less great leaders like Mahatma Gandhi, Motilal Nehru and C.R. Das, the role of Kamala Nehru is most significant. Born in a respectable Kashmiri family in Sitaram Bazar in Old Delhi, she was married in the Nehru family which had gained much influence and reputation on account of the legal practice of the highest order of Motilal Nehru as well as his established status in social and political circles of North India. The marriage of Kamala with Jawaharlal Nehru was indeed a festive occasion and the marriage party happended to live in Delhi for a few days. Kamala's ancestors as well as parents were affluent in every respect and their connections with the Nehru family developed in a natural way when Pandit Motilal Nehru happened to see Kamala and her parents.

The adjustment of Kamala Nehru at Anand Bhawan was remarkable in every sense. Already she was well-conversant with social etiquettes. The meals at Anand Bhawan were both Indian and European in style. Motilal Nehru lived in a high style and he provided all kinds of facilities to his son and daughter-in-law. Kamala Nehru could have nice company of Vijayalakshmi and Krishna at Anand Bhawan.

Jawaharlal Nehru did not show inclination for legal practice though his father wished that he should take advantage of his experience and knowledge of law. His mind was for something higher in life and for that he was yet to decide. His interest in Home Rule Movement was soon diverted to the Gandhian ideology when Gandhiji entered the portals of Anand Bhawan.

With the acceptance of Congress presidentship at Amritsar in 1919, Pandit Motilal Nehru brought about a remarkable change in the ideology of the Congress. His significant speech contained an anti-Raj stance as well as the future political programme to be launched by the Congress with the support and co-operation of the people. The Non-Co-operation Movement was launched at all India level and members of the Nehru family participated in it. At this point of time, Jawaharlal Nehru who was about thirty years old was deeply involved in the political affairs under the leadership of Mahatma Gandhi. Indiraji was hardly four or five years old and her parents and grand-father and grand-mother—all were busy in one way or the other, in the freedom struggle. Jawaharlal Nehru moved out among the villages in the United Provinces and apprised them of their poverty, economic condition, ideology of the Congress party and last but not the least about the attainment of Swaraj. His personal touch with the people had much effect on them and in a few years the United Provinces became a firm political base for the Nehru family as well as for all those who had links with Anand Bhawan.

Nehru's deep interest for the freedom struggle brought about a remarkable change among the members of his family at Anand Bhawan. Day in and day out, several people used to come for meetings and consultations. Naturally Swarup Rani Nehru, Kamala Nehru and other members of the family watched these developments with interest. A new wave of sincere patriotism was generated in them and soon they become part and parcel of the political movement. Undoubtedly the sacrifices they made were superb and influenced the women fold in several regions of our sub-continent.

In 1912, the year young Jawahar was to complete his studies in England and return to Allahabad, he had some correspondence with his father about his marriage.

Motilal urged Jawahar to leave the matter in his hands. Jawahar willingly did so, though he hoped that he would have an opportunity to see his future bride before he became engaged to her. From time to time Motilal sent him photographs of girls under consideration.

Jawahar Nehru once wrote to his father while at college in Cambridge : I have already written to you on the subject of my marriage and have left the matter entirely in your hands. You have not told me yet who the girl in question is. I might possibly have seen her or heard of her in the days of my infancy . . . . I am glad there is some chance of my not becoming engaged to the girl of your choice before I see her. I don't suppose my seeing her will make very much difference. I am not likely to become passionately found of her at first sight nor is there much chance of my disliking her violently. Still I shall feel more satisfied if the engagement took place after we had seen each other . . . . You express a hope that my marriage should be romantic. I should like it to be so but I fail to see how it is going to come about. There is not an atom of romance in the way you are searching girls for me and keeping them waiting till my arrival. The very idea is extremely unromantic. And you can hardly expect me to fall in love with a photograph . . . .

Another letter reveals Nehru's reaction to the photograph of a girl which had been sent to him. He was not impressed by the girl's looks or educational attainments. But he added that "education does not consist of passing exams or knowing English or mathematics. It is a mental state and if this is not present it matters little how many exams a person has passed."

It is evident that Motilal was glad that Jawahar had at least left the question of his marriage to him and wrote to Jawahar : I was glad to read what you said on the question of your marriage. That under the circumstances is the only correct view to take. I fully realise the importance of your seeing the girl yourself and will do my best to put off my definite reply on some pretext or another, seeing meanwhile that the interval is not wasted and the girl employs her time usefully. Two of the girls who at different times were considered very eligible for you are to be married in Allahabad this month. I mean Tej Behadur's daughter and Jainath's daughter. The first mention of Kamala as a prospective bride for Jawahar was made by Motilal in a letter written to Jawahar in April 1912. He said : "Braj (Brajlal Nehru) is now busy at work in your interest. He has seen a girl in Delhi and is pressing me to go and see her. He speaks of her as a most desirable acquisition for the Nehru family."

Motilal followed this letter with another soon after : "The day after I wrote last I suddenly made up my mind to go up to

Delhi for a day and see the little beauty. Brajlal had managed to have the little girl invited at a get-together given to us by a relation of Diwan Sahib. From what little I could see of the girl I found that Brajlal's description of her was perfectly accurate. So far as features go there is no other girl to approach her. She seemed to be extremely intelligent. The net result of my visit to Delhi is that one more girl is waiting for you."

And Jawahar answered : "As regards the Delhi girl, surely she is too young for me. I am ten years her senior and that is rather a big difference. I could not possibly marry her before she was 18 or 19, that is six or seven years hence. I would not mind waiting as I am not in a matrimonial state of mind at present."

Kamala's photograph had attracted Nehru and he had written to his father : "As for looks, who can help feeling keen enjoyment at the sight of a beautiful creature? And I think you are quite right in saying that the outer feature generally take after the inner person. And yet sometimes this is not the case. Beauty is after all skin deep. . ." Kamala, the "little Delhi beauty", was no more than 13 when Motilal went to see her in Delhi. He did not contemplate bringing a child daughter-in-law into his home, but since girls were married off quite young in the Kashmiri community he felt that the engagement could be held soon and the marriage a little later.

Krishna Huthee Singh wrote about Kamala thus : She was sixteen and very lovely and rather tall for an Indian girl. . . . Her hair was dark and she had large brown eyes and a very gentle disposition. It is surprising that so little has been written about Kamala, for she was one of the most beautiful women I knew or ever have known. . . . What made father like her, apart from her sweetness and beauty, was that she looked very healthy : My mother had been a semi-invalid most of her life and, though father treated her and taught us to treat her as a very precious delicate piece of China, he wanted a strong wife for his son.

"Motilal wanted the time between the engagement and marriage to be "usefully employed" by providing the prospective bride with education. Besides, he wanted her to acquire some of the accomplishment necessary for one who was to become a member of a house well known for its lavish hospitality and the wife of a handsome, well-educated and sophisticated young man who was to return to India after seven years at Harrow and

Cambridge and in London. A young man who was "more an Englishman than an Indian."

Kamala, used to a traditional Indian home, had a lot to learn to adjust herself to live in a highly westernised home with its cocktail rounds, horse riding, and tennis parties. For some months before they married Kamala came to live in Allahabad with her aunt, Senapati Mushran and her husband. She attended a few functions at Anand Bhawan.

Occasionally, Kamala and Jawahar would go out for a drive in the family car. And there was no doubt that they were silently attracted to each other. The English governess of the Nehru sisters was given an additional charge, that of grooming Kamala.

Those who knew Kamala in those early years before marriage remember her as a slim, tall (for a Kashmiri), and beautiful girl who wore simple cotton sarees. She did not wear jewels or use make-up like other girls of her age and position. Indeed, her striking beauty did not need any adornment. She was a serious, intense girl, intelligent and highly strung. The marriage of Jawahar and Kamala took place in Delhi on February 8, 1916. It was Vasant Panchami that day - the festival which heralds the coming of spring.

The wedding between 26-year-old Jawahar and 17-year-old Kamala was one of the most glittering events of the time. The Atals approached a neighbouring Kashmiri family by the name Haksar for the loan of their house for housing the wedding guests. This tall three-storeyed building stood very near Atal House. It had enormous halls and courtyards and could easily accommodate the hundreds of guests who would come with the bridgroom's party for the wedding ceremony. A special train from Allahabad brought the groom, his family, relations and friends - altogether 300 odd guests - to Delhi. Here many more guests joined the party. Several houses were requisitioned to accommodate them, yet the space available was not adequate. A tented "town" therefore came up just outside the walled city, and bore the sign, "Nehru Wedding Camp" written in flowers. For seven days and seven nights the festivities continued, many of them taking place at the wedding camp itself. Jawahar in his brocade sherwani and turban and Kamala in her pearl-studded saree made a breathtakingly handsome Kamala's saree had taken a group of dexterous-fingered craftsmen working on the verandahs of Anand Bhawan months to prepare."

3

Motilal Nehru and Kamala

7, Ferozepur Road
Lahore
30-6-1919

My dear Jawahar,

Malaviya arrived in Amritsar soon after I posted my letter of yesterday. We then visited the Jallianwala Bagh. It was a truly gruesome sight. In spite of the lapse of nearly 21/2 months after the incident there were more than one corpses to be seen floating and the wall in a highly decomposed state. We spent some time there and examined the whole place very carefully. This was done in a boiling heat. We then saw the notorious foot bridge and also burnt down buildings. Today was set apart for Gujranwala but both Malaviya and Shraddhanand were so much affected by the trail of yesterday that they decided to have some rest. We are discussing things today - tomorrow we go to Gujaranwala and I leave the day after.

There is no news of rain from the U.P. If it is anything like the weather we are experiencing here little Indira cannot possibly bear it. However, Kamala and Nan may be disgusted with Naini Tal they should stay there for another week or ten days. You will of course have to come down for the Ramnagar case for which I have to go back leaving Malaviya here. Your mother will join me at Delhi - Chander and Janak are going with me. You had better return to Allahabad on Friday. It is no use writing anything about what we have seen and heard here. I shall tell you all when we meet.

Love to all.

Your loving
Father

7, Ferozepur Road
Lahore
19-8-1919

My dear Jawahar,

Used as I am to rush things I have broken my own record on the occasion. There is not a minute to spare. Not even to write a few lines. I am dashing off these lines in the brief interval which a pelting rain has given me.

I approve generally of your arrangements about Solon and Betty. Enclosed is a letter from a Lahore doctor considered to be a specialist in Tuberculosis. He was going to Solon to give the injection to a Lahore patient and I took advantage of his visit to make sure of the house etc. I hope Kamala has shaken off the fright caused by Mukerjee.

I have just wired to you saying that Krishna Kant is not wanted. It is very unsafe to have the Editor of a paper in my party. It is impossible to expect him to keep anything to himself and resist the temptation of "Copy".

I have been to Amritsar twice and am taking Lahore and Amritsar on alternate days. There is a good deal of work to be done. I am going to Amritsar again tomorrow. If Purushottam turns up I shall make him get down at Amritsar and then send him off to Gujranwala.

I have wired to Harnam Singh that I cannot get back this week but will try to be in time for argument if sufficient notice is given to me of the date fixed. As for Ibrahim I have declined the responsibility of advising without knowing Nasim's reasons for such an extraordinary step. You do not say how Gurumukh has fared in the witness box. However the Ramnagar case is at present completely out of my mind and I shall go on with the work here unless called away for more substantial reasons than merely examining Ibrahim.

I have already written to Roshanlal about disinfecting etc. The enclosures will speak for themselves.

Your loving
Father

Please send all the Punjab Papers by the hand of the next man who comes here.

My chief concern at present is about the Nawal Kishore's Press claim. I do not see how we can propose an instalment arrangement and show fight at one and the same time. If we dispute his statements about his being a shareholder and the price we ought to send a cheque for the amount we admit to be due and dispute the rest of the claim. But there is no fund available to draw upon except my poor earnings and they will all be absorbed by this one claim. I have to find something like Rs. 50,000 by the end of April or the middle of May for the shares I have applied for in the British India Corporation Ltd. (the amalgamation scheme of the Cawnpore Mills). For this I was relying on the fees from this case. We cannot put off the N.K. Press beyond a week or ten days. Has the meeting of shareholders and the Directors been called yet? Please see that it is called at the earliest possible date. I shall try to be present.

I am enclosing the following :

(1) A letter from Dr. D.N. Ray in reply to the one I wrote from Allahabad. I have noted the directions which concern me. Please keep the letter carefully and follow it scrupulously in the cases of Kamala and Sarup. The ointment for the former is being sent by post parcel.

(2) The Temperature chart of Kamala returned from Calcutta. This should also be carefully preserved for future reference and a daily record should be kept of her temperature taken at least once a day in the afternoon.

(3) A letter from some Kashmiri blackguard evidently an enemy of Mahtab Ram.

Your loving
Father

Nirmal has just arrived with your letter and the "Ind." papers. I shall see what I can make of them and send you a copy if Nirmal can finish the typing tonight.

M.N.

I have examined the papers you have sent with Nirmal. They are very few which is of course due to the slipshod manner in which things are done in the "Ind." office. But one paper without which I can do nothing is the notice received from Bisheshar Nath Vakil to which I am supposed to reply on the material supplied by you. This notice was handed to Ladli and I have not seen it since. I have just wired to you for this and have to wait till it comes.

M.N.

I sent another wire a little earlier asking for some books. Much against my own and the client's inclinations Sircar has objected to C.R. Das cross examining Hariji. There was a long discussion in Court today and the order is to be passed tomorrow. I had looked up the whole law on the subject when my appearance in the Ramnagar case was objected to. The cases are noted in black fat notebook under the Ramnagar case and I have asked you and Shamji Mushran to send that notebook with the reports. I am not sure that the telegram will be intelligible to either of you but I was silly enough to say that I have such a note and Sircar insisted on my getting it. If you cannot send the notebook and the cases by tonight's train they will be too late. I am afraid I have not made this clear. Gokarannath wires saying that Gandhiji "held up" in Ahmedabad for the week beginning 1st April and the A.I.C.C. meeting should therefore be held in Bombay. I cannot understand how Gandhiji can attend at Bombay if he is "held up" in Ahmedabad. I have wired to ask Gandhiji if Delhi will suit him and have also wired Malaviyaji. On receipt of their replies I shall make up my mind.

I have had no news either about Mohan's son-in-law or Braj Kumar since my arrival here. How are they doing?

If Sircar's objection is allowed (though I do not think it ought to be) the case will have to be adjourned for at least a month if not more to enable Plff. to engage other Counsel. This will suit both Das and myself so far as our public engagements are concerned. In any case I must go to Allahabad for a couple of days either this week or the next. I have already told you that I shall take leave of my client for the Easter week. There is therefore no reason to despair of my going to Allahabad in the near future.

Chakravarty informs me that Kamala's temperature goes up to 99 degree every evening. This is a serious matter but you say nothing about it. I gave very peremptory directions to Kamala about keeping an accurate record of these fluctuations of the temperature and also of her weight. Please send me full particulars. I do hope she is following the directions of Dr. Roy.

Dr. Murarilal of Cawnpore stopped here for a few hours. His complaint was that the country had nothing in the way of a proper lead before it as to the Congress programme about reforms. This complaint is a just one. We must have a complete programme settled at the next meeting of the A.I.C.C. wherever it is held. Some drafts will be necessary. Who is going to make them? I am asking Gokarannath to write to the Provincial Secretaries to have the drafts ready to be considered at the All India meeting. Can you suggest any other course? There is any amount of work to be done but no workers. You cannot do everything single handed.

Your loving
Father

Gokaran has sent me the agenda for the next meeting of the A.I.C.C. It consists mainly of ministerial work but includes two or three important items for which a fuller meeting than the one we can expect on the 3rd April is desirable. It does not contain the most important item about which I gave special instructions to Gokaran, viz. the settlement of the Congress programme of work in connection with the Reforms. The time is all the short for getting the views of the various Provincial Committees on this important subject. Everything points to a postponement of the meeting.

I am glad Ram Chandra has turned up. You were quite right in assigning to him the role of an inspector. We cannot expect to get Hariji out of the witness box before the 26th as Das is trying all he is worth to take his vengeance on him for the objection. Sircar was stupid enough to take. We have then an important witness from Burma to put in and he is likely to take two days (27th and 29th). If Bholanath and Abbas turn up on the 29th I shall dispose of them before Easter and purchase my freedom for the holidays. If not I have either to stay here or spend a few days in Allahabad with them during the holidays. In any case I am afraid it is not possible for me to go to Allahabad before Easter.

The record of Kamala's temperature you have sent is disquieting. "Looking well" and "seeming to improve" are the very symptoms of her disease. The real test is absence of any rise in the temperature and gaining weight. Your report as to the former is discouraging and you say nothing about the latter. We must make up our minds to send her away for the hot weather to some place suitable for her. Sarup says that Rammo is expected on the 23rd. You had better got all the information about Burma from her but having regard to your engagements and mine I do not think it will be possible for either of us to accompany the party to Burma and I would not think of sending Kamala with the other ladies to a place not easily accessible to us. This is the most important question we have to settle.

I am enclosing a cheque for Jaugne and Scowen. Guzder's account has swelled up to over Rs. 8000. It is so old that you cannot possibly check it. I think it ought to be paid in full and the monthly bills in future to be properly checked. Durga Charan told me that their prices were awful. By paying Rs. 5000 now the account will be squared as there is 14 per cent dividend about to be declared which will come to about Rs. 2400.

The dinner shout has gone and I must close.

Your loving
Father

Have you any news of what is happening in the Bombay Suit against *The Independent?*

M.N.

There was a Lahore bill of some milliner who had made Kamala's fur-coat. Have you paid this?

I am afraid I shall have to wait for next month's pay to meet our respective overdrafts from the Allahabad Bank. Send me the Calcutta cheque book after having the pass book written up to date with a note of the balance available.

M.N.

Arrah
3-5-20

My dear Jawahar,

It has been definitely decided that I leave for Allahabad tonight and I have just wired to you to that effect. I shall spend tomorrow and the day after in Allahabad and leave for Sutna on the morning of the 6th by the Bombay mail.

I found Chakravarti and Knightley in Benaras. They will go back to Allahabad tomorrow. I do not know if there is any arrangement for my meals in Allahabad and have just wired to Raghbar Dayal to arrange for some sort of a cook.

It is not yet settled whether the Commission will be executed in Sutna or Rewah. I hope it will be the former which I am told is a heaven compared with Rewah. On return from the Commission I shall probably have to go to Calcutta to examine certain witnesses on our side. I shall particularly welcome this as I stand in need of consulting a good occulist. There is an appreciable weakness in the sight of my left eye and I should like to find out what it is due to. There is nothing to be surprised at in this as I have now arrived at the time of life when I must expect these things. I thought at one time that old age would have no effect on me but I have become ten years older during the last few months.

I have disposed of all the correspondence you gave me as well as all I received here up to date. They only letter I have not yet written is to Shridhar. The idea that it will reach him after a long time has delayed it even longer. I hope to write it in Allahabad. The reply to your cable to him is now over due. I am very anxious to know the latest news about him.

I have cabled £1000 to Nevill for publicity work in connection with the Report.

Anand Bhawan
Allahabad
6-5-20

My dear Jawahar,

The horses came back yesterday safe and sound not very much the worse for their adventure. I have instructed Ladli to claim a refund and damages—also to engage a box at once and send the horses insured for Rs. 2000 as soon as possible.

I have received your letter enclosing Amal Home's. Bepin has agreed to act as Editor-in-Chief (he loves this decription) on Rs. 500. His son to continue as Sub on Rs. 100 and his son in England to get £6 a month for weekly letters and cuttings etc.

from the London papers. Mohan's salary is now to be fixed. What is your opinion? He is working very hard. The Punjab men I hope will clear out in a few days and I have written to Harkishenlal to recall them.

I have just dictated a letter to the Ford Automobiles. It is being typed-copy will be sent to you later.

I am sorry to hear Indu is not well. She must have caught a chill. Kamala is very careless about her.

I am again hard pressed for time as a number of men turned up from early morning and wasted the whole morning.

Your Loving Father

Faizabad
1-7-20

My dear Jawahar,

The witness seems to be a never ending one but I have made up my mind to finish him this evening even at the cost of omitting a point or two. If I succeed I motor down to Lucknow tomorrow morning and stay with young Ohdedar for the day-see (Fathima) and Maqbul Hosain the Registrar of Jt. Stock Cos. and such others as come my way - proceed by the night train to Allahabad arriving there early next morning - spend the day in Allahabad and leave for Araah by the night train. It will not be possible for me to leave Arah district after this as the Commission for the Plffs. examination has been granted. The case will again be taken up in court on the 9th and the Commission will begin at Dumraon on the 12th. At the lowest estimate it will take the rest of the month. The argument will take anything from 4 to 6 weeks. I am thus booked to the middle of September.

I am expecting the "Ind" of today to see if they have complied with my directions about the special Pubjab Edition.

I expect your mother will be able to travel in another 10 days and you will be back in Allahabad by the middle of the month.

I hope Nan is all right now. Strother Smith gave it as his opinion which had been confirmed by experience that riding will do her good. But she must not ride the Arab.

Is Kamala still having any rise of temperature? How are Betty and the Priya Darshini. I hope the latter is taking her meals regularly.

Your loving
Father

Chestnut Lodge
Almora
5-6-21

My dear Jawahar,

I have had no news from home since I left.The only communication received was a telegram from Kamala enquiring after my health.

The stormy dry weather we are having here is retarding my recover. Except that it is not so hot the conditions are very similar to those prevailing in the plains - perhaps worse for me. Strong dusty winds alternate with sultry lulls - a perpetual haze overhangs the surrounding hill - the whole atmosphere is laden with dust and smoke from the forest fires which are still going on. Besides this I had considerably over-rated my recuperative powers. The conviction is now brought home to me that I am distinctly aging and I notice a marked weakening of almost all the functions of the body. I am certainly very much better than I was when I left Allahabad but nothing compared to what I had expected at the end of the first week of my stay here. It is impossible to expect a remarkable change for the better during the next few days though I hope I shall in a few days be able to have fairly long walks and the full course of my exercise. Things will also improve after a shower or two which is daily expected. The *Chota Barsat* of the hills is now over due.

I am at present at a loss to know what to do but will have to make up my mind within the next four days. The chances are that I shall decide to stay on and give up the Bombay meeting. It seems to me that nothing.

I must confess I have not much of a faith in your physical capacity to bear extreme heat. There is however no help for it. I do not think the Govt. have imagination enough to transfer you and some others similarly situated to some hilljail - I hear the Almora jail is quite as commodious as any other District jail and is run all the year round unlike the Naini Tal jail which is merely a lock-up and is closed at the end of the season. If they did that we should shored (sic) not have had to give up the house taken at Almora. I am really more concerned about the health of poor little Indu who is paying for the sins of her father and grandfather. But your mother and Kamala would not listen to any proposal for a change while you are broiling in the heat of Lucknow. They are sure to visit you one of these days. Try to persuade them for the sake of poor little child to have even so short a change at any hill station they like. Now that you are safely disposed of for some time the conditions which obtained till recently do not apply any longer. Six weeks or so would bring the roses back to Indu's cheeks and she would be quite different to the pale languid thing she is now. I cannot advise Naini Tal as I know it does not agree with your mother and she is likely to be bed ridden all the time. She is low as she has been on former occasions. But either Mussoorie or Almora ought to do - perhaps the latter will suit best. There are not many visitors to Almora and the house we were negotiating for is probably still available. However I simply suggest the idea. You can discuss it with the others when they come. I am quite alive to the difficulties they will put forward but by the side of Indu's health I do not attach very great importance to them.

As for the family visiting me here it is entirely useless to incur the risks of N' Tal. Six weeks is not a very long time and I can join them soon after my release wherever they are.

They proposed to remove Murarilal to this jail to attend on me. I was first half willing but on reconsideration have definitely declined the favour with thanks. I am quite comfortable and am keeping fairly well. There is only one more injection to take to complete the course and it was hardly worthwhile to incur the obligation of having allowed the attendance of the doctor under whose treatment I entered upon this course of treatment.

Nan and Ranjit are thinking of going to Allahabad. I do not think it is wise to undertake a long journey in this weather. They ought to wait till the rains are established.

Remember particularly that you should not publish either the Govt. letter or your reply on any account whatever until the prosecution is either actually commenced or definitely abandoned. It will be very bad tactics to rush into print before the happening of either of these events.

I am in a state of suspense about both your movements and mine as I do not know what has actually happened so far and whether you are coming here or I have to go back before the 6th.

I see that I was not right in guessing that you were the donor of the *Gupt dan* as you say you wanted to transfer *your* war bonds for Rs. 5000 which were not Kamala's. I had no recollection of any such war bonds but in the view that I take of these securities they are as much hours as the securities standing in my name are mine - the truth being that they all rightfully belong to third parties.

So Mrs. Sarla Devi has succeeded in creating the theatrical effect she was hungering for by parting with a few worthless trinkets, valuing them at a considerable sum and saying that the other jewellery she had was converted when her husband was in Jail. I wonder what the good folk in Calcutta and Bombay who helped her with large sums of money directly and through Malaviyaji say to the latter statement, but they probably do not know that not even half of what they paid was actually parted with Mrs. Sarla and that a very large portion of what she actually parted with will go back to her as soon as I can call a meeting of the old Punjab Sub-committee of the Congress. This will be among the first items of business to claim my attention on my return. It is no use relying on Malaviyaji. I am going to call the meeting as General Secretary of the Congress. With love.

Your loving
Father

Lucknow
3-4-22

My dear Jawahar,

I have received all the things sent through Uma.

The health of the family gives cause for anxiety. As you know Dr. Sarcar is not a man in whom I place any great confidence. I have allowed him to look after the family for what of a better and more reliable man on whom you could count at all times and for all diseases. You have to keep an eye over him and if you find his treatment is not doing much good you should change it. He is something of a faddist in certain matters. In case a change of treatment becomes necessary you will have to fall back on allopathy as there is no other homoeopath who can be trusted even to the extent that Sarcar can.

I am glad you think the work is proceeding satisfactorily all round. You must have good reason to make an exception of Cawnpore from the general rule of suspension of picketing of cloth shops. I hope it is not a mere case of *Zid versus Zid* which always ends in trouble.

I note your programme. The taking of Kamala and Betty with you on your tour in this weather with plague and influenza raging all round does not seem to me to be very wise. I do not know how poor Indu is to be disposed of. It will go hard with her in either case. If she is taken with the party she will have to share all the inconveniences of travelling. If she is left behind with two old grannies she will be very lonely.

4

Nehru's Historic Reminiscences

My marirage took place in 1916 in the city of Delhi. It was on the Vassanta Panchami day which heralds the coming of spirng in India. That summer we spent some months in Kashmir. I left my family in the valley and, together with a cousin of mine, wandered for several weeks in the mountains and went up the Ladakh road. This was my first experience of the narrow and lonely valleys, high up in the world, which lead to the Tibetan plateau. From the top of the Zoji-la pass we saw the rich.verdant mountain sides below us on the side and the bare bleak rock on the other. We went up and up the narrow valley bottom flanked on each side by mountains, with the snow-covered tops gleaming on one side and little glaciers creeping down to meet us. The wind was cold and bitter but the sun was warm in the day time, and the air was so clear that often we were misled about the distnace of objects, thinking them much nearer than they actually were. The loneliness grew; there were not even trees or vegetation to keep us company - only the bare rock and the snow and ice and, sometimes, very welcome flowers. Yet I found a strange satisfaction in these wild and desolate haunts of nature; I was full of energy and a feeling of exaltation.

I had an exciting experience during this visit. At one place on our march beyond the Zoji-la pass - I think it was called Matayan - we were told that the cave of Amaranath was only eight miles away. It was true that an enormous mountain all covered with ice and snow lay in between and had to be crossed, but what did that matter? Eight miles seemed so little. In our enthusiasm and camp (which was situated at about 11,500 feet altitude) and with a small party went up the mountain. We had a local shepherd for a guide. We crossed and climbed several glaciers, roping ourselves up, and our troubles increased and breathing became a little difficult. Some of our porters, lightly laden as they were, began to bring up blood. It began to snow and the glaciers became terribly slippery; we were fagged out and every step meant a special effort. But still we persisted in our foolhardy attempt. We had left our camp at four in the morning and after twelve hours' almost continuous climbing we were rewarded by the sight of a huge ice-field. This was a magnificent sight, surrounded as it was by snow-peaks, like a diadem or an amphitheatre of the gods. But fresh snow and mists soon hid the sight from us. I do not know what our altitude was but I think it must have been about 15,000 to 16,000 feet, as we were considerably higher than the cave of Amaranath.

We had now to cross this ice-field, a distance probably of half a mile, and then go down on the other side to the cave. We thought that as the climbing was over, our principal difficulties had also been surmounted, and so, very tired but in good humour, we began this stage of the journey. It was a tricky business as there were many crevasses and the fresh snow often covered a dangerous spot. It was this fresh snow that almost proved to be my undoing, for I stepped upon it and it gave way and down I went a huge and yawning crevasse. It was a tremendous fissure and anything that went right down it could be assured of safe keeping and preservation for some geological ages. But the rope held and I clutched to the side of the crevasse and was pulled out. We were shaken up by this but still we persisted in going on. The crevasses, however, increased in number and width and we had no equipment or means of crossing some of them. And so at last we turned back, weary and disappointed, and the cave of Amaranath remained unvisited.

The higher valleys and mountains of Kashmir fascinated me so much that I resolved to come back again soon. I made many a plan and worked out many tour, and one, the very thought of which filled me with delight, was a visit to Manasarovar, the wonder lake of Tibet, and snow-covered Kailas near by. That was eighteen years ago, and I am still as far as ever from Kailas and Manasarovar. I have not even been to visit Kashmir again, much as I have longed to, and ever more and more I have got entangled in the coils of politics and public affairs. Instead of going up mountains or crossing the seas I have to satisfy my wanderlust by coming to prison. But still I plan, for that is a joy that no one can deny even in prison, and besides what else can one do in prison? And I dream of the day when I shall wander about the Himalaya and cross them top reach that lake and mountain of my desire. But meanwhile the sands of life run on and youth passes into middle age and that will give place to something worse, and sometimes I think that I may grow too old to reach Kailas and Manasarovar. But the journey is always worth the making even though the end may not be in sight.

"Yea, in my mind these mountains rise,
Their perils dyed with evening's rose;
And still my ghost sits at my eyes
And thirsts for their untroubled snows."

Walter de la Mare.

When I came out of gaol in October, both political and economic conditions seemed to me to be crying our for a no-tax campaign in rural areas. The economic difficulties of the agriculturists were obvious enough. Politically, our civil disobedience activities, though still flourishing everywhere, were getting a bit stale. People went on going to gaol in small numbers, and sometimes in large groups, but the sting had gone from the atmosphere. The cities and the middle classes were a bit tired of the hartals and processions. Obviously something was needed to liven things up, a fresh infusion of blood was necessary. Where could this come from except from the peasantry? - and the reserve stocks there were enormous. It would again become a mass movement touching the vital interests of the masses, and, what was to me very important, would raise social issues.

We discussed these matters, my colleagues and I, during the brief day and a half I was at Allahabad. At short notice we convened a meeting there of the executive of our Provincial Congress Committee, and, after long debate, we decided to sanction a no-tax campaign, making it permissive for any district to take it up. We did not declare it ourselves in any part of the province, and the Executive Council made it apply to zamindars as well as tenants, to avoid the class issue if possible. We knew, of course, that the main response would come from the peasantry.

Having got this permission to go ahead, our district of Allahabad wanted to take the first step. We decided to convene a representative kisan or peasants' conference of the district a week later, to give the new campaign a push. I felt that I had done a good first day's work after release from gaol. I added to it a big mass meeting in Allahabad city, where I spoke at length. It was for this speech that I was subsequently convicted again. And then, on October 13th, Kamala and I went off to Mussoorie to spend three days with father. He was looking just a little better, and I was happy to think that he had turned the corner and was getting well. I remember those quiet and delightful three days well; it was good to be back in the family. Indira, my daughter, was there; and my three little nieces, my sister's daughters. I would play with the children and sometimes we would march bravely round the house in a stately procession, led flag in hand, by the youngest, aged three or four, singing *Jhanda uncha rahe hamara,* our flag song. And those three days were the last I was to have with father before his fatal illness came to snatch him away from me.

Expecting my re-arrest soon, and desiring perhaps to see a little more of me, father suddenly decided to return to Allahabad also. Kamala and I were going down from Mussoorie on the 17th October to be in time for the Peasant Conference at Allahabad on the 19th. Father arranged to start with the others on the 18th, the day after us.

We had a somewhat exciting journey back, Kamala and I. At Dehra Dun an order under Section 144 Criminal Procedure Code was served on me almost as I was leaving. At Lucknow we got off for a few hours, and I learnt that another order under Section 144 awaited me there, but it was not actually served on me, as the police officer could not reach me owing to the large crowds. I was presented with an address by the Municipality, and then we left by car for Allahabad, stopping at various places *en route* to address some peasant gathering. We reached Allahabad on the night of the 18th. The morning of the 19th brought yet another order under Section 144 for me! The Government was evidently hot on my trail and my hours were numbered. I was anxious to attend the kisan conference before my re-arrest. We called this conference a private one of delegates only, and so it was, and did not allow outside Rs to come in. It was every representative of

Allahabad District, and, as far as I remember, about 1600 delegates were present. The conference decided very enthusiastically to start the no-tax campaign in the district.

There was some hesitation among our principal workers, some doubt about the success of such a venture, for the influence and the power of the big zamindars to terrorise, backed as this was by the Government, was very great, and they wondered if the peasantry would be able to withstand this. But there was no hesitation or doubt in the minds of the sixteen hundred and odd peasants of all degrees who were present, or at any rate it was not apparent. I was one of the speakers at the conference. I do not know if thereby I committed a breach of the Section 144 order which had forbidden me from speaking in public.

I then went to the station to receive my father and the rest of the family. The train was late, and, immediately after their arrival, I left them to attend a public meeting, a joint affair of the peasants, who had come from the surrounding villages, and the townspeople. Kamala and I were returning from this meeting, thoroughly tired out, after 8 p.m. I was looking forward to a talk with father, and I knew that he was waiting for me, for we had hardly spoken to each other since his return. On our way back our car was stopped almost in sight of our house, and I was arrested and carried off across the river Jumna to my old quarters in Naini. Kamala went on, alone, to Anand Bhawan to inform the waiting family of this new development; and, at the stroke of nine, I re-entered the great gate of Naini Prison.

After eight days' absence I was back again in Naini, and I rejoined Syed Mahmud, Narmada Prasad and Ranjit Pandit in the same old barrack. Some days afterwards I was tried in prison on a number of charges, all based on various parts of that one speech I had delivered at Allahabad, the day after my discharge. As usual with us, I did not defend myself, but made a brief statement in court. I was sentenced for sedition under section 124A to 18 months' rigorous imprisonment and a fine of Rs. 500; under the Salt Act of 1882 of six months and a fine of Rs. 100; and under Ordinance VI of 1930 (I forget what this Ordinance was about) also to six months and a fine of Rs. 100. As the last two were concurrent, the total sentence was two years' rigorous imprisonment and, in addition, five months in default of fines. This was my fifth term.

My re-arrest and conviction had some effect on the tempo of the civil disobedience movement for a while; it put on a little spurt and showed greater energy. This was largely due to father. When news was brought to him by Kamala of my arrest, he had a slightly unpleasant shock. Almost immediately he pulled himself together and banged a table in front of him saying that he had made up his mind to be an invalid no longer. He was going to be well and to do a man's work, and not to submit weakly to illness. It was a brave resolve, but unhappily no strength of will could overcome and crush that deep-seated disease that was eating into him. Yet for a few days it worked a marked change, to the surprise of those who saw him. For some months past, ever since he was at Yeravda, he had been bringing up blood in his sputum. This stopped quite suddenly after his resolve of his, and for some days it did not reappear. He was pleased about it, and he came to see me in prison and mentioned this fact to me in some triumph.

It was unfortunately a brief respite, for the blood came later in greater quantities and the disease reasserted itself. During this interval he worked with his old energy and gave a push to the civil disobedience movement all over India. He conferred with many people from various places and issued detailed instructions. He fixed one day (it was my birthday in November) for an all-India celebration at which the offending passages from my speech, for which I had been convicted, were read out at public meetings. On that day there were numerous lathi charges and forcible dispersals of processions and meetings, and it was estimated that, on that day alone, about five thousand arrests were made all over the country. It was a unique birthday celebration.

Ill as he was, this assumption of responsibility and pouring out of energy was very bad for father, and I begged of him to take absolute rest. I realised that such rest might not be possible for him in India, for his mind would always be occupied with the ups and downs of our struggle and, inevitably, people would go to him for advice. So I suggested to him to go for a short sea voyage towards Rangoon, Singapore, and the Dutch Indies, and he rather liked the idea. It was arranged that a doctor friend might accompany him on the voyage. With this object in view he went to Calcutta, but his condition grew slowly worse and he was unable to go far. In a Calcutta suburb he remained for seven weeks, and the whole family joined him there, except Kamala, who remained in Allahabad for most of the time, doing Congress work.

My re-arrest had probably been hastened because of my activities in connection with the no-tax campaign. As a matter of fact few things could have been better for that campaign than my arrest on that particular day, immediately after the kisan conference, while the peasant delegates were still in Allahabad. Their enthusiasm grew because of it, and they carried the decisions of the conference to almost every village in the district. Within a couple of days the whole district knew that the no-tax campaign had been inaugurated, and everywhere there was a joyful response to it.

Our chief difficulty in those days was one of communication of getting people to know what we were doing or what we wanted them to do. Newspapers would not publish our news for fear of being penalised and suppressed by Government; printing presses would not print our leaflets and notices; letters and telegrams were censored and often stopped. The only reliable method of communication open to us was to send couriers with dispatches, and even so our messengers were sometimes arrested. The method was an expensive one and required a great deal of organisation. It was organised with some success, and the provincial centres were in constant touch with headquarters as well as with their principal district centres.

It was not difficult to spread any information in the cities. Many of these issued unauthorised news-sheets, usually cyclostyled, daily or weekly, and there was always a great demand for them. Four our public notifications, one of the city methods was by beat of drum; this resulted usually in the arrest of the drummer. This did not matter, as arrests were sought, not avoided. All these methods suited the cities and were not easily applicable to the rural areas. Some kind of touch was kept up with principal village centres by means of messengers and cyclostyled notices, but this was not satisfactory, and it took time for our instructions to percolate to distant villages.

The kisan conference at Allahabad got over this difficulty. Delegates had come to it from practically every important village in the district and, when they dispersed, they carried the news of the fresh decisions affecting the peasantry, and of my arrest in connection with them, to every part of the district. They became, sixteen hundred of them, effective and enthusiastic propagandists for the no-tax campaign. The initial success of the movement thus became assured, and there was no doubt that the peasantry as a whole in that area would not pay their rent to begin with, and not at all unless they were frightened into doing so. No one, of course, could say what their powers of endurance would be in face of official or zamindari violence and terrorism.

Our appeal had been addressed both to zamindars and tenants not to pay; in theory it was not a class appeal. In practice most of the zamindars did pay their revenue, even some who sympathised with the national struggle. The pressure on them was great and they had more to lose. The tenantry, however, stood firm and did not pay, and our campaign thus became practically a no-rent campaign. From the Allahabad district it spread to some other districts of the United Provinces. In many districts it was not formally adopted, but in effect tenants withheld their rents or, in many cases, were wholly unable to pay them owing to the fall in prices. As it happened, neither Government nor the big zamindars took any widespread action to terrorise the recalcitrant tenantry for several months. They were not sure of their ground, as they had the political struggle with civil disobedience on the one side, and the economic slump, resulting in agricultural distress, on the other. The two merged into each other, and the Government was always afraid of an agrarian upheaval. With the Round Table Conference in session in London, they were not keen on adding to their troubles in India or on giving a still more striking demonstration of 'strong' government.

A planned basis for the raising of mankind to higher material and cultured levels, to a cultivation of spiritual values, of co-operation, unselfishness, the spirit of service, the desire to do right, goodwill and love - ultimately a world order. Everything that comes in the way will have to be removed, gently if possible, forcibly if necessary. And there seems to be little doubt that coercion will often be necessary. But if force is used it should not be in the spirit of hatred or cruelty, but with the dispassionate desire to remove an obstruction. That will be difficult. It is not an easy task; there is no easy way, and the pitfalls are numerous. The difficulties and pitfalls do not disappear by our ignoring them, but by realising their true nature and facing them boldly. All this sounds fanciful and Utopian, and it is highly unlikely that many people will be moved by these noble motives. But we can keep them in view and stress them, and it may be that gradually they will lessen the hatreds and passions that fill most of us.

Our method must lead to this goal and be based on these motives. But we must also realise that human nature being what it is, in the mass, it will not always respond to our appeals and persuasions, or act in accordance with high moral principles. Compulsion will often be necessary, in addition to conversion, and the best we can do is to limit this compulsion and use it in such a manner that its evil is lessened.

I was not flourising in Alipore Gaol. My weight had gone down considerably, and the Calcutta air and increasing heat were distressing me. There were rumours of my transfer to a better climate. On May 7th I was told to gather my belongings and to march out of the gaol. I was being sent to Dehra Dun gaol. The drive through Calcutta in the cool evening air was very pleasant after some months of seclusion, and the crowds at the big Howrah station were fascinating. I was glad of my transfer, and looked forward to Dehra Dun with its nearby mountains. On arrival I found that all was not as it used to be nine months earlier, when I had left it for Naini. I was put in a new place, an old cattle-shed cleaned up and fitted out.

As a cell it was not bad, and there was a little veranda attached to it. There was also a small yard adjoining, about fifty feet in length. The cell was better than the ancient one I had had previously in Dehra, but soon I discovered that other changes were not for the better. The surrounding wall, which had been ten feet high, had just been raised, especially for my benefit, by another four or five feet. The view of the hills I had so looked forward to was completely cut off and I could just see a few tree-tops. I was in this gaol for over three months, and I never had even a glimpse of the mountains. I was not allowed to walk outside in front of the gaol, as I used to, and my little yard was considered quite big enough for exercise.

These and other new restrictions were disappointing, and I felt irritated. I grew listless and disinclined to take even the little exercise that my yard allowed. I had hardly ever felt quite so lonely and cut off from the world. The solitary confinement began to tell on my nerves, and physically and mentally I declined. On the other side of the wall, only a few feet away, I knew there was freshness and fragrance, the cool smell of grass and soft earth, and distant vistas. But they were all out of reach and my eyes grew weary and heavy, faced always by those walls. There was not even the usual movement of prison life, for I was kept apart and by myself.

After six weeks the monsoon broke and it rained in mountains; we had twelve inches of rain during the first week. There was a change in the air and whispering of new life; the temperature came down and the body felt relaxed and relieved. But there was no relief for the eyes or the mind. Sometimes the iron door of my yard would open to allow a warder to come in or go out, and for a few seconds I had a sudden glimpse of the outside world - green fields and trees, bright with colour and glistening with pearly drops of rain - for a moment only, and then it all vanished like a flash of lighting. The door was hardly ever fully opened. Apparently the warders had instructions not to open it if I was anywhere near, and even when they opened it, to do so just a little. These brief glimpses of greenery and freshness were hardly welcome to me. That sight produced in me a kind of nostalgia, a heartache, and I would even avoid looking out when the door opened.

But all this unhappiness was not really the fault of the gaol, though it contributed to it. It was the reaction of outside events - Kamala's illness and my political worries. I was beginning to realise that Kamala was again in the grip of her old disease, and I felt helpless and unable to be of any service to her. I knew that my presence by her side would have made a difference.

Unlike Alipore, Dehra Dun gaol allowed me a daily newspaper, and I could keep in touch with political and other developments outside. In Patna the All-India Congress Committee met after nearly three years (for most of this time it was unlawful), and its proceedings were depressing. It surprised me that no attempt was made at this first meeting, after so much that had happened in India and the world, to analyse the situation, to have full discussions, to try to get out of old ruts. Gandhiji seemed to be, from a distance, his old dictatorial self - "If you choose to follow my lead you have to accept my conditions," he said. His demand was perfectly natural, for one could not both have him and ask him to act against his own deeply-felt convictions. But there seemed too much of imposition from above and too little of mutual discussion and hammering out a policy. It is curious how Gandhiji dominates the mind and then complains of the helplessness of people. Few people, I suppose, have had more loyal devotion and obedience on the mass-scale than he has had, and it seems hardly fair to blame the masses for not coming up to the high standard he had set for them. At the Patna meeting he did not even stay till the end, as he had to continue his Harijan tour. He told the A.I.C.C. to be business-like and to adopt the resolutions placed before them by the Working Committee with speed, and then he went away.

It is probably true that prolonged discussions would not have improved matters. There was a confusion and want of clarity among the members, and though many were prepared to criticise, there were hardly any constructive suggestion. Under the circumstances this was natural, for the burden of the struggle had already fallen on these leaders from various provinces and they were a little tired and mentally not fresh. Dimly it was felt that they had to cry halt, civil disobedience had to be stopped; but what then? Two groups took shape : one desiring purely constitutional activities through the legislatures, the other thinking rather vaguely along socialistic lines. The majority of the members belonged to neither of these groups. They disliked a reversion to constitutionalism, and at the same time socialism frightened them a little and seemed to them to introduce an element which might spilt their ranks. They had no constructive ideas, and the one hope and sheet-anchor they possessed was Gandhiji. As of old, they turned to him and followed his lead, even though many of them did not wholly approve of what he said. Gandhiji's support of the moderate constitutional elements gave them dominance in the Committee and the Congress.

All this was to be expected. But the reaction took the Congress further back than I had thought. At no time during the last fifteen years, ever since the advent of non-co-operation, had Congress leaders talked in this ultra-constitutional fashion. Even the Swaraj Party of the middle 'twenties, which itself was the result of a reaction, was far in advance of the new leadership, and there were no such commanding personalities now as the Swaraj Party had. Many persons who had studiously kept aloof from the movement so long as it was risky to join it, now streamed in and assumed importance.

The proscription of the Congress was ended by the Government and it became a legal organisation. But many of its associated and subsidiary bodies continued to be illegal, such as its volunteer department, the Seva Dal, as also a number of Kisan Sabhas, which were semi-independent peasant unions, and several educational institutions and youth leagues, including a children's organisation. In particular the 'Khudai Khidmatgars', or the Frontier Redshirts, and they are called, were still outlawed. This organisation had become a regular part of the Congress in 1931, and represented it in the Frontier Province. Thus, although the Congress had completely drawn off the direct action part of the struggle and had reverted to constitutional ways, the Government kept on all special laws meant for civil disobedience, and even continued the proscription of important parts of the Congress organisation. Special attention was also paid to the suppression of peasant organisations and labour unions, while, it was interesting to note, high Government officials went about urging the zamindars and landlords to organise themselves. Every facility was offered to these landlords' organisations. The two major ones in the United Provinces have their subscriptions collected by official agency, together with the revenue or taxes.

I am afraid I have never been partial to the Hindu or Moslem communal organisation, but an incident made me feel particularly bitter towards the Hindu Mahasabha. One of its secretaries actually went out of the way to approve of the continuation of the ban on the "Redshirts", and to part Government on the back for it. This approval of the deprivation of the most elementary of civil rights, at a time when there was no aggressive movement on, amazed me. Apart from this question of principle, it was well known that these Frontier people had behaved wonderfully during these years of struggle; and their leader, Khan Abdul Ghaffar Khan, one of the bravest and straightest men in India, was still in prison - a State prisoner kept confined without any trial. It seemed to me that communal bias could hardly go further, and I expected that more prominent leaders of the Hindu Mahasabha would hasten to disown their colleague on this matter. But, so far as I could discover, not a single one of them said a word about it.

I was much upset by this Hindu Sabha secretary's statement. It was bad enough in itself, but to my mind it appeared as a symbol of the new state of affairs in the country. In the heat of the summer afternoon I dozed off, and I remember having a curious dream. Abdul Ghaffar Khan was being attacked on all sides and I was fighting to defend him. I woke up in an exhausted state, feeling very miserable, and my pillow was wet with tears. This surprised me, for in my waking state I was not liable to such emotional outbursts.

My nerves were obviously in a bad way in those days. My sleep became troubled and disturbed, which was very unusual for me, and all manner of nightmares came to me. Sometimes I would shout out in my sleep. Once evidently the shouting had been more vigorous than usual, and I woke up with a start to find two gaol warders standing near my bed, rather worried at my noises. I had dreamed that I was being strangled.

About this time a resolution of the Congress Working Committee had also a painful effect on me. This resolution was passed, it was stated, "in view of the loose talk about the confiscation of private property and necessity of class war", and it proceeded to remind Congressman that the Karachi Resolution "neither contemplates confiscation of private property without just cause or compensation, nor advocacy of class war. The Working Committee is further of the opinion that confiscation and class war are contrary to the Congress creed of non-violence". The resolution was loosely worded and exhibited a certain amount of ignorance on the part of the farmers as to what class war was. It was obviously aimed at the newly formed Congress Socialist Party. There had, as a matter of fact, been no talk of confiscation on the part of any responsible member of this group; there had, however, been frequent reference to the existence of class war under present conditions. The Working Committee's resolution seemed to hint that any person believing in the existence of this class conflict could not even be an ordinary member of the Congress. Nobody had ever accused the Congress of having turned Socialist or of being against private property. Some members of it held those opinions, but now it appeared that they had no place even in the rank and file of this all-embracing national organization.

It had often been stated that the Congress represented the nation, including every group and interest in it, from prince to pauper. National movements frequently make that claim, meaning thereby presumably that they represent the great majority of the nation and that their policy is for the good of all interests. But the claim is on the face of it untenable, for no political organisation can represent conflicting interests without reducing itself to a flabby and unmeaning mass with no distinctive and distinguishing features. The Congress is either a political party with a definite (or vague) aim and philosophy of achieving political power and of utilising it for the national good, or it is just a benevolent and humanitarian organisation with no views of its own and wishing well to everybody. It can represent only those who are in general agreement with that aim and philosophy, and those who oppose this are likely to be considered by it an anti-national or anti-social and reactionary elements whose influence must be checked or eliminated, in order to give effect to its own philosophy. It is true that a national anti-imperialist movement offers a wide basis for agreement, as it does not touch the social conflicts. And so the Congress did represent in anything degrees the vast majority of the people of India, and it within its fold all manner of mutually differing groups who agreed only on the anti-imperialist issue, and even in regard to this there were great differences in stress. Those who, on this basic issue of anti-imperialism, held a contrary opinion kept out of the Congress and sided, also in varying degrees, with the British Government. The Congress thus became a kind of permanent All-Parties Congress, consisting of large numbers of groups shading into each other and held together by one common faith and the dominating personality of Gandhiji.

The Working Committee subsequently tried to explain its resolution on class war. The importance of that resolution lay not so much in its language or what it definitely laid down, as in fact that it was yet another indication of the way Congress was going. The resolution had obviously been inspired by the new parliamentary wing of the Congress aiming at gaining the support of men of property in the coming election to the Legislative Assembly. At their instance the Congress was looking more and more to the Right and trying to win over the moderate and conservative elements in the country. Soothing words were being addressed even to those who had been hostile to the Congress movements in the past and had sided with the Government during the continuance of civil disobedience. A clamorous and critical Left wing was felt to be a handicap in this process of conciliation and 'conversion', and the Working Committee's resolution, as well as many other individual utterances, made it clear that the Congress Executive were not going to be moved from their new path by this nibbling from the Left. If the Left did not behave it would be sat upon and eliminated from the Congress ranks. The manifesto issued by the Parliamentary Board of the Congress contained a programme which was far more cautious and moderate than any that the Congress had sponsored during the past fifteen years.

The Congress leadership, quite apart even from Gandhiji, consisted of many well-known persons with bright records in the national struggle for freedom, men honoured throughout the country for their integrity and fearlessness. But the new orientation of policy brought into the second ranks, and even the front rank, of Congress many individuals who could hardly be described as idealists. In the Congress ranks there were, of course, large numbers of idealists, but the door for careerists and opportunists was now more open than it has ever been before. Apart from Gandhiji's enigmatical and elusive personality, which dominated the scene, the Congress seemed to process two faces : a purely political side was developing like a caucus, and the other aspect was that of a prayer meeting, full of pietism and sentimentality.

One the Government side there was an air of triumph, in no way concealed, at what they considered the success of their policy in suppressing civil disobedience and its offshoot. The operation had been successful, and for the moment it mattered little whether the patient lived or died. They proposed to continue the same policy, with minor variations, even though the Congress had been for the moment brought round to some extent. They knew that such changes in national policy could only be temporary so long as the basic problem remained, and any relaxation on their part might lead to a more rapid growth than otherwise. Perhaps they also thought that in continuing to suppress the more advanced elements in the Congress or in the labour and peasant ranks, they would not greatly offend the more cautious leaders of the Congress.

To some extent my thoughts in Dehra Dun gaol ran along these channels. I was really not in a position to form definite opinions about the course of events, for I was out of touch. In Alipore I had been almost completely out of touch, in Dehra a newspaper of the Government's choice brought me partial and sometimes one-sided news. It is quite possible that contacts with my colleagues outside and a closer study of the situation would have resulted in my varying my opinion in some degree. Distressed with the present, I began thinking of the past, of what had happened politically in India since I began to take some part in public affairs. How far had we been right in what we had done? How far wrong? It struck me that my thinking would be more orderly and helpful if I put it down on paper. This would also help in engaging my mind in a definite task and so diverting it from worry and depression. So in the month of June 1934 I began this 'autobiographical narrative' in Dehra Dun gaol, and for the last eight months I have continued it when the mood to do so has seized me. Often there have been interval when I felt no desire to write; three of these gaps were each of them nearly a month long. But I managed to continue, and now I am nearing the end of this personal journey. Most of this has been written under peculiarly distressing circumstances when I was suffering from depression and emotional strain. Perhaps some of this is reflected in what I have written, but this very writing helped me greatly to pull myself out of the present with all its worries. As I wrote, I was hardly thinking of an outside audience; I was addressing myself, framing questions and answering them for my own benefit, sometimes even drawing some amusement from it. I wanted as far as possible to think straight, and I imagined that this review of the past might help me to do so.

Towards the end of July, Kamala's condition rapidly deteriorated, and within a few days became critical. On August 11th I was suddenly asked to leave Dehra gaol, and that night I was sent under police escort to Allahabad. The next evening we reached Prayag station in Allahabad and there I was informed by the District Magistrate that I was being released temporarily so that I might visit my ailing wife. It was six months to a day from the time of my arrest.

My release was temporary. I was given to understand that it was for a day or two or for such longer period as the doctors might think absolutely necessary. It was a peculiar position, full of uncertainty, and it was not possible for me to settle down to anything. A fixed period would have enabled me to know how I stood, and I would have tried to adjust myself to it. As it was, any day, at any moment, I might be taken back to prison.

The change was sudden and I was wholly unprepared for it. From solitary confinement to a crowded house with doctors, nurses, and relatives. My daughter Indira had also come from Santiniketan. Many friends were continually coming to see me and enquire after Kamala's health. The style of living was quite different; there were home comforts, better food. And colouring all this background was anxiety for Kamala's serious condition.

There she lay frail and utterly weak, a shadow of herself, struggling feebly with her illness, and the thought that she might leave me became an intolerable obsession. It was eighteen and a half years since our marriage, and my mind wandered back to that day and to all that these succeeding years had brought us. I was twenty-six at the time and she was about seventeen, slip of a girl, utterly unsophisticated in the ways of the world. The difference in our ages was considerable, but greater still was the difference in our mental outlook, for I was far more grown-up than she was. And yet with all my appearance of wordly wisdom I was very boyish, and I hardly realised that this delicate, sensitive girl's mind was slowly unfolding like a flower and required gentle and careful tending. We were attracted to each other and got on well enough but our backgounds were different and there was a want of adjustment. These maladjustments would sometimes lead to friction and there were many petty quarrels over trivialities, boy-and-girl affairs which did not last long and ended in a quick reconciliation. Both had a quick temper, a sensitive nature, and a childish notion of keeping one's dignity. In spite of this our attachment grew, though the want of adjustment lessened only slowly. Twenty-one months after our marriage, Indira, our daughter and only child, arrived.

Our marriage had almost coincided with new developments in politics, and my absorption in them grew. They were the Home Rule days, and soon after came Martial Law in the Punjab and Non-Co-operaiton, and more and more I was involved in the dust and tumble of public affairs. So great became my concentration in these activities that, all unconsciously, I almost overlooked her and left her to her own resources, just when she required my full co-operation. My affection for her continued and even grew, and it was a great comfort to know that she was there to help me with her soothing influence. She gave me strength, but she must have suffered and felt a little neglected. An unkindness to her would almost have been better than this semi-forgetful, casual attitude.

And then came her recurring illness and my long absences in prison, when we could only meet at gaol interviews. The Civil Disobedience Movement brought her in the front rank of our fighters, and she rejoiced when she too went to prison. We grew ever nearer to each other. Our rare meetings became precious, and we looked forward to them and counted the days that intervened. We could not get tired of each other or stale, for there was always a freshness and novelty about our meetings and brief period together. Each of us was continually making fresh discoveries in the other, though sometimes perhaps the new discoveries were not to our liking. Even our grown-up disagreements had something boyish and girlish about them. After eighteen years of married life she had still retained her girlish and virginal appearance; there was nothing matronly about her. Almost she might have been the bride that came to our house so long ago. But I had changed vastly, and though I was fit and supple and active enough for my age - and, I was told, I still possessed some boyish traits - my looks betrayed me. I was partly bald and my hair was grey, lines and furrows crossed my face and dark shadows surrounded my eyes. The last four years with their troubles and worries had left many a mark on me. Often, in these later years when Kamala and I had gone out together in a strange place, she was mistaken, to my embarrassment, for my daugher. She and Indira looked like two sisters.

Eighteen years of married life! But how many long years out of them had I spent in prison-cell, and Kamala in hospitals and sanatoria? And now again I was serving a prison sentences and out just for a few days, and she was lying ill, struggling for life. I felt a little irritated at her for her carelessness about her health. And yet how could I blame her, for her eager spirit fretted at her inaction and her inability to take her full share in the national struggle. Physically unable to do so, she could neither take to work properly nor to treatment, and the fire inside her wore down the body. Surely she was not going to leave me now when I needed her most? Why, we had just begun to know and understand each other really; our joint life was only now properly beginning. We relied so much on each other, we had to much to do together.

So, I thought as I watched her from day to day and hour to hour.

Colleagues and friends came to see me. They told me of much that had happened of which I was unaware. They discussed current political problems and asked me questions. I found it difficult to answer them. It was not easy for my mind to get away from Kamala's illness, and after the isolation and detachment of gaol I was not in a position to face concrete questions suddenly. Long experience had taught me that it is not possible to appraise a situation from the limited information available in gaol. Personal contacts were necessary for a proper mental reaction, otherwise the expression of opinion was likely to be purely academic and divorced from reality. It seemed also unfair to Gandhiji and my old colleagues of the Congress Working Committee for me to say anything definite regarding Congress policy before I had had the opportunity to discuss everything with them. My mind was full of criticism of much that had been done, but I was not prepared to make any positive suggestions. Not expecting to come out of prison just then I had not thought along these lines.

I had also a feeling that in view of the courtesy shown by the Gandhiji in allowing me to come to my wife, it would not be proper for me to take advantage of this for political purposes. I had given no undertaking or assurance to avoid any such activity, nevertheless I was continually being pulled back by this idea.

I avoided issuing any public statements except to contradict false rumours. Even in private I refrained from committing myself to any definite line of policy, but I was free enough with my criticisms of past events. The Congress Socialist Party had recently come into existence, and many of my intimate colleagues were associated with it. So far as I had gathered, its general policy was agreeable to me, but it seemed a curious and mixed assemblage and, even if I had been completely free, I would not have suddenly joined it. Local politics took up some of my time, for in Allahabad, as in several other places, there had been an extraordinarily virulent campaign during the election for the local Congress Committees. No principles were involved, it was purely a question of personalities, and I was asked to help in settling some of the personal quarrels that had arisen.

I had no desire whatever to go into these matters, nor had I the time. In spite of this some of the facts came to my notice and caused me great distress. It was surprising that people should get so vastly excited over local Congress elections. Among the most prominent were those who had retired during the struggle for various private reasons. With the withdrawal of civil disobedience those reasons ceased to have weight, and they emerged suddenly and carried on a fierce and often vulgar campaign against each other. It was extraordinary how the ordinary canons of decency were forgotten in the passionate desire to down the other party. I was especially grieved at the fact that Kamala's name and even her illness had been exploited for the purposes of these local elections.

Among the wider questions that were discussed was the Congress decision to contest the coming election to the Legislative Assembly. Many of the younger groups opposed this decision because they thought it was a return to parliamentary and compromising methods, but they suggested no effective alternative. Some of these opponents on grounds of high principle had, curiously enough, no objection to organisations other than the Congress running the elections. Their object seemed to be to leave the field clear to communal organisations. I felt disgusted with the local squabble and the kind of politics which were rapidly developing. I felt out of tune with them and a stranger in my own city of Allahabad. What could I do, I wondered, in this environment when the time came for me to attend to such matters?

I wrote to Gandhiji about Kamala's condition. As I thought I would be going back to prison soon and might have no other chance to do so, I gave him also some glimpse into my mind. Recent events had embittered and distressed me greatly, and my letter carried a faint reflection of this. I did not attempt to suggest what should be done or what should not be done; all I did was to interpret some of my reactions to what had happened. It was a letter full of barely suppressed emotion, and I learnt subsequently that it pained Gandhiji considerably.

Day after day went by and I waited for the summons to prison or some other intimation from Government. From time to time I was informed that further directions would be issued the next day or the day after. Meanwhile the doctors were asked to send a daily bulletin of my wife's condition to Government. Kamala had slightly improved since my arrival.

It was generally, believed, even by those who are usually in the confidence of the Government, that I would have been fully discharged but for two impending events - the full session of the Congress that was taking place in October in Bombay and the Assembly Elections in November. Out of prison I might be a disturbing factor at these, and so it seemed probable that I might be sent back to prison for another three months and then discharged. There was also the possibility of my not being sent back to gaol, and this possibility seemed to grow as the days went by. I almost decided to settle down.

It was the eleventh day after my release, August 23rd. The police car drove up and the police officer came upto me and told me that my time was up and I had to accompany him to Naini Prison. I bade good-bye to my people. As I was getting into the police car my ailing mother ran up again to me with arms outstretched. That face of hers hunted me for long. Shadow is itself unrestrained in its path while sunshine, as an incident of its very nature, is pursued a hundredfold by nuance. Thus is sorrow from happiness a thing apart; the scope of happiness, however, is hampered by the aches and hurts of endless sorrows.

I was back again in Naini Prison, and I felt as if I starting a fresh term of imprisonment. In and out, out and in; what a suttlecock I had become! This switching on and off shook up the whole system emotionally and it was not easy to adjust oneself to repeated changes. I had expected to be put in my old cell at Naini to which a previous long stay had accustomed me. There were some flowers there, originally planted by my brother-in-law, Ranjit Pandit, and a good veranda. But this old Barrack No. 6 was occupied by a detenu, a State prisoner, kept confined without trial or conviction. It was not considered desirable for me to associate with him, and I was therefore placed in another part of the gaol which was much more closed in and was devoid of flowers or greenery.

But the place where I spent my days and nights mattered little, for my mind was elsewhere. I feared that the little improvement that had taken place in Kamala's condition would not stand the shock of my re-arrest. And so it happened. For some days it was arranged to supply me in prison with a very brief doctor's bulletin daily. This came by a devious route. The doctor had to telephone it to the police headquarters and the latter then sent it on to the prison. It was not considered desirable to have any direct contacts between the doctors and the gaol staff. For two weeks these bulletins came to me, sometimes rather irregularly, then they were stopped although there was a progressive deterioration in Kamala's condition.

Bad news and the waiting for news made the days intolerably long and the nights were sometimes worse. Time seemed almost to stand still or to move with desperate slowness, and every hour was a burden and a horror. I had never before had this feeling in this acute degree. I thought then that I was likely to be released within two months or so, after the Bombay Congress Session, but those two months seemed an eternity.

Exactly a month after my re-arrest a police officer took me from prison on a brief visit to my wife. I was told that I would be allowed to visit her in this way twice a week, and even the time for it was fixed. I waited on the fourth day-no one came for me; and on the fifth, sixth, seventh. I became weary of waiting. News reached me that her condition was becoming critical again. What a joke it was, I thought, to tell me that I would be taken to see her twice a week.

At last the month of September was over. They were the longest and most damnable thirty days that I had ever experienced.

Suggestion were made to me through various intermediaries that if I could give an assurance, even an informal assurance, to keep away from politics for the rest of my term I would be released to attend on Kamala. Politics were far enough from my thoughts just then, and politics I had seen during my eleven days outside had disgusted me, but to give an assurance! And to be disloyal to my pledges, to the cause, to my colleagues, to myself! It was an impossible condition, whatever happened. To do so meant inflicting a mortal injury on the roots of my being, on almost everything I held sacred. I was told that Kamala's condition was becoming worse and worse and my presence by her side might make all the difference between life and death. Was my personal conceit and pride greater than my desire to give her this chance? It might have been a terrible predicament for me, but fortunately that dilemma did not face me in that way at least. I knew that Kamala herself would strongly dispprove of my giving any undertaking, and if I did anything of the kind it would shock her and harm her.

Early in October I was taken to see her again. She was lying almost in a daze with a high temperature. She longed to have me by her, but as I was leaving her, to go back to prison, she smiled at me bravely and beckoned to me to bend down. When I did so, she whispered : "What is this about your giving an assurance to Government? Do not give it!"

During the eleven days I was out of prison it had been decided to send Kamala, as soon as she was a little better, to a more suitable place for treatment. Ever since then we had waited for her to get better, but instead she had gone down-till and now, six weeks later, the change for the worse was every marked. It was futile to continue waiting and watching this process of deterioration, and it was decided to send her to Bhowali in the hills even in her present condition.

The day before she was to leave for Bhowali I was taken from prison to bid her good-bye. When will I see her again? It wondered. And will I see her at all? But she looked bright and cheerful that day, and I felt happier than I had done ere long.

5

Jail Life : The Anxiety

Nearly three weeks later I was transferred from Naini Prison to Almora district gaol so as to be nearer to Kamala. Bhowali was on the way, and my police escort and I spent a few hours there. I was greatly pleased to note the improvement in Kamala, and I felt her, to continue my journey to Almora, with a light heart. Indeed, even before I had reached her, the mountains had filled me with joy.

I was glad to be back in these mountains, and as our car sped along the winding road the cold morning air and the unfolding panorama brought a sense of exhilaration. Higher and higher we went : the gorges depended : the peaks lost themselves in the clouds : the vegetation changed till the firs and pines covered the hill-sides. A turn of the road would bring to our eyes suddenly a new expanse of hills and valleys with a little river gurgling in the depths below. I could not have my fill of the sight and I looked on hungrily, storing my memory with it, so that I might revive it in my mind when actual sight was denied.

Clusters of little mountains huts clung to the hill-sides, and round about them were tiny fields made by prodigious labour on every possible bit of slope. They looked like terraces from a distance, huge steps which sometimes went from the valley below right up almost to the mountain top. What enormous labour had gone to make nature yield a little food to the sparse population! How they toiled unceasingly only to get barely enough for their needs! Those ploughed terraces gave a domesticated look to the hillsides and they contrasted strangely with the bleaker or the more wooded slopes.

It was very pleasant in the daytime and, as the sun rose higher, the growing warmth brought life to the mountains and they seemed to lose their remoteness and become friendly and companionable. But how they change their aspect with the passing of day! How cold and grim they become when "Night with giant strides stalks o'er the world" and life hides and protects itself and leaves wild nature to its own. In the semi-darkness of the moonlight or starlight the mountains loom up mysterious, threatening, overwhelming, and yet almost insubstantial, and through the valleys can be heard the moaning of the wind. The poor traveller shivers as he goes his lonely way and sense hostility everywhere. Even the voice of the wind seems to mock him and challenge him. And at other times there is no breath of wind or other sound, and there is an absolute silence that is oppressive in its intensity. Only the telegraph wire perhaps hum faintly, and the stars seem brighter and nearer than ever. The mountains look down grimly, and one seems to be face to face with a mystery that terrifies. With Pascal one thinks : *"La silence eternal de ces espaces infini m'effraie"*. In the plains the nights are never quite so soundless; life is still audible there, and the murmuring and humming of various animals and insects break the stillness of the night.

But the night with its chill and inhospitable message was yet distant as we motored along to Almora. As we neared the end of our journey, a turn in the road and a sudden lifting of the clouds brought a new sight which I saw with a gasp of surprised delight. The snowy peaks of the Himalayas stood glistening in the far distance, high above the wooded mountains that intervened. Calm and inscrutable very seemed, with all the wisdom of past ages, mighty sentinels over the vast Indian plain. The very sight of them cooled the fever in the brain, and the petty conflicts and intrigues, the lusts and falsehoods of the plains and the cities seemed trivial and far away before their eternal ways.

The little gaol of Almora was perched up on a ridge. I was given a lordly barrack to live in. This consisted of one huge hall, fifty-one feet by seventeen, with a katcha, very uneven floor, and a worm-eaten roof which was continually coming down in little bits. There were fifteen windows and a door, or rather little there were so many barred openings in the walls, for there were no doors or windows. There was thus no lack of fresh air. As it grew colder some of the window-openings were covered with coir matting. In this vast expanse (which was bigger than any yard at Dehra Dun) I lived in solitary grandeur. But I was not quite alone, for at least two score sparrows had made their home in the broken-down roof. Sometimes a wandering cloud would visit me, its many arms creeping in through the numerous openings and filling the place with a damp mist.

Here I was locked up every evening at about five, after I had taken my last meal, a kind of high tea, at four-thirty; and at seven in the morning my barred door would be unlocked. In the daytime I would sit either in my barrack or outside in an adjoining yard, warming myself in the sun. I could just see over the enclosing walls the top of a mountain a mile or so away, and above me I had a vast expanse of blue sky dotted with clouds. Wonderful shapes these clouds assumed, and I never grew tired of watching them. I fancied I saw them take the shape of all manner of animals, and sometimes they would join together and look like a mighty ocean. Or they would be like a beach, and the rustling of the breeze through the deodars would sound like the coming in of the tide on a distant seafront. Sometimes a cloud would advance boldly on us, seemingly solid and compact, and then dissolve in mist as it came near and finally enveloped us.

I preferred the wide expanse of my barrack to a narrow cell, though it was lonelier than a smaller place would have been. Even when it rained outside I could walk about in it. But as it grew colder its cheerlessness became more marked, and my love for fresh air and the open abated when the temperature hovered about the freezing-point. The new year brought a good fall of snow to my delight, and even the drab surroundings of prison became beautiful. Especially beautiful and fairy-like were the deodar trees just outside the gaol walls with their garment of snow.

I was worried by the ups and downs of Kamala's condition, and a piece of bad news would upset me for a while, but the hill air calmed me and soothed me and I reverted to my habit of sleeping soundly. As I was on the verge of sleep I often thought what a wonderful and mysterious thing was sleep. Why should one wake up from it? Suppose I did not wake at all?

Yet the desire to be out gaol was strong in me, more than I had ever felt before. The Bombay Congress was over, and November came and went by and the excitement of the Assembly election also passed away. I half expected that I might be released soon.

But then came the surprising new of the arrest and conviction of Khan Abdul Ghaffar Khan and the amazing orders passed on Subhas Bose during his brief visit to India. These orders in themselves were devoid of all humanity and consideration; they were applied to one who was held in affection and esteem by vast numbers of his countrymen, and who had hastened home, in spite of his own illness, to the deathbed of his father-to arrive too late. If that was the outlook of the Government there could be no chance of my premature release. Official announcement later made this perfectly clear.

After I had been a month in Almora gaol I was taken to Bhowali to see Kamala. Since then I have visited her approximately every third week. Sir Samuel Hoare, the Secretary of State for India, has repeatedly stated that I am allowed to visit my wife once or twice a week. He would have been more correct if he had said once or twice a month. During the last three and a half months that I have been at Almora I have paid five visits to her. I do not mention this as a grievance, because I think that in this matter the Government have been very considerate to me and have given me quite unusual facilities to visit Kamala. I am grateful to them for this. The brief visits I have paid her have been very precious to me and perhaps to her also. The doctors suspended their regime for the day of my visit to some extent, and I was permitted to have fairly long talks with her. We came ever nearer to each other, and to leave her was a wrench. We met only to be parted. And sometimes I thought with anguish that a day might come when the parting was for good.

My mother had gone to Bombay for treatment, for she had not recovered from her ailment. She seemed to be progressing. One morning in mid-January a telegram brought a wholly unexpected shock. She had had a stroke of paralysis. There was a possibility of my being transferred to a Bombay prison to enable me to see her, but as there was a little improvement in her condition I was not sent.

January has given place to February, and there is the whisper of spring in the air. The bulbul and other birds are again to be seen and heard, and tiny shoots are mysteriously bursting out of the ground and gazing at this strange world. Rhododendrons make blood-red patches on the hill-sides, and peace and plum blossoms are peeping out. The days pass and I count them as they go, thinking of my next visit to Bhowali. I wonder what truth there is the saying that life's rich gifts follow frustration and cruelty and separation. Perhaps the gifts would not be appreciated otherwise. Perhaps suffering is necessary for clear thought, but excess of it may cloud the brain. Gaol encourages introspection, and my long years in prison have forced me to look more and more within myself. I was not by nature an introvert but prison life, like strong coffee or chnine, leads to introversion. Sometimes, to amuse myself, raw an outline of Professor McDougall's cube for the asurement of introversion and extroversion, and I gaze at to find out how frequent are the changes from one interpreter to another. They seem to rapid.

I followed from the newspapers supplied to me the proceedings of the Bombay session of the Congress. I was naturally interested in its politics and personalities. Twenty years' intimate association had tied me up so closely with it that my individuality had almost become merged in it, and far stronger than the claims of office and responsibility were the invisible bonds that tied me to that great organisation and to thousands of my old comrades. And yet I felt it difficult to get excited over its proceedings; in spite of some important decisions the whole session seemed to me a dull affair. The subjects that interested me were hardly discussed. What would I have done if I had been there, I wondered. I did not know for certain; I could not say how I would have reacted to the new conditions and my surroundings. And I saw no reason why I should force my mind to come to a difficult decision in prison when such a decision was wholly unnecessary then. The time would come when I would have to face the problems of the day and decide on my course of action. It was needless folly to anticipate that decision, even in the recesses of my mind, for circumstances would change before that choice was forced on me.

The two outstanding features of the Congress, as far as I could make out from my distant and secluded abode on the mountains, were : the dominant personality of Gandhiji and the exceedingly poor show that the communal opposition under Pandit Madan Mohan Malaviya and Mr. Aney put up. To all who have knowledge of the inner workings of the Indian massmind, as well as the middle-class mind, it was no surprise to find that Gandhiji continues to be far and away the master figure in India. Government officials and some secluded politicians often imagine, making the wish the father to the thought, that he is played out in the political field or, at least, that his influence has greatly declined. And then when he that any other life involving a renunciation of these ideals and a tame submission to superior force, would have been a wasted existence, full of discontent and inner sorrow.

To me these years have brought one rich gift, among many others. More and more I have looked upon life as an adventure of absorbing interest, where there is so much to learn, so much to do. I have continually had a feeling of growing up, and that feeling is still with me and gives a zest to my activities as well as to the reading of books, and generally makes life worthwhile.

In writing this narrative I have tried to give my moods and thoughts at the time of each event, to represent as far as I could my feelings on the occasion. It is difficult to recapture a past mood, and it is not easy to forget subsequent happenings. Later ideas thus must inevitably have coloured my account of earlier days, but my object was, primarily for my own benefit, to trace my own mental growth. Perhaps what I have written is not so much an account of what I have been but of what I have sometimes wanted to be or imagined to be.

Some months ago Sir C.P. Ramaswamy Aiyar stated in public that I did not represent mass-feeling, but that I was all the more dangerous because of my sacrifices and idealism and the fervour of my convictions, which he characterised as 'self-hypnotisation.' A person suffering from self-hypnosis can hardly judge himself and in any event, I would not presume to join issue on this personal matter with C.P. We have not met for many years, but there was a time long ago, when we were joint secretaries of the Home Rule League. Since then much has happened, and C.P. has risen by ascending spirals to dizzy heights and I have remained of the earth, earthy. There is little now in common between us except our common nationality. He is today a full-blooded apologist of British rule in India, especially during the last few years; and admirer of dictatorship in India and elsewhere, and himself a shining ornament of autocracy in an Indian State. We disagree about most things, I suppose, but we agree on one somewhat trivial subject. He is absolutely right when he says that I do not represent mass-feeling. I have no illusions on that point.

Indeed, I often wonder if I represent any one at all, and I am inclined to think that I do not, though many have kindly and friendly feelings towards me. I have become a queer mixture of the East and West, out of place everywhere, at home nowhere. Perhaps my thoughts and approach to life are more akin to what is called Western than Eastern, but India clings to me, as she does to all her children in innumerable ways; and behind me lie, somewhere in the subconscious, racial memories of a hundred, or whatever the number may be, generation of Brahmans. I cannot get rid of either that past inheritance or my recent acquisition. They are both part of me, and, though they help me in both the East and the West, they also create in me a feeling of spiritual loneliness not only in public activities but in life itself. I am a stranger and alien in the West. I cannot be of it. But in my own country also, sometimes, I have an exile's feeling.

The distant mountains seem easy of access and climbing, the top becomes, but as one approaches, difficulties appear, and the higher one goes the more laborious becomes the journey and the summit recedes into the clouds. Yet the climbing is worth the effort and has its own joy and satisfaction. Perhaps it is the struggle that gives value to life, not so much the ultimate result. Often it is difficult to know which is the right path; it is easier sometimes to know what is not right, and to avoid that is something after all. If I may quote, with all humility, the last words of the great Socrates : "I know not what death is - it may be a good thing, and I am not afraid of it. But I do know that it is a bad thing to desert one's past, and I prefer what may be good to what I know to be bad."

The years I have spent in prison! Sitting alone, wrapped in my thoughts, how many seasons I have seen go by following each other into oblivion! How many moons I have watched wax and wane, and the pageant of the stars moving along inexorably and majestically! How many yesterdays of my youth lie buried here; and sometimes I see the ghosts of these dead yesterdays rise up, bringing poignant memories, and whispering to me : "Was it worthwhile?" There is no hesitation about the answer. If I were given the chance to go through my life again, with my present knowledge and experience added, I would no doubt try to make many changes in my personal life : I would endeavour to improve in many ways on what I had previously done, but my major decisions in public affairs would remain untouched. Indeed, I could not vary them, for they were stronger than myself, and a force beyond my control drove me to them.

It is almost exactly a year since my conviction; a year has gone by out of the two years of my sentence. Another full year remains, for there are no remission this time, as simple imprisonment carries no such deductions. Even the eleven days that I was out in August last have been added on to the period of my sentence. But this year too will pass, and I shall go out and then? I do not know, but I have a feeling that a chapter of my life is over and another chapter will begin. What this is going to be I cannot clearly guess. The leaves of the book of life are closed.

Badenweiler, Schwarzwald,

October 25, 1935

In may last my left Bhowali for further treatment in Europe. After departure there were no more visits to Bhowali for me, no more fortnightly outings and drives on the mountain roads. I missed them, and Almora gaol seemed to be drearier than before.

News came of the Quetta earthquake, and for a while all else was forgotten. But not for long, for the Government of India does not allow us to forget it or its peculiar ways. Soon we learnt that Rajendra Prasad, the Congress President, and the man who knew more about earthquake relief work than almost any other person in India, was not permitted to go to Quetta and help in relief. Nor could Gandhiji or any other public man of note. Many Indian newspapers had their securities confiscated or writing articles on Quetta.

Everywhere the military mentality, the police outlook - in the Assembly, in civil government, in bombing on the Frontier. Almost it would seem that the British Government in India is permanently at war large sections of the Indian people.

The police are a useful and a necessary force, but a world full of policemen and the police bludgeon may not, perhaps, be a desirable place to live in. It has often been said that an unrestrained use of force degrades the user of it as it humiliates and degrades the object of it. Few things are more striking today in India than the progressive deterioration, moral, and intellectual, of the higher services, more especially the Indian Civil Service. This is most in evidence in the superior officials, but it runs like a thread throughout the service. Whenever occasion arises for making a fresh appointment to the higher ranks, the person who represents the new spirit best is inevitably chosen.

On September 4, I was suddenly discharged from Almora Gaol as news had come that my wife's condition was critical. She was under treatment in Badenweiler in the Schwarzwald in Germany. My sentence was 'suspended', I was told, and I was released five and half months before my time. I hurried to Europe by air.

Europe in turmoil, fearful of war and tumult and with economic crises always on the horizon; Abyssinia invaded and her people bombed; various imperialist systems in conflict and threatening each other; and England, the greatest of the imperialist Powers, standing up for peace and the League Covenant while it bombs and ruthlessly oppresses its subject peoples. But here in the Black Forest it is calm and peaceful, and even the swastika is not much in evidence. I watch the mists steal up the valley and hide the distant frontier of France and cover the landscape, and I wonder what lies behind them.

Five and a half years ago, sitting in my prison barrack in the Almora district gaol, I wrote the last line of the autobiography. Eight months later I added a postscript from Badenweiler in Germany. That autobiography, published in England, had a kindly reception from all manner of people in various countries, and I was glad that what I had written had brought India nearer to many friends abroad and had made them appreciate, to some extent the inner significance of our struggle for freedom.

My publisher recently asked me to add a new chapter to the book in order to bring it further up to date. His request is reasonable and I could not deny it. And yet I have found it no easy matter to comply. We live in strange times, when life's normal course has been completely upset. But a more serious difficulty confronted me. I wrote my autobiography entirely in prison, cut off from outside activity. I suffered from various humours in prison, as every prisoner does, but gradually I developed a mood of introspection and some peace of mind. How am I to capture that mood now, how am I to fit in with that narrative? As I glance through my book again, I feel almost as if some other person had written a story of long ago. The five years that have gone by have changed the world and left their impress upon me. Physically I am older of course, but it is the mind that has received shock and sensation again and again and had hardened, or perhaps matured. My wife's death in Switzerland ended a chapter of my existence and took away much from my life that had been part of my being. It was difficult for me to realise that she was no more and I could not adjust myself easily. I threw myself in my work, seeking some satisfaction in it, and rushed about from end to end in India. Even more than in my earlier days, my life became an alternation of hug crowds and intensive activity and loneliness. My mother's death later broke a final link with the past. My daughter was away studying at Oxford, and later under treatment in a sanatorium abroad. I would return to my home from my wanderings almost unwillingly, and sit in that deserted house all by myself, trying even to avoid interviews there. I wanted peace after the crowds.

But there was no peace in my work or my mind, and the responsibility that I had to shoulder often oppressed me very greatly. I could not align myself with various parties and groups; I did not even fit in with my closest colleagues. I could not function as I wanted to, and at the same time I prevented others from functioning as they wanted to. A sense of suppression and frustration grew and I became a solitary figure in public life, through vast crowds came to hear me and enthusiasm surrounded me.

I was affected more than others by the development of events in Europe and the Far East. Munich was shock hard to bear and the tragedy of Spain became a personal sorrow to me. As these years of horror succeeded one another, the sense of impending catastrophe overwhelmed me, and my faith in a bright future for the world became dim.

And now the catastrophe has come. The volcanoes in Europe spit fire and destruction, and here in India I sit on the edge of another volcano, not knowing when it may burst. It is difficult to tear myself away from the problem of the moment, to develop the mood of retrospection and survey these five years that have gone by, and write calmly about them. And even If I could do so, I would have to write another big book, for there is so much to say. I shall endeavour therefore, as best I may, to refer briefly only to certain events and development in which I have played a part or which have affected me.

I was with my wife when she died in Lausanne on February 28, 1936. A little before news had reached me that I had been Elected president of the Indian National Congress for the second time. I returned to India by air soon after and on my way, in Rome, I had a curious experience. Some days before my departure a message was conveyed to me that Signor Mussolini would like to meet me when I passed through Rome. In spite of my strong disapproval of the Fascist regime, I would ordinarily have liked to meet Signor Mussolini and to find out for myself what a person who was playing such an important part in the world's affairs was like. But I was in no mood for interviews then. What came in my way even more was the continuance of the Abyssinian campaign and my apprehension that such an interview would inevitably be used for purposes of Fascist propaganda. No denial from me would go far. I remembered how Mr. Gandhiji, when he passed through Rome in 1931, had a bogus interview in the *Giornale d'Italia* fastened on to him. I remembered also several other instances of Indians visiting Italy being used, against their wishes, for Fascist propaganda. I was assured that nothing of the kind would happen to me and that our interview would be entirely private. Still I decided to avoid it and I conveyed my regrets to Signor Mussolini.

I could not avoid going through Rome, however, as the Dutch K.L.M. airplane I was travelling by spent a night there. Soon after my arrival in Rome, a high official called upon me and gave me an invitation to meet Signor Mussolini that evening. It had all been fixed up, he told me. I was surprised and pointed out that I had already asked to be excused. We argued for an hour, till the time fixed for the interview itself, and then I had my way. There was no interview.

I returned to India and plunged into my work. Within a few days of my return I had to preside over the annual session of the National Congress. For some years, which I had spent mainly in prison, I had been out of touch with development. I found many changes, new alignments, a hardening on party lines within the Congress. There was an atmosphere of suspicion and bitterness and conflict. I treated this lightly, having confidence in my own capacity to deal with the situation. For a short while I seemed to carry the Congress in the direction I wanted it to go. But I realised soon that the conflict was deep-rooted and it was not so easy, to charm away the suspicion of each other and the bitterness that had grown in our ranks. I thought seriously of resigning from the presidentship but, realising that this would only make matters worse, I refrained.

Again and again, the next few months, I considered this question of resignation. I found it difficult to work smoothly with my own colleagues in the Congress executive, and it became clear to me that they viewed my activities with apprehension. It was not so much that they objected to any specific act but they disliked the general trend and direction. They had justification for this as my outlook was different. I was completely loyal to Congress decisions but I emphasized certain aspects of them, while my colleagues emphasized other aspects. I decided finally to rising and I informed Gandhiji of my decision. In the course of my letter to him I wrote that "since my return from Europe I have found that the meetings of the Working Committee exhaust me greatly; they have a devitalising effect on me and I have almost the feeling of being much older in years after every fresh experience. I should not be surprised if this feeling was also shared by my colleagues of the Committee. It is unhealthy experience and it comes in the way of effective work.

Soon afterwards a far-away occurrence, unconnected with India, affected me greatly and made me change my decision. This was the news of General Franco's revolt in Spain. I saw this rising, with its background of German and Italian assistance, developing into a European or even a world conflict. India was bound to be drawn into this and I could not afford to weaken our organisation and create an internal crisis by resigning just when it was essential for us to pull together. I was not wholly wrong in my analysis of the situation, though I was premature and my mind rushed to conclusions, which took some years to materialise.

The reaction of the Spanish War on me indicates how, in my mind, the problem of India was tied up with other world problems. More and more I came to think that these separate problems, political or economic, in China, Abyssinia, Spain, Central Europe, India, or elsewhere, were facets of one and the same world problem. There could be no final solution of any one of them till this basic problem was solved. And in all probability there would be upheaval and disaster before the final solution was reached. As peace was said to be indivisible in the present day world, so also freedom was indivisible, and the world could not continue for long part free, part unfree. The challenge of fascism and nazism was in essence the challenge of imperialism. They were twin brothers, with this variation, that imperialism functioned abroad in colonies and dependencies, while fascism and nazism functioned in the same way in the home country also. If freedom was to be established in the world not only fascism and nazism had to go but imperialism had to be completely liquidated.

This reaction of foreign events was not confined to me. Many others in India began, to some extent, to feel that way, and even the public was interested. This public interest was kept up by thousands of meeting and demonstration that the Congress organised all over the country in sympathy with the people of China, Abyssinia, Palestine and Spain. Some attempts were also made by us to send aid, in the shape of medical supplies and food, to China and Spain. This wider interest in international affairs helped to raise our own national struggle to a higher level, and to lessen somewhat the narrowness which is always a feature of nationalism. But, inevitably, foreign affairs did not touch the life of the average person, who was absorbed in his own troubles. The peasant was full of his growing difficulties, his appalling poverty, and of the many burdens that crushed him. The agrarian problem was, after all, the major problem of India and the Congress had gradually evolved an agrarian programme, which though going far, yet accepted the present structure.

It appears from your letter that you may also again be coming here. But at this point the letter has been cut, so nothing more can be known. Anyhow, if you come, I shall be very happy; and if you do not come, then it would be better still. Coming to jail again is to be doubly blessed. I say to perhaps because in the terminology of jail I am a 'second timer'. I am very proud when

I think of my good fortune. In my statement I referred to this. But one very significant aspect I had not thought it proper to mention in that statement because that was my personal affair and I did not like to state it to strangers. The reason for my being happy and being amazed at my good fortune was this, that I have got a father and mother who always placed a lofty ideal before me and always added to my strength and spirit. And my other near relations also have, according to the same ideal, tried to serve the nation. How many persons are there with such good fortune in the whole world? You have written something about renouncing the world. In a way it is correct; but in another, and probably in the real sense, I have seen the real world now and I am enjoying it fully. The earlier world now seems absolutely insignificant and useless. Now I understand a little what Jesus meant when he asked us to forsake the world and save the soul.

Do not conclude from all this that I am lost in metaphysical and philosophical matters and am running away from the ordinary, worldly, and state. Reading your letter some such ideas cropped up for a while and I have written them down. Ordinarily the time here is passed in children's games.

This letter has now become too long. The superintendent will be hard put to it to read it all. I have come to know that he has some special interest in my letters. This time he may get a bit tired!

With very much love,

Your loving son
Jawahar
(Prisoner No. 4126)

What are Jivan and Nikkoo doing these days?

To Father

District Jail
Lucknow
August 17, 1922

My dear Father,

I received a letter from Kamala (dated 12th), together with a note from mother, this afternoon and I hasten to write my allotted letter. It is already more than two weeks since I wrote my last letter, although it was not sent till much later. I do not know if the two weeks will be computed from the date of my sending the letter to the office or from the date of despatch. On the last occasion it took five days for the letter to be finally posted. I wonder what transpired during those five days. Was the poor letter lying unheeded and uncared for in a pigeon-hole of the office or in a file on the Superintendent's table? Or was it carefully and anxiously scanned and scrutinised , and perhaps translated, by the official hierarchy in this jail, lest a world or sentence should offend against His Majesty's Regulations or bring into contempt the King Emperor's representative even down to the Naibs and the apprentices who have been supplied for our behoof and betterment by a benign government? And how did it ultimately emerge from this scrutiny? Was it cut up and censored and sent to you in this turncated from? That a least you must know. Unhappily, I have to remain in the dark and hence may err again. It would be more sensible to enlighten me and point out the offending passages. But who am I to teach sense to the powers that be? I can continue to behave as of old and write whatever suggests itself to me regardless of the blue pencil or the scissors of the office. And so I proceed. I can certainly propose, even though the disposal may be in the hands of the worthy Superintendent. For a change, I am writing in English. Incidentally, this may suit the Superintendent also and save the trouble of translation etc.

I am sending this letter to you and to Allahabad as I do not know definitely the programme of mother and Kamala. Apparently they are not clear about it themselves. Kamala says they might return to Allahabad about the 25th or early in September with Nan.

In my last letter to Kamala I had written that I am happy that we got a sound reason for stopping the interviews, and had referred to Bapuji and others. This, I hear, the jail authorities have interpreted and declared to others as meaning that I have no complaint in jail, and it is only out of consideration for Gandhiji that I do not want to have interviews. This is completely wrong. It is, of course, my opinion that the greater the hardship imposed upon us, the greater the benefit, for it will make us stronger. For this reason I liked the hardship of having no interviews. I also thought that we should curb our becoming much too social. It is better to remain prepared for all eventualities in the future.

In jail everyone has a chance of acquiring sound self-discipline. But even if I had wanted to stop interviews, I would not have done it unless forced to do so. Just because of my whims I do not wish mother and others to be put to hardship. It is now more than a month since I saw anyone from outside. I have not been to any other barrack even during this period. My horizon is my barrack wall. From there the sun rises and there it sets. I am very happy all the same. I have gained a lot during this month. So long as the sky, the stars and the moon are visible there is no reason why I should be idle. These days, in particular, the beauty of the rains is seen almost every day, and it is delightful to watch the mutli-coloured clouds. The superintendent says that no beautiful or good thing should be allowed inside the jail (by accident he has said some things very true - very few of the nobler things of the world can enter here - truth, mercy, love etc., are stopped at the gate!). But it is a consolation that the jail authorities have not power to keep God and His nature out of jail.

What you have written about our not meeting each other has made me sad. I am confident that I shall see you and see you soon. What are a few months in the life of a person? And you have yet to complete your second half century. This idea (of not seeing me again) you have been thinking about for long. After gaining Swaraj we have much to do and Swaraj is now, I am sure, very close at hand, the progress made by us in the last year and a half surprises me. We have put life into a dead body. What is left now? There may probably not have another example of such stupendous progress in the whole world. We, who are engaged in the struggle, cannot see it clearly; but the rest of the world sees it and is amazed. I for one am very confident.

What use is it to see you for a short while? I don't feel satisfied seeing you for a few minutes, nor can we talk much.But you are always before my mind's eyes.

I have just come to know that some of our books are with Mahadeva Desai and Purshottam. I will enquire. But as far as I know Mahadeva has very few books. He is in another barrack. Ranga Iyer is in Fyzabad. He may now soon be released. What are you going to do about him?

Love to all. Give my love to Umar Sobhani. Indira must be very happy at Bombay.

This letter goes care of the address of Shankarlal. To what address should I sent the next letter? You may be somewhere near Madras at that time. I intend writing to Kamala this time and if no other address is sent to me, then to her also I will write care of Shankarlal. Writing letters from here reminds me of writing from abroad. From there I had to write every week and from here once every two weeks. I had had this habit of regular letter-writing for seven to eight years, so now I do not mind this.

Adab to Hakim Sahib. I still have a desire to serve him. He told me that he would call me to Delhi but he has not done so. Instead of Delhi I have reached the District Jail, Lucknow!

Have you taken any decision regarding the law books? My opinion is that if they are not disposed of quickly they will be damaged and become useless. You, me or anyone else like us cannot check the lists or ascertain their price. Give this job to some bookseller. I think, when you go to Calcutta, you should talk to Cambray to correct the lists, ascertain their price and, better still, buy the books. He may not pay much. But still, it will be better if we get rid of these law books. Cambray may pay a thousand or two less. But, if you do not sell them off immediately to him, the loss incurred would be ten times more and the problem would be with us all the time. But please keep any law books which have literary or political significance, such as political and State trials, books on constitutional law, etc.

If a man from Cambray comes, please ask him to make a list of the other books also and arrange them properly. They are in a very bad state these days as there is no one to look after them. The books are scattered in every room. My room is full of them. If you or I need any book it is found with great difficulty or is not traceable at all. Many books which I had asked for, it seems, are not traceable, though I am positive that they are there. I have sent here an extremely old edition (1887) of Bryce's Holy Roman Empire, but the new edition must be somewhere in the house. If lists are properly prepared and the books arranged in some order on the shelves, it will be convenient and you too would be able to find them easily.

I used to get from abroad the Nation and the New Statesman every week. I do not know if they are still received. If they do come, then please send them to me. I do not think the superintendent will have any objection. If they are not being received for abroad, then do not please renew the subscription. Please keep sending the modern Review. I want to see the issues of both June and July.

All the things sent by Kamala from Delhi to me as well as the rolls of cotton, two mats, etc., have reached me.

I do not need any money. I can cash a cheque whenever I want. I do not know the state of my bank account; perhaps I have an overdraft. I have asked Kamala, but she has not answered this question.

A day after my arrest there was to be an attachment of goods at Anand Bhawan to realise my fine. What happened to that? Have Rs. 100 been realised?

I had asked for a few notebooks, but I no longer need them. I am getting good notebooks made in the jail itself.

Our charkhas are working well but still I want to have the new style charkha from Sabarmati Ashram. I asked Maganlal Bhai last March to sent me one, but he has not done so. Please write to him to send me a charkha direct to the jail address. Particular care should be taken of the spindle. He should also send one of the carding machines made in the Ashram.

You were planning to retain Ram Chandra. Is he working as your Secretary?

I am learning Urdu these days, and hope to write to you soon in Urdu. Please send me an Urdu dictionary. Ram Narain Lal published one, and it should be in Anand Bhawan.

I am worried to know that Nanni is not improving in health. You wrote that she may not be able to go to Bombay. If she cannot go to Bombay from Ahmedabad, how will she return to Allahabad?

All the political prisoners from Agra have now come here - Joseph, Mahadev, Bal Krishna Kaul and others. Bal Krishna is to be released in a few days.

I am so pleased to read about you in the newspaper. We are all very attentively following your programme and been greatly impressed with the whole-heartedness of your efforts. I am only worried about your health. If you looked after it, then you could work better than many young men.

Polak was here a couple of days back to see me and Devdas but as we had stopped interviews, we refused to see him. I do not know what reported to him and how he took it. He is an extreme moderate these days, and perhaps could not understand our principle. I do not want him to think that we were annoyed with him and so did not meet him.

You need not worry at all about my health. I am looking after it carefully and I think jail life will do it some good. It is not so hot now, and the heat affected me very little. At Allahabad you may remember, I did not have a fan in my office. When I had got used to that heat and could stand it easily, this is nothing. The nights are pretty cold and during the day also there is often a pleasant breeze. Sometimes, of course, it is humid, but I am not worried about that. So please do not send me any kind of fan. A fan, if it arrived, would disturb me. Most fans I do not like and small electric fans too are no good. But even if there be any good fan, I do not want it. I find the accumulation of luggage in the barrack a nuisance.

I received the books sent by you. I have now got the following :

1. Memoirs of Babar
2. Sarkar's Shivaji
3. Bernier's Travels
4. Vincent Smith's Akbar
5. Manucci's Storia do Mogor - 4 vols.
6. Bryce's Holy Roman Empire
7. Poems of Keats
8. Poems of Shelley
9. Tennyson's Idylls of the King
10. Arnold's Light of Asia
11. Havell's Aryan Rule in India (this came separately)
12. Pater's Renaissance (received yesterday)

I had asked for many other books which are in Anand Bhawan but have not yet been sent. Perhaps nobody could find them, but please look for them again. I do not want these books to be bought again. I am certain that the books whose names I have written are in Anand Bhawan. Please tell Nand Kishore to look for them carefully once more. The names are given in my previous letter, so there is no need to list them again.

I have not as yet got the almirah for books. The earlier it comes the better, otherwise the books may be damaged. The almirah should be small and fitted with a lock. Kishan Bhai is probably not in Lucknow these days, for otherwise he would have arranged for this. It will be difficult for Govind Malaviya to send the almirah from Allahabad. Please ask Shiv Raj Narayan, Mohanlal Saxena or Ram Chandra (if any of these be in Lucknow) and they will procure it for me.

I had heard about The Independent and Upson. You did very well by making over all the responsibility to others. Upson's salary seems to be a bit high, but sitting here I can't say anything. I hope the new manager will be better. Economy should be fully observed.

I have received your detailed programme and so am sending this letter to Bombay to the address of Shankarlal. After Bombay and Poona, I think, mother and Kamala should come back to Allahabad and rest for a few days. It does not seems necessary just yet for Kamala to go to Calcutta. There will be many other chances later to see the city. The weather also is not good there these days and her going will cause inconvenience to you.

Please meet Grimwood Mears. I hear he is very cross with me and he also gave his opinion against me in my case. Had it come up before him, he would have extended the term of imprisonment. I have for a long time been expecting him to take action against new and to debar me from the courts. I would like to give him a bit of my mind.

I had asked for the statement and accounts from the Allahabad Bank, Calcutta, for income tax purposes and consult Birju Bhai. You would have done whatever was necessary regarding the income tax. As for the shares, please do consult Jamna Lalji. Send a copy of the statements to Burju Bhai also. There is hardly any scope for dividing the shares or changing the ownership. I do not remember whether we got the money from the British India Corporation Ltd. Please enquire from the bank, and if we have not got the money, then write to the Corporation.

I heard from Miss Hooper yesterday about her going back to Allahabad. She is coming to town soon and I hope to see her then.

I have already written to you on the subject of my marriage and have left the matter entirely in your hands. You have not told me yet who the girl in question is. I might possibly have seen her or heard of her in the days of my infancy.

It is good of Sir Robert Aikman to be so impressed by my manners. Personally I do not think that is a very great compliment to me. It shows that I must be particularly inane person if there is nothing more shrinking about me than my manner. Even as regards the latter some people differ from Sir Robert. I happened to come across Mrs. Kazim Hussein at some function or other last summer. I had not seen her for years and of course did not recognise her. She apparently thoughts that I had intentionally cut her, and she told some people afterwards that I was a conceited prig and wanted taking down a peg or two. Her husband, whom I had previously met and spoken to, fortunately had a different opinion of me, and stood up for me. Poor Mrs. Kazim Hussein is not quite all there since the death of her daughter.

I suddenly developed a violent cough last week which prevented me from sleeping for a night or two. I don't know what it was due to, but I have hardly smoked since then and it is very much better now.

With love,

from your loving son
Jawahar

I hope you had yourself photographed in your court dress. I should like to have a copy of it.

To Father

30 Gloucester Terrace
Dec. 22nd, 1911

My dear Father,

. . . . As regards my marriage, you know my views well enough and it is hardly necessary for me to repeat them here. I do not, and cannot possibly, look forward with relish to the idea of marrying a girl who I do not know. At the same time I acknowledge that your solution of the difficulty is the only one, if it is taken for granted that I am to marry a Kashmiri girl. And on the whole, I think, it would not be particularly pleasing to most people concerned if I married a non-Kashmiri. If she was the Blue Bird you were in search of it would be a different matter, but Blue Birds are as rare in the non-Kashmiris as in the Kashmiris. If you are intent on my getting engaged to the girl you mention I have no objection to offer. Only I should like you to put off till I have seen her. That ought not to disarrange matters very much as I expect to be back in India before long. If you think you cannot manage this then you are welcome to do as you wish and I shall abide by your decision. . . .

With love,

From your loving son
Jawahar

To Father

30 Gloucester Terrace W.
29-12-11

My dear Father,

Your last letter came from Delhi and contained an account of the State entry. Your next I hope will be about the Durbar itself, and will contain all about the Gaekwar incident. The papers here have said a lot about it but none of them given a complete account. I think it was silly of the Gaekwar to do as he did, and sillier still to humbly apologise for it after he had done it. But silliest of all was his justification to the *Times.*

I have made up my mind to leave London for a few days at least and am going to Matlock in Derbyshire tomorrow I may stay there for a week or more. In any case I shall be back by the 15th when the bar lectures begin. I wanted to go for Christmas but I have been rather hard up lately and could not make up my mind to go. The result was I had a perfectly sickening Christmas here and resolved to go out of town for the New Year at any cost. I have borrowed money for the purpose and thereby again increased my debts which were gradually lessening themselves. At the present moment, you will be surprised to hear, I believe I owe about $150! I am afraid I have no money sense. The more I attempt to economise the less I succeed in doing so. I do not know how much I have spent in the course of this year, but I know it must be far more than I have ever done before. And yet I have never been flush and have always been trying to economise for the last 12 or 14 months! It is a jolly good thing that I am returning home soon, otherwise I might conceivably get into trouble.

Wednesday, April 23

Had an unwelcome visitor-a scorpion-in my cell. Can't make out where he came from - There is so much sweeping and cleaning going on.

The way a jail is run in India is not unlike the British Govt. of India. There is great efficiency in the apparatus of the govt. - which goes to strengthen the hold of the govt. of this country - and little or no care of the human material of the country. Outwardly this jail must appear efficiently run and to some extent this must be true. But no one seems to think that the main purpose of the prison must be to improve and help the unhappy individuals who come to it. Break them! That is the idea - So that by the time they go out they may not have an atom of spirit left in them.

Monday, 28 April

Two weeks!

All round me I have prisoners sentenced to life imprisonment. Many of them have already spent ten or fifteen years in jail - some over twenty. For years and years they have not seen a child or a woman or even horse or a dog. What a terrible outlook! A lifer! As I was walking outside my barrack early this morning a CO asked me : What of us lifers? Will swaraj take us out of this hell?

Mostly they come in the gang cases. In each case a hundred or more may be convicted mostly for life or 20 years. Some of them are probably guilty but even so a life sentence is terrible. But most must be innocent - It is quite enough to look at them and say that they have not got spirit enough for big crime. Usually they get sentenced in batches on the evidence of some approvers.

My cook is a lifer - a more harmless individual it is difficult to imagine. His story is that some distant relative wanted to rape his widowed daughter and in a fit of rage he stuck a knife into him. He is over 60 now and has been in jail for two or three years or more.

The Sup. casually told me today that my bed is going to be changed up in future! It was an amazing proposition and it took me by surprise. It appears that this precautionary measure is not for my sake but for the sake of the other five convicts in my barrack, lest they use my bed to climb over the wall. How they can do so with me in the bed it is a little difficult to imagine. So from tonight onwards when my bed is taken out of the cell, it will forthwith be chained.

Thursday, May Day

I am very worried about Classes. A and B and C. It is annoying enough to sit idly no active work when people outside are working away for all they are worth. I sit and read when mother and Kamala and Nan and Betty picket in the hot sun! It is even more annoying to find that I am the only person here in Naini Jail getting this Class A treatment. Even Narmada Prasad has not been given it. I understand he will have to put on prison clothes and do prison work. This is getting on my nerves and I can't stand it. I hinted as much to father in yesterday's letter. I shall wait for my interview with him in two or three days. Afterwards, I shall write to the Govt. or the Sup.

I have given up sleeping in the afternoon. The news from outside during the last few days has made me feel too excited to sleep. It seems such a futile way of spending any part of the day. I feel very proud and happy at the part mother and Kamala and Nath and Betty are taking in the campaign. Altogether the country seems to be doing splendidly. How can this wonderful energy and enthusiasm fail? Oh! to be in the fray and not to sit idly by, behind high walls.

Wednesday, 7 May

A painful incident, but not unusual in jails, took place today. I do not know all the facts but it appears that the new assistant jailer, Chhatar Singh, who has recently come from Agra, has not made himself very popular. Within a few days in his attempts to cow down the prisoners in the barrack entrusted to him he had them beaten repeatedly with shoes, etc. Today he produced someone before the Supt. for some petty jail offence and it is doubtful if there was any offence. Some punishment was given, fetters or some such thing. On coming out of the Supt.'s room, in the head jailer's office this man suddenly hit Chhatar Singh. He had not a shadow of a chance. The head jailer immediately gave the order to the *pukkas, lambardars,* etc. to fall on him came! But for us man is naturally more interesting than all the great animals that existed before him; he is interesting because he brought a new thing with him which the others do not seem to have had. This was mind curiosity the desire to find out and learn. So from the earliest days began man's quest. Observe a little baby, how it looks at the new and wonderful world about it; how it begins to recognize things and people; how it learns. Look at a little girl; if she is a healthy and wide-awake person she will ask so many questions about so many things. Even so, in the morning of history when man was young and the world was new and wonderful, and rather fearsome to him, he must have looked and stared all around him, and asked questions. Who was he to ask except himself? There was no one else to answer. But he had a wonderful little thing - a mind - and with the help of this, slowly and painfully, he went on storing his experience and learning from them. So from the earliest times until today man's quest has gone on, and he has found out many things, but many still remain, and as he advances on his trail, he discovers vast new tracts stretching out before him, which show to him how far he is still from end of this quest if thee is such an end.

What has been this quest of man, and whether does he journey? For thousands of years men have tried to answer these questions. Religion and philosophy and science have all considered them, and given many answers. I shall not trouble you with these answers, for the sufficient reason that I do not know most of them. But, in the main, religion has attempted to give a complete and dogmatic answer, and has often cared little for the mind, but has sought to enforce obedience to its decisions in various ways. Science gives a doubting and hesitating reply, for it is of the nature of science not to dogmatize, but to experiment and reason and rely on the mind of men. I need hardly tell you that my preferences are all for science and the methods of science.

We may not be able to answer these questions about man's quest with any assurances, but we can see that quest itself has taken two lines. Man has looked outside himself as well as inside; he has tried to understand Nature, and he has also tried to understand himself. The quest is really one and the same, for man is part of Nature. 'Know thyself', said the old philosophers of India and Greece; and the Upanishads contain the record of the ceaseless and rather wonderful strivings after this knowledge by the old Aryan Indians. The other knowledge of Nature has been the special province of science, and our modern world is witness to the great progress made therein. Science, indeed, is spreading out its wings even farther now, and taking charge of both lines of this quest and co-ordinating them. It is looking up with confidence to the most distant stars, and it tells us also of the wonderful little things in continuous motion - the electrons and protons - of which all matter consists.

The mind of man has carried man a long way in his voyage of discovery. As he learnt to understand Nature more he has utilized it and harnessed it to his own advantage, and thus he has won more power. But unhappily he has not always known how to use this new power, and he has often misused it. Sciences itself has been used by him chiefly to supply him with terrible weapons to kill his brother and destroy the very civilization that he has built up wish so much labour.

Friday, 29 July

I feel angry again today. I have seen in the paper that the govt. have revised their own sentence on Ranjit about stoppage of interviews. Originally it was for a month. Now the stoppage is for three months and correspondence also banned! Heigh ho! What disgusting meanness. Perhaps this enhanced punishment is due to my writing and making a fuss - but I did not write about Ranjit's interviews at all. I wrote only about the insult to mother. Or perhaps Ranjit has himself written a stiff letter to govt. Feel like swearing. This is the dept. of the noble Nawab of Chhatari, Home Member!

I am quite sure now that I shall not have interviews with Kamala, mother and Indu for a long time now till I am discharged. The govt. has got too much of a swelled head to confess a mistake; and I have got too much of a swelled head to tolerate any slight. It is already a month and a half since I met Kamala and mother.

Thursday, 22 September

What a capacity Bapu has got for giving shocks to people! A week ago - on the 14th - I read about his decision to 'fast unto death' in disapproval of the separate electorates given by Ramsay MacDonald's award to Depressed Classes. Suddenly all manner of ideas rushed into my head - all kinds of possibilities and contingencies rose up before me - and upset my equilibrium completely. For two days nearly I was in darkness with no light to show the way out, my heart sinking when I thought of some results of Bapu's action. The personal aspect was powerful enough and I thought with anguish that I might not see him again. It was on board ship that I saw him last, over a year all the time. Ranjit apparently had a lot to say about Kamala, etc. but under the circumstances he refrained. This put me out still further. I am sure I must have looked disagreeable and given mother and Ranjit the impression that I was unhappy. What a thing to do! Having misbehaved in the morning, I cursed myself all day for it and felt thoroughly depressed. Temperature went up to 99°F. Probably due to the exitement and subsequent depression. Before going to sleep wrote a long letter to Kamala with a note to Indu - Bad night.

I sent my letter to Kamala this morning to the Supt. It contained a rather strongly and sarcastically worded description of the double supervision on my interview yesterday. The police official specially came in for a bit of frank expression of opinion on my part - I wonder if the Supt. will object to any part of the letter. . . .

Father's *barsi* today - I am fasting the whole day and till tomorrow monring - 36 hours. I am not quite clear why I should fast but I was so annoyed with myself on February 6 when even Indu fasted and I did not, that I have to do something of the kind now - my companions are also more or less fasting.

I have been thinking a great deal of father lately. Not because of the *barsi* but because I am in jail. Almost all my latest memories of him are jail memories, and being again in prison my mind goes back to him again and again.

Wednesday, 9 March

Of all the ordinary prisoners with us the lowest in the social scale - the sweeper-is the smartest, cleanest and most intelligent looking. He is the only person who can read Hindi with some ease. And the most unintelligent and illiterate are the two Brahmans! I have given a Hindi book to Shibbu the sweeper and primers to others - not the Brahmans who are not very keen about learning anything. Every evening after they are locked up Shibbu and the others sit round a miserable lamp and try to read - Shibbu being the teacher. This is done after work hours, after lock up in the barrack for the night. Still the warder objected to it and threatened to report to the jailer!

7 April

To Vijaya Lakshmi Pandit and Krishna Hutheesing

What is the good of going to jail if one does not improve in health and weight! Prison is the best of universities if only one knows how to take naturalist, that is lover of nature, and flowers and animals. I found it delightful to read his beautiful prose and to gallop with him (in imagination alas!) over the boundless plain, and to rejoice with him when the golden flower sang, and to go in search of birds' eggs and rare flowers, and live in the open air with the sky and the earth companions and friends. All manner of birds and beasts meet one in his pages-ostriches and flamingos and strange frogs and curious snakes. Strange that this fascinating book of childhood was written by Hudson when he was nearly eighty years in far away London. How his childhood lived for him even in his old age! Even the beautiful title of the book - *Far Away and Long Ago* - is full of wistfulness and longing for the days that were past.

As I read Hudson, I began to think, also rather wistfully, of my own boyhood and especially of the horses I had had and the fine rides I used to have. How splendid it is to gallop away, the horse's feet spurning the ground, and the cold wind rushing past you! It is long since I have ridden or possessed a horse to ride, and you, my dear, have had no decent chance at all. But if we cannot ride horses we can ride the wind and the whirlwind and they are even swifter.

17 November

To the Superintendent, District Jail, Dehra Dun

I thank you for showing me the letter from the U.P. Government dated November 12, 1932 regarding my interviews and the treatment to be given to my mother and wife. I am obliged to the government for their assurance that it is far from their intention 'that any insult should be offered to "my" relations or for the matter of that, to any Indian lady'. As this is the official policy of government I should like them to consider why and how it was that insult was offered to my mother and wife on 27 May, 1932 by the jailer of the Allahabad District Jail, who shouted at them angrily and offensively for some time and then hustled them out of his jail. In the course of her sixty and odd years of life my mother has not had to face such treatment on any other occasion and from any other person, and I trust that government will appreciate that it is natural for me to resent such treatment of my mother in her old age. The shock to her was considerable, and, although circumstances and domestic affliction have hardened her, she shrinks even now from the idea of having a jail interview. Almost her sole remaining attachments in life are to her children, and all three of them happen to be in prison. Yet for five months now she has not seen them. I have tried to include her at least to visit my sisters in the Lucknow Central Prison. But she has not agreed, partly because of the Allahabad Jail incident and the action government took on it, and partly because of some new jail regulations according to which she must sit far apart and must not touch even her daughters during interviews.

I would also request government to consider what actually happened in the Allahabad District Jail on May 27 . . . .

I am writing at length about this incident not merely for a personal reason, although I have suffered enough during the last five months, but on wider grounds also. If government are still of the opinion that they have acted correctly in awarding the punishments I have nothing further to say to them. If however they feel, as I think they must, that they were misled and thus made to err, they should at least say so.

This little incident has a wider significance. Government rely completely on their jail officials for the conduct of their jail, and each official relies on the one below him. Thus when any untoward occurrence takes place in jail, the government version of it made public or stated by the Home Member with all due solemnity in the Council Chamber, can be traced back to a petty jail official whose account, having passed through various channels, has at last reached the top and been adopted by it. It is not checked or verified in any satisfactory manner, for the only persons who might help in doing so are the prisoners who cannot be encouraged in this way. So It happens that government often make statements which all the world in jail, including both official and prisoner, know perfectly well to be wholly untrue or largely exaggerated. On the basis of these reports and statements government proceed to punish people in the name of discipline. The other side is seldom even heard and even when it reaches the ears, it is not listened to. The petty breach of discipline may have been provoked by deliberate insult and attempt to humiliate, but this is not know outside the high walls of prison, although it might be notorious enough inside that limited world.

I would therefore request government to give me the same treatment which they are now giving to my colleagues who were till lately in Fyzabad jail.

I regret that this letter has become so long. I have felt deeply on the matters referred to in this letter and I have come to the conclusion that I owed it to government and to myself to write fully and frankly. I have tried to do so after careful though in what I hopes is restrained and unadorned language. May I beg of you to send this letter of mine to the U.P. Government and to communicate to me any answer that you may receive in regard to it?

Friday, November 25

I feel weary and tired and stale. Thoughts of Kamala's illness, and Indu, far away, and all the world going awry, and knaves and scoundrels in the seats of authority shouting and haranguing and threating, and good men silent, and fools, oh! so many of them everywhere!

November 29

To Indira Nehru

Boys and girls are taught history in schools by means of dull uninteresting books. But the real way to learn history is to see the nation's art and music and literature. But of course the best way of all for you is to wait of the great history I am writing for you!

Do you know, when I was at Ellora seven or eight years ago, I went for a strange quest. It struck me that all the thousand of statues of men there were beardless. Beards evidently were not in fashion in those days. Then I hunted and hunted and discovered once full-grown beard. I wonder if you will finds it - or you may do better than I did, and find several.

January 5, 1933

To Mahatma Gandhi

The stopping of interviews has made me retire a little more into myself but I have had pleasing and friendly neighbours - the Himalayas. The sight of their outline against the sky, and now their summits and sides covered with fresh snow, have meant a great deal to me. They seem to rouse in me ancient memories of the long ago when perhaps my ancestors wandered about the mountains of Kashmir and played in their snow and glaciers. I have had companions here but largely I have been left to myself, and I have grown a little contemplative, in defiance of heredity and family tradition and personal habit! But that is a thin veneer which I am afraid will rub off at little provocation. How can the Ethiopian change his skin?

March 7

To Mahatma Gandhi

Thanks you for your letter and the first two copies of *Harijan*. I read through the *Harijan* of course with interests, and was delighted to see the old rapier touch of overmuch kindness and inexhaustible patience which extinguishes, or as you say neutralizes, the opponent. I pity the poor Sanatanists. With their anger and abuses and frantic cursing, they are no match of this kind of subtle attack. And yet the power of stupidity and conservatism and entrenched privilege in this world is amazing. Even mahatmas and saints cannot easily upset this combination unless circumstances have prepared the ground. Have you read Benard Shaw's *Saint Joan* - the play about Joan of Arc? If not I wish you would do so, and especially the preface of the play. It is quite a little thing and will not take much time. A short while ago I sent a copy of the book to Indu and you could easily commander it from her.

The tribe of Sanatanists is of course doomed because they are relics of a bygone age. Their very anger shows the extent of the danger that confronts them. Under strain all tolerance disappears, and their intolerance at present is a sign of the great strain you are putting on them. It is all very well for the likes of Sapru and me (a curious combination!) to talk pompously and in a superior way of our tolerance in matters of religion when neigher of us has any religion worth talking about; or for us to bless the movement for temple entry when neither has the remotest desire to go within a hundred miles of a temple except, so far as I am concerned, to see the architecture and the statuary! But touch either of us on some particular subject and you will find the raw side and there will be little of tolerance then. Who is more intolerant than you are in certain matters? The fact is real tolerance hardly exists; what goes under the name of tolerance is indifference. What we do not value we make a virtue of tolerating in others. A person who is not prepared to be aggressively intolerant about something or another is a pretty useless individual. So I fell a little sympathy - of an inverted kind - for the Sanatanists. They value something for which they are prepared to fight. The issue is clarified. The dangerous people are always those who are dodging and avoiding difficulties in an effort to ignore them or forget them, or are looking at them with one eye only!

Of course, if you will stir up stagnant matter there will be a bad smell, and the Hindu social structure has stangnated long enough in all conscience. My own remedy for a stagnant pool would be to drain it completely and let the sun dry and purify the bottom and the sides. Cool fresh water can then be poured in and arrangements made for it to keep running on, so that there may be no stagnation again. Superficial drawing can never clean the accumulations of filth at the bottom. But you are emptying the tank to some extent and maybe we shall see the bottom! . . .

But I must protest against the apology for an envelope in which your letter came. If Vallabhbhai is responsible for it, much as I love him, I must make it clear that envelop-making is not his strong line. Or perhaps the fault is not entirely his when the raw material he is supplied which comes from the waste-paper-basket.

Forgive me for my superficiality. I like my diamonds smooth and polished. You have shown us the art and style of living life in the grand manner. That is the real thing, but why should we ignore style and art in the little things of life? Most of us cannot reach the snowy heights. Would you deprive us of the flowers in the valleys?

Sunday, March 12

It is Holi today - all through the morning I heard sounds of revelry outside. Shouting and singing and dancing. I felt what a good festival Holi was and I felt a trifle lonely to be sitting all by myself when the world was dancing outside. I felt so even though I take no part in Holi outside. What then must the average prisoner feel on this day? He must be terribly homesick and lonesome. Holi is a holiday in jail which means that the prisoners are kept locked up nearly the whole day, there being no work for them.

In the afternoon suddenly, as I was dozing my dhobi (who is not a prisoner) turned up to pay a Holi visit to me! It was a surprise, an extraordinarily pleasant surprise. We embraced and he sprinkled some *gulal* on me and presented me with a plateful of really good sweets. I was greatly touched.

Strange how suddenly a physical longing for the soft things of life comes on me - pleasant surrounding, good friends, agreeable women, interesting conversation. Reading a newspaper yesterday I came across some names of old acquaintances - and their pictures were there - and the old days when I was a student in England came before me - and a certain nostalgia - We live in different worlds and I have not seen some of them for a score of years. The dhobi who came to visit me is nearer to me than the princes and princesses of old.

Sunday, March 26

Just as I was picking out a new razor blade to shave - my best, news came that Kamala was not coming today but tomorrow. The day suddenly seemed very long. I had a bright idea that I might wash and clean up everything including the *newar* and which has been given to me and which badly needs a wash. So the day was spent in rubbing and scrubbing, and taking the bed to pieces and washing the *newar* (several hundred feet of it) and generally in fairly continuous physical activity. We - two other convicts and I began at 8 in the morning. At 1 was quite exhausted and we broke off. After an hour or so we started again and did not finish finally till about 6 in the evening. Far the greater part of the time was spent on the bed or rather in cleaning the *newar* and then drying it and lastly weaving it on the bed.

May 5

To Mahatma Gandhi

I suppose it is this close confinement that affects the nerves. And then when any news comes in letters or newspaper that I do not like it upsets me far more than it should. Kamala is again in the trip of her old disease and this news has oppressed me. Indu does not write to me and I get very angry. So during the last few days I have been full of irritation against Kamala and Indu and the world generally. Curious when one is in a bad mood how one finds excuses for it and picks at otherwise trivial matters in the past. It is not Kamala's fault that she is again laid up. What is the poor girl to do? But this means that I shall be lonelier here than ever. And my mind goes back to all the petty grievances I have had against her in the past and dwells on them and this increases my ill-humour. I fight against this with little success while it lasts. Gradually it goes away. If I have to write a letter during this fit of ill-humour the letter is bound to be a harsh and unfriendly one. I wrote yesterday to Kamala and others. I had not quite recovered and in spite of all my efforts my letter was harsh and I am afraid will pain her.

Indu has passed her exam and must be excited and expecting congratulations and the like. Instead I have not even written to her! . . . .

Back of all this in my mind I suppose is dissatisfaction at the political situation and this finds its way out in domestic entanglements and worries which I would hardly notice otrhewise.

June 15

To Indira Nehru

About Vakil's suggestion that you might take Soniben's cottage at Santiniketan and set up a separate establishment there with a cook, etc., I am afraid I do not agree at all. I dislike very much the idea of your keeping apart from the 'common herd' and requiring all manner of special attention, just as the Prince of Wales does when he goes to school or college. This seems to me to savour of vulgarity and snobbery. It is a bad beginning to make in any place to shout out to the people there that they are inferior beings and you are a superior person requiring special and particular treatment. Do you think any self respecting boy or girl would came to make friends with you under these circumstances? And what would the teachers and professors, who run the college there, feel? Would they not feel that they had been insulted to some extent by our having made our own arrangement over their heads? No, this kind of thing will never do. Wherever we go we must keep on a level with our surroundings and not imagine that we are better or superior. It is better not to go to a place than to go as a superior person. If you ever desire to work among village folk or for factory workers, how do you think you would like with them or visit them? As a society lady with a scented handkerchief to keep off the bad smells, occasionally patronizing them or doling out charity to them? That is not the way to meet your kind or to do human service. This method of charity and condescension irritates me exceedingly and I have no use for it.

I think I have told that it has long been my desire that a part of your education - and every boy's and girl's education - should consist of real honest work in a factory or in the fields. Unfortunately this cannot be arranged in India under present conditions but this idea of mine will give you some notion of what I think of education. If you want to work in a factory, do you think you could do so as a superior person living apart and in a much better way than the others? The idea is absurd. The very object of going there is to learn from the sufferings, discomforts and misery which surround and wrap up the great majority of people; to see the drama of real life; to become akin to a small extent at least with the masses; to understand their viewpoint; and to get to know how to work so as to raise them and get them out of their misery. This cannot be done by people who live in cotton-wool but by those who can face the sun and the air and hard living. However, all this does not arise at present and much will depend on what ideals in life you have. I cannot impose my ideals on you. If you want to make your life Worthwhile you will have to decide for yourself what your life-philosophy should be.

Tuesday, 26 June

How old I am getting! My hair is turning grey at a great pace, it is already mostly grey and I have developed quite a distinguished (?) elderly look. The world passes on and goes ahead, while I and so many like me - sit silent and inactive and grow older and older. Life stops in Jail in many ways but age creeps on. My eyes grow dull from staring at the walls. They are beginning to sag - like father's.

June 28

Last night I was sitting reading in the verandah near my bed. I took some books to my cell passing the narrow space between the bed and the wall. On returning the same way I suddenly stopped within two feet of a little snake lying coiled up at the base of the wall opposite my bed. I must have passed it in the first instance, within six inches of it.

The decency of the snake is not attacking me had a favourable effect on me and I sat on my bed for long watching it. The warder came and suggested killing it. I told him to give the poor thing a chance. But it would not take advantage of the chance and only moved about a little in the small verandah. I tried even to push it on with the help of a mosquito net pole - I do not use the net but this bamboo was there - but it would not make an effort to escape. There was only one way in and out from my little yard - a small hole for a drain. It must have come that way.

After nearly an hour another warder came for the night and the time for lights out approached. It was difficult to allow the snake to remain in the yard with two warders, apart from myself. A proposal was again made to put an end to it and I reluctantly agreed. It was stunned - I thought it had died - and I promptly put it in a glass jar. This morning to my surprise I found it very much alive. I tried to feed it with milk. I compared its marks with those on the chart and came to the conclusion that it was a krait, a very poisonous snake. It was about 20 inches long and not fully grown. This evening it died after making violent efforts to get out of the jar. I propose keeping it in spirit.

Extracts from the Prison Diary with Letters
12 February - 12 August, 1934

Friday, August 24

In and out - out and in! After eleven days of freedom back I came to Naini prison. Eleven days of meeting crowds of friends, discussions and of course Kamala's illness. Eleven days of comfortable living. And now I am back to the loneliness of solitary jail life.

Wednesday, October 3

I was taken to her today again for 3 hours because Bidhan had come - How much weaker she looked - a shadow. Gone downhill since last I saw her ten days ago. Bidhan seeing her after ten days, said her condition had greatly deteriorated. She is to wait no longer here in the hope of getting better and then going elsewhere for treatment. She is going soon to Bhowali - perhaps in another four or five days. When will I see her again? Will I see her at all? Brave little girl. She smiled at me as I was coming away though her temperature was 103.4 and she was in daze. And even in this condition she said : do not give an assurance to govt.! How she longs to have me out and by her but not at the price of undertakings to the government.

I feel both heavy and empty since my return to my barrack and so lonely and weary.

I gave Kamala today Edgar Allan Poe's lines :

Thou wast all that to me, love,
For which my soul did pine -
A green isle in the sea, love,
A fountain and a shrine,
All wreathed with fairy fruits and flowers,
And all the flowers were mine.
And all my days are trances
And all my nightly dreams
Are where thy grey eye glances,
And where thy footsteps gleams -
In what ethereal dances,
By what eternal streams.

They seemed to represent my feelings.

Saturday, January 12, 1935

A terrible and unexpected shock. Early in the morning a telegram came from Nan from Allahabad that Jivraj Mehta had telephoned from Bombay to say that mother had had a stoke of paralysis and was unconscious. Nan was going immediately to Bombay. I held together for a while and then came the thought that I had seen the last of mother. Her face, charged with pain and emotion, as she said goodbye to me on 23 August, when I was rearrested and carried off to Naini, rose up before me vividly. As I was getting in the police car she run up again to me with arms outstretched. That face haunted me. How she loved me and was wrapped up in me. She would ask my advice in the most trivial things and hold on to even a suggestion as if it was the final and inescapable truth. How she had suffered because of my long absences in prison and how she had bravely faced and endured not only this agony but the physical pain of a police lathi charge. She did this more for her love of father and me than for any principle. And yet there was also the pride not to submit.

I collapsed and wept and found some difficulty in pulling myself together. Poor little mother - what a tortured life she had led for many years - all her children in prison and so much happening that was painful. And now the end had come suddenly. Perhaps it was as well that it was sudden and perhaps painless. She would not recover from this stroke of paralysis at her age and in her weak state.

But it was hard to think that I would not see her again. I grow lonelier than ever. The home that father had built up so lovingly goes to pieces. Kamala lies ill in Bhowali - a long long illness with no cure in prospect, mother lying unconscious in Bombay, I in Almora Jail . . . .

I have shivered all day although it has not been as cold as usual. The wind is moaning through the pine trees a dismal note full of desolation. Or is it my mind that is desolate? I am losing most of the footholds I had. India, Allahabad - the mental bonds that tied me to them seem to loosen and I feel like an exile who cannot even took forward to a home anywhere. The morning wind is a fit accompaniment to my mood. I am weary but there is no rest.

February 4

To Indira Nehru

The clouds are my favourite companions here and I watch them daily. Sometimes they pay me a visit in the shape of mist and they fill my barrack with a damp and sticky feeling, but it is not so bad. Usually they are high up assuming the most fantastic shapes. I fancy I see shapes of animals in them, elephants and camels and lions, and even little pigs. Or they resemble the porpoises that hop about in the sea, or fish lying side, almost like sardines in a tin. And then they would change suddenly and coalesce and look like a mighty ocean, and at other times like a beach. The wind rustling through the deodars helps the illusion for it sounds like the tide coming in and the waves breaking on a distant sea-front. It is a great game, this watching of the clouds. Once I saw some whiffs of them floating about and I was immediately reminded of Sir Prabhashankar Pattani's peroxide beard. It was really a remarkable likeness and I was highly amused and laughed to myself for a long time. Have you seen this famous beard? It is worth seeing. Puphi - the elder one - knows it well and so you had better tell her of my experience here.

February 22

To Indira Nehru

Why does one read books? To instruct oneself, amuse oneself, train one's mind, etc., etc. - Certainly all this and much more. Ultimately it is to understand life with its thousand facets and to learn how to live life. Our individual experiences are so narrow and limited, if we were to rely on them alone we would also remain narrow and limited. But books give us the experiences and thoughts of innumerable others, often the wisest of their generation, and lift us out of our narrow ruts. Gradually as we go up the mountain sides fresh vistas come into view, our vision extends further and further, and a sense of proportion comes to us. We are not overwhelmed by our petty and often transient loves and hates and we see them for what they are - petty and hardly noticeable ripples on the immense ocean of life. For all of us it is worthwhile to develop this large vision for it enables us to see life whole and to live it well. But for those who chrish the through of rising above the common herd of unthinking humanity and playing a brave part in life's journey, this vision and sense of proportion are essential to keep us on the right path and steady us when storms and heavy winds bear down on us.

Sunday, March 3

How curious is life! I seem to be learning its mysterious ways still and my wonder grows. It is overwhelming at times and how it mocks! I have returned from Bhowali full of strange thoughts and feelings which I hardly dare put down in black and white. There is a sense of emptiness and loneliness and yet there is also some relief from the tension of past days. At least I feel I know what the trouble is which caused this tension. Understanding is often painful but it is better than a blind search for something which eludes one. And yet I do not know - so many fresh mysteries crop up. So many dark alleys leading I know not where. What can one do except to keep calm and preserve.

It is an old habit, that shouting and groaning in sleep. Kamala used to tell me about it. In prison I used to do it sometimes. I remember how, during the Cripps negotiations, one night I was more than usually noisy and Rajan dashed into my room to find out what ailed me.

There is an old childhood dream which I remember. It came to me repeatedly with variations. Some horried creatures was pursuing me, something that I could not clearly see or visualize, and I ran my fastest away from it. I ran and ran but always it was close behind me. Ultimately I entered a building and mounted a high tower. There near the top I looked myself from the inside in a room. But there was a high window or a skylight and to my exceeding horror I saw a huge hand come through this window and stretch itself out towards me. It was only a hand with an arm attached, nothing more. There was no escape possible for me from that room. The hand approached, came nearer and nearer, and then I awoke in a cold sweat, shivering with fright and horror . . . .

For the past few years or so the nightmares have usually something to do with a feeling of oppression, of being unable to do what I want to do. I want to move and my limbs do not obey me. I want to shout and warn someone and my throat is parched and dry and no voice comes out of it, or just a hoarse grunt . . . .

What is all this due to? What old suppressions? Is it sex? - Partly perhaps, though I do not think this is the primary cause. Is it the feeling of helplessness and oppression due to political causes? Perhaps.

Wednesday, July 5

We have now read most of the correspondence that passed between Bapu and the govt. Not quite all yet, as the newspapers have not given everything. A fully cyclostyled record has reached Vallabhbhai but I have not read it so far. My first impressions confirmed. Generally a feeling of satisfaction but mixed with occasional irritation - why should it be necessary to have to explain what he said and wrote previously - and at such great length? Because of non-violence and the metaphysical aspects of satyagraha, a certain almost theological element of casuistry creeps in sometimes.

But this approach apart, Bapu has done a good job and he has laboured hard at it. He has cleared many cobwebs and explained his own thinking and action. In that thinking there is that inevitable tug of war between moral considerations and practical problems, and occasionally there is a contradiction which cannot be resolved, at least by me. But such contradictions are, I suppose, inherent in life's problems. What appears odd to us in his manner of approach.

Suppose he had been as explicit in 1942 as he is now - what a lot of difference this might have made. Not that he has said anything new. Much of all this he had told us previously but the public did not know it. It is after all a question of emphasis.

By this correspondence and his last letter to Wavell, he has made it very clear how anxious he is to have a settlement, and yet he has stuck to his fundamentals. Wavell's refusal to meet him is now so obviously wrong from any point of view, except the imperialist one of crushing Congress, that reactions in India and abroad are bound to be against it.

The position is that the Congress has been cleared of many false charges and the basic conflict between nationalism and imperialism has been brought to the surface. That cannot be resolved just yet and practical solutions are hardly possible now.

Saturday, August 5

Three weeks since I wrote last in this journal. Three weeks of growing perturbations and mental distress. I wrote then that I was not put out at all by various developments and the two proposals Bapu had made, though I disagreed with much that he had said and the manner of saying and doing. Well, I take all that back. I am very much put out, angered and out of temper.

The floods of statements, interviews, correspondence, etc., that have emanated from Bapu, and the very frequent utterances of Rajagopalachari, have overwhelmed me and others and I feel stifled and unable to breathe normally. For the first time in these two years I have a sensation of blankness and sinking of heart. Today I have been writing to Indu my usual Saturday letter. I found some difficulty in doing so and could hardly finish my sentences.

Jinnah with his insolence has contributed to this, and so also the debate in the House of Commons and the general attitude of the British press - But after all that is to be expected. It is Bapu's response to all this that bowls me over . . . .

My mind goes back : the conflicts in the Working Committee in 1936-37 - that revealing incident, after the Calcutta AICC in 1937 as a French poet once said, as we gaze into the eyes of our dearest and nearest we find that a stranger is looking at us.

How to bridge the gap between the dreams that fill us and the reality that is so different? How to do it? How? It seems easy when one is young and full of enthusiasm. In our pride of youth we care little for walls and obstacles. It is good that we should feel that way for a while at least during our span of life before weariness and dissolution come. It is good to cling to and lengthen that period of youth. And therefore I wrote to you some time back not to hurry, to linger awhile on the way. And when you pass on to a fuller and more complex life, carry something of the breath of youth with you, something of its idealism, but in place of its egotism try to widen your humanity. Only then can we endeavour to bridge that gap. At best that bridge is a ramshackle affair, liable to collapse at the first touch of storm and tempest. But the effort is always worthwhile; it brings its own reward. And there seems no other way.

A Letter to Bharati Sarabhai, 25 November, 1935

A PRIVATE PERSON

Subhas Bose, I found, had taken to describing himself as a writer. Being more modest, I could not quite bring myself to do that. But what am I? In a recent application for a passport, I decided to call my profession 'public affairs', whatever that might mean. I suppose the term is wide enough to cover a multitude of activities, good and evil. And yet, in spite of public exhibitions and the like, I have never ceased to feel a singularly private person.

A Letter to Goshiben Captain, 28 December, 1935

KAMALA

In the long autumn evenings I sat by myself in my room in the pension, where I was staying, or sometimes went out for a walk across the fields or through the forest. A hundred pictures of Kamala succeeded each other in my mind, a hundred aspects of her rich and deep personality. We had been married for nearly twenty years, and yet how many times she had surprised me by something new in her mental or spiritual make-up. I had known her in so many ways and in latter years, I had tried my utmost to understand her. That understanding had not been denied to me, but I often wondered if I really knew her or understood her. There was something elusive about her, something fay-like, real but unsubstantial, difficult to grasp. Sometimes, looking into her eyes, I would find a stranger peeping out at me.

Except for a little schooling, she had had no formal education; her mind had not gone through the educational process. She came to us as an unsophisticated girl apparently with hardly any of the complexes which are said to be so common now. She never entirely lost that girlish look, but as she grew into a woman her eyes acquired a depth and a fire, giving the impression of still pools behind which storms raged. She was not the type of modern girl, with the modern girl's habits and lack of poise; yet she took easily enough to modern ways. But essentially she was an Indian girl and more particularly, a Kashmiri girl, sensitive and proud, childlike and grown-up, foolish and wise. She was reserved to those she did not know or did not like, but bubbling over with gaiety and frankness before those she knew and liked. She was quick in her judgement and not always fair or right, but she stuck to her instinctive likes and dislikes. There was no guile in her. If she disliked a person, it was obvious, and she made no attempt to hide the fact. Even if she had tried to do so, she would probably not have succeeded. I have come across few persons who have produced such an impression of sincerity upon me as she did.

I thought of the early years of our marriage when, with all my tremendous liking for Kamala, I almost forgot her and denied her, in so many ways, that comradeship which was her due. For, I was then like a person possessed, giving myself utterly to the cause I had espoused, living in a dream world of my own, and looking at the real people who surrounded me as unsubstantial shadows. I worked to the utmost of my capacity and my mind was filled to the brim with the subject that engrossed me. I gave all my energy to that cause and had little left to spare.

And yet I was very far from forgetting her, and I came back to her again and again as to a sure haven. If I was away for a number of days the thought of her cooled my mind and I looked forward eagerly to my return home. What indeed could I have done if she had not been there to comfort me and give me strength, and thus enable me to recharge the exhausted battery of my mind and body?

I had taken from her what she gave me. What had I given to her in exchange during these early years? I had failed evidently and, possibly, she carried the deep impress of those days upon her. With her inordinate pride and sensitiveness she did not want to come to me to ask for help, although I could not have given her that help more than anyone else. She wanted to play her own part in the national struggle and not be merely a hanger on and a shadow of her husband. She wanted to justify herself to her own self as well as to the world. Nothing in the world could have pleased me more than this, but I was far too busy to see beneath the surface, and I was blind to what she looked for and so ardently desired. And then prison claimed me so often and I was away from her, or else she was ill. Like Chitra in Tagore's play, she seemed to say to me : 'I am Chitra. No goddess to be worshipped, nor yet the object of common pity to be brushed aside like a moth with indifference. If you deign to keep me by your side in the path of danger and daring, if you allow me to share the great duties of your life, then you will know my true self.' But she did not say this to me in words and it was only gradually that I read the message of her eyes.

In the early months of 1930 I sensed her desire and we worked together, and I found in this experience a new delight. We lived for a while on the edge of life, as it were, for the clouds were gathering and a national upheaval was coming. Those were pleasant months for us, but they ended too soon, and early in

April, the country was in the grip of civil disobedience and governmental repression, and I was in prison again.

Most of us menfolk were in prison. And then a remarkable thing happened. Our women came to the front and took charge of the struggle. Women had always been there, of course, but now there was an avalanche of them, which took not only the British government but their own menfolk by surprise. Here were these women of the upper or middle classes, leading sheltered lives in their homes - peasant women, working-class women, rich women - pouring out in their tens of thousands in defiance of government order and the police lathi. It was not only that display of courage and daring, but what was even more surprising was the organizational power they showed.

Never can I forget the thrill that came to us in Naini prison when news of this reached us, the enormous pride in the women of India that filled us. We could hardly talk about all this among ourselves, for our hearts were full and our eyes were dim with tears.

. . . . In this upheaval Kamala had played a brave and notable part and on her inexperienced shoulders fell the task of organizing our work in the city of Allahabad when every known worker was in prison. She made up for that inexperience by her fire and energy and, within a few months, she became the pride of Allahabad.

We met again under the shadow of my father's last illness and his death. We met on a new footing of comradeship and understanding. A few months later when we went with our daughter to Ceylon for our first brief holiday, and our last, we seemed to have discovered each other anew. All the past years that we had passed together had been but a preparation for this new and more intimate relationship.

We came back all too soon and work claimed me and, later, prison. There was to be no more holidaying, no working together, not even being together, except for a brief while between two long prison terms of two years each which followed each other. Before the second of these was over, Kamala lay dying.

When I was arrested in February 1934, on a Calcutta warrant, Kamala went up to our rooms to collect some clothes for me. I followed her to say goodbye to her. Suddenly she clung to me and, fainting, collapsed. This was unusual for her as we had trained ourselves to take this jail-going lightly and cheerfully and to makes as little fuss about it as possible. Was it some premonition she had that this was our last more or less normal meeting?

Two long prison terms of two years each had come between me and her just when our need for each other was greatest, just when we had come so near to each other. I thought of this during the long days in jail, and yet I hoped that the time would surely come when we could be together again. How did she fare during these years? I can guess but even I do not know, for during the jail interviews, or during a brief interval outside there was little normality. We had to be always on our best behaviour lest we might cause pain to the other by showing our own distress. But it was obvious that she was greatly troubled and distressed over many things and there was no peace in her mind. I might have been to some help, but not from jail.

All these and many other thoughts, came to my mind during my long solitary hours in Badenweiler. I did not shed the atmosphere of jail easily; I had long got used to it and the new environment did not make any great change. I was living in the Nazi domain with all its strange happenings which I disliked so much, but Nazism did not interfere with me. Three were few evidences of it in the quiet village in a corner of the Black Forest.

Or perhaps my mind was full of other matters. My past life unrolled itself before me and there was always Kamala standing by. She became a symbol of Indian women, or of woman herself. Sometimes she grew curiously mixed up with my ideas of India that land of ours so dear to us, with all her faults and weaknesses, so elusive and so full of mystery. What was Kamala? Did I know her? Understand her real self? Did she know or understand me? For, I too was an abnormal person with mystery and unplumbed depths within me, which I could not myself fathom. Sometimes I had thought that she was a little frightened of me because of this. I had been, and was, a most unsatisfactory person to marry. Kamala and I were unlike each other in some ways, and yet in some other ways very alike; we did not complement each other. Our very strength became a weakness in our relations with each other. There could either be complete understanding, a perfect union of minds, or difficulties. Neither of us could live a humdrum domestic life, accepting things as they were.

Among the many pictures that were displayed in the bazars in India, there was one containing two separate pictures of Kamala and me, side by side, with the inscription at the top, *adarsha jori,* the model or ideal couple, as so many people imagined us to be. But the ideal is terribly difficult to grasp or to hold. Yet I remember telling Kamala, during our holiday in Ceylon, how fortunate we had been in spite of difficulties and differences, in spite of all the tricks life had played upon us, that marriage was an odd affair, and it had not ceased to be so even after thousands of years of experience. We saw around us the wrecks of many a marriage or, what was no better, the conversion of what was bright and golden into dross. How fortunate we were, I told her, and she agreed, for though we had sometimes quarrelled and grown angry with each other we kept that vital spark alight, and for each one of us life was always unfolding new adventure and giving fresh insight into each other.

The problem of human relationships, how fundamental it is, and how often ignore in our fierce arguments about politics and economics. It was not so ignore in the old and wise civilizations of India and China, where they developed patterns of social behaviour which, with all their faults, certainly gave poise to the individual. That poise is not in evidence in India today. But where is it in the countries of the West which have progressed so much in other directions? Or is poise essentially static and opposed to progressive change? Must we sacrifice one for the other? Surely it should be possible to have a union of poise and inner and outer progress, of the wisdom of the old with the science and the vigour of the new. Indeed we appear to have arrived at a stage in the world's history when the only alternative to such a union is likely to be the destruction and undoing of both.

From *The Discovery of India* (1946)

6

Role in History

Born on 1st August, 1899 in the famous Atal family, Kamala Nehru was ten years younger to Jawaharlal Nehru. The head of the family, Pandit Kishan Lal served as an official in the princely courts of Jaipur and Jodhpur in Rajasthan and Rewa in Central India. He was Private Secretary to the Maharaja of Jaipur. Thus he gained high social status among the Kashmir families.

Jawaharmul was the fifth son of Kishan Lal Atal. He was adopted by a Kaul family and adopted his surname as Kaul. He had a cloth shop at Nai Sarak and a flour mill in the same area of Old Delhi. His wife Rajpati was a nobel lady having religious bent of mind. Kamala had two brothers and two sisters and all led a comfortable life in the huge campus of the Atal House.

So long as Kamala Nehru lived, she saw to it that her daughter's educational career should not suffer. In Anand Bhawan the atmosphere was surcharged with hectic political activities in 1920s and 1930s. The family witnessed two deaths of prominent persons - Motilal Nehru and Swarup Rani Nehru. Jawaharlal Nehru was very often in jail. Kamala Nehru showed keenness in domestic environments inspite of her illness and political affiliations.

Kamala Nehru received much respect from the people of India. A trust was created with the patronage of Gandhiji. Several institutions were inaugurated in her memory. The famous Kamala Nehru Hospital in Allahabad was started and in Delhi, the Kamala Nehru College is one of the reputed institutions under Delhi University. Several parks, roads and other public places were named in her memory. Several women organisations pay her rich tributes till this day.

Kamala Nehru was hardly thirty six when she was taken away by the cruel current of death. Undoubtedly it was a great personal loss to Jawaharlal Nehru at a time when he was deeply engrossed in the complexities of numerous political developments in our sub-continent. At this paint of time when the end of the second Civil Disobedience Movement had raised several issues during the Viceroyalty of Lord Willingdon, Nehru's family life was shattered. He felt lonely, but a practical person as he was he faced difficult situations with courage and determination.

KAMALA NEHRU DEAD

All India Mourns Her Loss Today

Deepest Sympathy Felt for Pt. Jawaharlal

"She represented all that was best in oriental womanhood"

—Mayor Nariman

GLOOM IN ASSEMBLY CIRCLES : LEADERS' TRIBUTES

The "Hindustan Times" deeply regrets to announce the Death of Mrs. Kamala Nehru at Lausanne Yesterday Morning.

According to a Geneva message, Mrs. Nehru's body will be cremated there and ashes brought to India.

The news has cast a gloom throughout the country. Business was suspended in Indian quarters in Bombay, Lahore and Allahabad and Delhi will observe a day of móurning, today.

"The tragic news will come as a great shock to the whole country. Kamala Nehru represented all that was best in ancient and modern oriental womanhood. Our hearts go in sincere sympathy and condolence to the bereaved husband, Pandit Jawaharal Nehru."

This tribute of Mayor Nariman of Bombay is typical of the general feeling of sympathy and regret throughout the country.

Geneva, Feb. 28. Mrs. Kamala Nehru died at 5 a.m. today. It is understood Mrs. Nehru's body will be cremated and ashes taken to India.

—Reuter

DELHI PLUNGED IN MOURNING

Delhi, Friday. The news of Mrs. Kamala Nehru's death spread like wild fire in the city. Anxious telephone enquiries were made at the "Hindustan Times", for confirmation of the sad news.

Our representative who went round the streets, found that quite a large number of shops were promptly closed on receipt of the sad news.

The Congress leaders held an emergent meeting and decided that Delhi should observed 'hartal' tomorrow (Saturday). The decision was announced by beat of drum.

PROCESSION AND MEETING

It has been decided to take out a mourning procession at 2 p.m.

A meeting convened in the Hindu College to hear Mr. Chaman Lal's lecture on Japan was converted into a mourning meeting. Professor Gupta, who presided, broke the sad news to the audience, who were shocked.

The following resolution, moved by the chair was passed, the audience standing :

"This meeting of the students of colleges and members of the public expresses its profound sense of grief and loss at the sad death of Shrimati Kamala Nehru and conveys its heartfelt sympathies to the Nehru family."

DELHI TO OBSERVE HARTAL TODAY

Mourning Procession to Start at 2 P.M. from Clock Tower

Mass Meeting at 4 P.M. in the Queen's Gardens

Mr. Jugal Kishore Khanna, General Secretary, District Congress Committee writes :

The country has just received the sad news of the sudden death of Shrimati Kamala Nehru, who had been ailing for the past several months. It is difficult to estimate the loss which the country has suffered by this sad and untimely demise of the wife of the president-elect of the Indian National Congress.

Saturday, the 29th of February, 1936, will be observed a day of a general mourning in Delhi. All business should be suspended in Old and New Delhi and the suburbs.

A bare-headed silent procession will start from the Clock Tower at 2 p.m. and will terminate in a public meeting to be held at 4.30 p.m. in the Azad Park, Queens Gardens, Delhi.

It is expected that the people of Delhi will share the grief by observing complete 'hartal' and joining the procession and public meeting.

PASSING AWAY OF MRS. KAMALA NEHRU

Leaders Shocked

Dr. M.A. Ansari, Mrs. Sarojini Naidu, Mr. Asaf Ali, Mr. Satyamurti, Dr. Bhagwan Das and other Congress leaders were shocked to hear the news and sent telegrams to Pandit Jawaharlal Nehru expressing their deep sorrow and sympathy in his loss which they described as a national loss.

MRS. NAIDU'S GRIEF

Mrs. Naidu burst into tears when the news was broken to her by our representative and she said : "She was like a little sister to me, what else can I say in this hour of grief!"

Mr. and Mrs. Asaf Ali also associated themselves with her feelings.

HOSTEL STUDENTS MOURN

An extraordinary meeting of the Main Hostel Association was held this evening when the following resolution was adopted, all standing :

"This meeting of the Main Hostel Association, Hindu College, places on record its deep sense of grief at the sad and untimely demise of Shrimati Kamala Nehru, and while praying for the soul of the deceased, conveys its heartfelt sympathies to the bereaved family."

EXHIBITION OPENING POSTPONED

In view of Mrs. Kamala Nehru's sad death the formal opening of the All-India Industrial Exhibition Delhi, which was fixed for February 29, 1936, has been abandoned and it will now commence from the 1st of March, 1936.

NEW HOSTEL MEETING

The New Hostel (Hindu College) Association assembled in a meeting records its deep and sincere grief at the most lamentable demise of Mrs. Kamala Nehru.

The anniversary celebration of the New Hostel of Hindu College has been postponed till further notice.

CONGRESS M.L.A.'S SORROW

Condolence Resolution at Party Meeting

The News of Mrs. Kamala Nehru's death was received in Delhi when the Assembly adjourned after presentation of budget. The Congress Party which met to transact some routine business passed a condolence resolution and adjourned. A cable is being sent to Pandit Jawaharlal Nehru expressing the party's grief.

When the news was conveyed to Mr. Nariman, Mayor of Bombay, and president of the B.P.C.C., he was shocked to hear it and said :

"The tragic news will come as a great shock to the whole country. Particularly at this juncture when the country was preparing to accord a grand reception to Pandit Jawaharlal Nehru, President-elect of the Indian National Congress.

"The young promising life has been cut off and sacrificed at a premature age at the sacred altar of freedom of the country."

Mr. Nariman added :

"With her death, has passed away a most pleasing, fascinating, noble and above all a most patriotic nationalist personality in modern times. Above all Kamala Nehru represented all that was best in ancient and modern oriental womanhood. Our hearts go in sincere sympathy and condolence to the bereaved husband, the family and the orphan child.

'BRAVE WIFE OF A BRAVE LEADER'

Interviews by the "United Press" on the death of Mrs. Kamala Nehru, Mr. K.M. Munshi, said : "Mrs. Kamala Nehru's death is a national calamity. She was one of the finest specimens of Indian womanhood in her generation. The country's heartfelt sympathy goes out to Pandit Jawaharlal Nehru in his sad bereavement."

Mr. S. Brelvi said : "The whole country share Pandit Jawaharlal Nehru's loss in the death of Mrs. Kamala Nehru. The brave wife of a brave leader of India and the memory of self-sacrificing devotion to the country will continue to inspire women in India for generation."—United Press.

A BRIEF LIFE SKETCH

"An embodiment of sacrifice, full of life and cheer in spite of years of continued sufferings," such was Kamala Nehru whom cruel Nature snatched away from Mother India. She was born in 1899 in the city of Delhi. Her mother Shrimati Rajpati Kaul, regarded her as the most affectionate child in the family.

Though she had no school or university education, her family education was such that she was selected by the promising Barrister Pandit Jawaharlal to be his companion.

They were married in 1916 and hardly had they enjoyed a few years of family life when the Non-co-operation Movement began in 1920 and the Nehru family plunged headlong into it.

Kamala used to keep indifferent health even before her marriage and suffered from as severe attack of headache for years.

Due to Pandit Jawaharlal's numerous imprisonment, her illness grew worse and she was taken to Switzerland in 1927 for treatment.

In the Civil Disobedience Movement in 1930, she played a very prominent part in the movement, after the arrest of Pandits Motilal and Jawaharlal and visited hundreds of towns and villages in ill-health. She was 'Dictator' of U.P. for some months and was ultimately arrested, sentenced and sent to Lucknow Jail, where she refused special treatment.

Since her return from jail she was keeping ill-health all these years except during the brief period around Karachi Congress session, when she was in her best spirits and used to entertain pressmen with sweets, fruits, etc.

The story of how cheerfully she bore her illness for the last four years in well-known to all her countrymen and women.

GANDHI'S MESSAGE

Mrs. Vijaya Lakshmi Pandit has received the following messages :

From Gandhiji :

"Just received a message about Kamala's death. Sympathies of all of us are with you. All of you must be brave. Love. Bapu."

From Mrs. Sarojini Naidu :

"Deeply share your grief. Sarojini."—A.P.I.

The news of the death of Mrs. Jawaharlal Nehru has come with almost starting suddenness. She was due to have sailed with her husband early in March, her health, in the opinion of her physicians, having sufficiently improved. A later message indicated that there had been a setback and that their return to India would be delaying by 10 days. But few were prepared for the tragedy that was imminent. As the devoted wife and helpmate of Jawaharlal, she must be said to have influenced the career of the Pandit in no small measure. The enthusiasm with which she espoused the cause of the Congress and courted imprisonment during the civil disobedience movement, was an inspiration to the rest of the country. The illness which has now ended in her all-too-early demise was contracted when she was a prisoner.

Like the true daughter of India that she was, she declined special treatment in jail and insisted on sharing the rigours of prison life with her comrades who were denied special facilities. The sympathy of the whole country will go to Pandit Jawaharlal and Mrs. Swaruprani Nehru in their terrible bereavement. As a woman Kamala Nehru was typically Indian tolerant and modest but with an outlook catholic enough to include the whole world. She was barely 36 years old at the time of her death and within this small compass had made thousands of friends in India and abroad who will fell her loss as an intensity personal one. In company with the rest of India, we extend our sympathy to Pandit Jawaharlal and other members of the family in this hour of sorrow.

SPONTANEOUS HARTAL OBSERVED IN THE CITY

Markets Closed : School Deserted
Thousands Join Silent Mourning Procession
Delhi's Tribute to Kamala Nehru

Within the last 24 hours no less than two dozen condolence meetings were held in Delhi and New Delhi in connection with the death of Kamala Nehru. All markets including cloth, cotton, bullion and iron were closed throughout the day. All colleges and most of the schools except the St. Stephen's College, were deserted.

MOURNING PROCESSION

At 2 p.m. several thousand persons including women, students, labourers, merchants and people of all trades and professions assembled at the Clock Tower and formed themselves into a procession, which started at 2 p.m. and passed through the main streets of Delhi and terminated at the Queen's Garden at 4 p.m. where a meeting was held with Shrimati Sarojini Naidu in the chair.

Touching tributes to the memory of Shrimati Kamala Nehru were paid by Pandit Indra, Mr. Asaf Ali, Pandit Govind Vallabh Pant (Deputy Leader of the Congress Party in the Assembly), Shrimati Parvati Devi, Pandit Neki Ram Sharma and Mr. Paliwal. The meeting was most representative and was attended by members of all communities.

RESOLUTIONS OF CONDOLENCE

Pandit Indra moved a resolution expression heartfelt sorrow at the death of Shrimati Kamala Nehru and conveying condolences and sympathies of half a million citizens of Delhi to Pandit Jawaharlal Nehru, President-elect of the Congress and assuring him that the death of Kamala Nehru was not only his personal loss but that the whole nation shared his grief. The resolution further conveyed sympathies of the people of Delhi to Shrimati Rajpati Kaul, mother of Kamala Nehru and other members of the Nehru family.

EMBODIMENT OF WOMANHOOD

The mover sad that Shrimati Kamala Nehru had played a great part in making Pandit Nehru, a brave warrior. Kamala was a true embodiment of Indian womanhood. She lived for the ideals of her husband and with her last breath must have prayed for the success of his efforts.

CABLE TO JAWAHARLAL

The Secretary, Provincial Congress Committee, has sent a cable to Pandit Jawaharlal at Lausanne and a telegram to Mrs. Vijialakshmi Pandit at Allahabad, expressing Delhi's sorrow at the unexpected demise of Kamala Nehru.

AT THE TIBBIA COLLEGE

A meeting of the students of the Tibbia College Hostel was held last night and a resolution expressing deep sorrow at the death of Kamala Nehru was passed. A telegram expressing sympathy was sent to the members of the bereaved family.

Various institutions including the Delhi Bar Association, the Muslim League, the Arabic College Union, the Insurances Associations, the Ramjas College and several other institutions held emergent meetings and passed resolutions of condolence.

AT SHAHDARA

At Shahdara complete hartal was observed today and a mass meeting was held at 7 p.m. where tributes were paid to the memory of Kamala Nehru.

COMMERCIAL COLLEGE UNION

Grief Over Mrs. Nehru's Death

An extraordinary meeting of the Commerical College Union was held on the 29th of February, 1936 to place on its record their sense of deep sorrow at the sad and untimely demise of Shrimati Kamala Nehru.

The meeting conveyed its heartfelt sympathy to the bereaved husband and family.

EMBODIMENT OF WOMANHOOD

The mover said that Shrimati Kamala Nehru had played a great part in making Pandit Nehru, a brave warrior. Kamala was a true embodiment of Indian womanhood. She lived for the ideals of her husband and with her last breath must have prayed for the success of his efforts.

She sacrificed her life and pleasures and told Pandit Nehru not to stay by her side but to leave for India to serve his country. Kamala was not only the wife of a patriot, but a staunch patriot herself and her own record of sacrifices in the struggle for the country's freedom was glorious.

"ROYAL WEDDING RECALLED"

Mr. Asaf Ali, seconding the resolution, recalled the day when the "royal wedding party" arrived from Allahabad 17 years ago with great pomp and show to celebrate the marriage of a promising barrister with a true daughter of Delhi, who proved to be a loyal wife, a dutiful mother and a brave daughter of Mother India. He wished and prayed that our sisters and daughters of today would walk in her footsteps.

PANDIT G.B. PANT'S TRIBUTE

Pandit Govind Vallabh Pant said that Kamala was a sister to him and the shock was so great that he could not speak. He wondered how Jawaharlal could have borne the shock all alone, thousands of miles away from his country. The history of the Nehru family, he added, would add to bright chapter to the history of India.

REVIVED ANCIENT TRADITIONS

Shrimati Parvati Devi paid a very touching tribute and said : Kamala knew how to live for her country and she also proved that the weaker sex could bravely fight for the country. She had once again revived the ancient traditions of the brave women of India.

"SPURNED RICHES"

Pandit Neki Ram said that Kamala spurned riches and pleasure and devoted her enthusiasm for the cause of the country. The speaker felt sure that Kamala's sould would be reborn in India to complete her mission of seeing India free.

HINDU MAHASABHA'S CONDOLENCE

Bhai Parmanand, M.L.A., Bhikshu Ottama, vice-presidents of the Hindu Mahasabha, and Lal Narain Datta, Treasurer, have conveyed their heartfelt condolence to Pahdit Jawaharlal Nehru and Mata Swarup Rani Nehru.

SIR MOHD. YAKUB'S TRIBUTE

"My heart goes out in sympathy to Pandit Jawaharlal Nehru on the sad demise of his devoted and talented wife. To fill the role of Pt. Jawaharlal's wife was by no means an easy task and it must be admitted that Mrs. Kamala Nehru fully proved equal to the task. She not only maintained but also enhanced, to a great extent, the status of India's womanhood by her loyalty, courage and endurance and leaves behind her a noble example worthy of being followed by the rising generation of her sex." - A.P.I.

MAULANA SHAUKAT ALI

Maulana Shaukat Ali, M.L.A., has sent the following telegram to Mrs. Pandit at Allahabad :

"Begam Mohammed Ali and myself offer our heartfelt sympathies in regard to the sad death of our brave sister."- A.P.I.

COUNTRY MOURNS KAMALA NEHRU'S LOSS

Condolence Meetings and 'Hartals'

Allahabad. There is a general 'hartal' and spontaneous

suspension of business throughout the city today in honour of the memory of late Mrs. Kamala Nehru.

A notification has been issued by the local Municipal Committee for the closure of all Municipal offices and schools.- United Press.

NAGPUR'S GRIEF

The Nagpur Municipal Committee adjourned its meeting this morning without transacting any business as a mark of respect to the memory of Mrs. Kamala Nehru.

A resolution was adopted expressing sympathy with Pandit Jawaharlal Nehru in his bereavement.

By another resolution the committee recorded his grief at the death of Sir Dinshaw Wacha. - United Press.

'HARTAL' IN LAHORE

As a mark of respect to the memory of late Mrs. Kamala Nehru the city is observing complete 'hartal' today. All the shops in the Indian quarters including Anarkali, Gowalmandi and Nisbet Road and in the Hindu and Muslim quarters within the city walls are closed.

Prominent Muslim leaders including Maulana Zagar Ali, who have issued appeal asking Muslims to observe 'hartal' today, personally went round the city this morning to see that the Muslim shops are closed.

Students and staff of several schools and colleges held meeting and adopted resolutions conveying condolence to Pandit Jawaharlal Nehru and the bereaved family. - United Press.

S.C. BOSE'S TRIBUTE

Calcutta. "Pandit Jawaharlal Nehru has lost his partner in life - the real partner in all his life-giving activities, one who did not fall even when she was hovering between life and death to remained him that the country's necessity was greater than hers" said Mr. Sarat Chandra Bose interviewed on the death of Mrs. Kamala Nehru.

"Although Kamala Nehru's health had recently been causing anxiety her friends and relatives were still hoping that she would get over the critical period to be with us sometime longer" said Dr. B.C. Roy and added born in a rich family and brought up amidst wealth and luxury she was refusing everything espoused a life of austerity, even of penury, in order to get in touch with the poor starving and suffering millions of her people. - A.P.I.

KARACHI'S GRIEF

Markets to Remain Closed

The news of Mrs. Kamala Nehru's death has cast a gloom in the city. Doctor Choitram, president of the Sind Provincial Congress Committee, has wired the following to Mrs. Saruprani Nehru :

"Accept heartfelt condolence. Mother India lost one of her bravest and noblest daughters. Country shares your grief."

Kazi Khuda Bux, interviewed said, it was the saddest news at this juncture.

Mr. Lalji Mehrotra, a prominent business man declared that it was not merely a great loss to the country, but greater personal loss.

Though this evening "At Home" in connection with the inauguration of new premises of Indian Merchants' Association would not be totally abandoned, illuminations and bands were given up. A requisition is being sent in to close municipal offices. All markets will remain closed from 2 p.m. tomorrow. - A.P.I.

CALCUTTA PAPERS'S TRIBUTES

All nationalist papers here record the death of Mrs. Kamala Nehru with feelings of profound regret.

The "Advance" says, "India has lost in her death a remarkable woman, who personified some of the best traits of Indian womanhood"

The "Amrit Bazar Patrika" writes "The news of her death will no doubt cause profoundest sorrow to those in this country and abroad, who knew her, admired her virtues and appreciated the great sacrifices she made for the freedom of the country. She was an accomplished lady in the truest sense of the world."

The vernacular papers like the "Anand Bazar Patrika" and the "Basumati" also speak in the same strain and testify to her great sacrifices for the country.

The "Forward" says, "She was not only a source of inspiration to her husband, but she tolled with him for the freedom of the country and shared his sufferings. Truly she offered herself as sacrifice to Mother India." – United Press.

BOMBAY MARKETS CLOSED

Mrs. Kamala Nehru's death has cast a gloom over Bombay grain markets, were closed today. The Marwari Chamber of Commerce passed a condolence resolution and closed their office today. The Hindustani Native Merchants' Association and its members are observing hartal.

Several others have paid tributes to the memory of the late Mrs. Kamala Nehru, including Shrimati Kamladevi Chattopadhyaya, Dr. Hardikar and Mr. Jashed Mehta.

Mr. K.F. Nariman, Mayor of Bombay, has cabled to Pandit Jawaharlal Nehru : "Bombay is shocked to hear the sad news and tenders its respectful condolences."

A public meeting will be held on the Chowpati under the presidency of Mr. Bhulabhai Desai when prominent Congress leaders and others will address. - United Press.

AT HAPUR

The shocking news of Mrs. Kamala Nehru's death was heart on the radio last night and spread like wild fire early this morning. Every one seemed grief-stricken at the catastrophe and anxious enquiries were made in Congress circles. A spontaneous hartal was observed.

AT BAREILLY

The sad news of Mrs. Kamala Nehru's death was received in Bareilly this morning with great shock. Profound sympathy for Pandit Nehru is being felt in all quarters.

AHMEDABAD'S SORROW

The Ahmedabad Municipality passed last night a condolence resolution on the death of Mrs. Kamala. Nehru, stating that the deceased was a jewel among women. The President, Mr. G.V. Mavlankar, referred to her as one of the brave-hearted women of India. A 'hartal' is being observed in the city today and a public meeting of the citizens will be convened this evening to express sorrow at the death of Mrs. Nehru. - A.P.I.

DR. TAGORE'S CONDOLENCE

Calcutta. Dr. Rabindra Nath Tagore has sent the following cable to Pandit Jawaharlal Nehru on the death of Mrs. Kamala Nehru :

"Please accept my heartfelt condolence. She shared your heroism in her life and in her death she leaves an undying glory of that heroism."

The Ashram at Shantiniketan remained closed today as a mark of respect to her memory. - United Press.

C.R.'S TRIBUTE

Bombay. A glorious tribute to the courage and patriotism of Mrs. Kamala Nehru was paid by Mr. C. Rajagopalachari, who is here on a brief private visit to see his daughter, who was recently ailing and has just been discharged from the hospital. He said :

"Though the sudden collapse was not unexpected, the actual fact is ever different from the worst fears. The bereaved family stands in no need of help from outside to bear the calamity with courage. I have no doubt the domestic grief will redouble Pandit Jawaharlal's passion for public service. The golden memory of Kamalaji's brave life and service in India's struggle will serve as an ever-living power-house for the all-Indian womanhood for courage and patriotism, converting deaths into life."

MR. MOITRA'S CABLE TO PT. NEHRU

Calcutta, Mr. Surendra Mohan Moitra, a member of the Congress Working Committee, representing Bengal, has sent the following cable to Pandit Jawaharlal Nehru :

"Stunned by the tragic news of the sudden demise of your illustrious wife. May God give you sufficient strength to bear the burden imposed by the country upon you." - United Press.

Dr. B.C. RAY'S TRIBUTE

Calcutta. Interviewed by the "United Press" in connection with the sad news of the death of Mrs. Kamala Nehru, Dr. B.C. Ray, under whose treatment she had been for considerable period said :

"The end of Mrs. Kamala Nehru was not quite unexpected. During the past few months, she has been hovering upon between life and death. She almost fought like a Trojan against the illness which ultimately overpowered her. She had a frail constitution but a indomitable spirit. During her brief but eventful political life on the occasion of the enforced absence of her husband and father-in-law, she took upon herself the leadership of the Congress in her province and with a grim determination took upon herself the duties which a person with lesser courage and will, would have found difficult. She never considered for herself her health, her comforts even the happiness of home life when she was called upon to do her duties by her toliting and suffering countrymen.

"She has lived and died a conqueror, because I verily believe that for her death had no sting. She has left to her husband to carry on the work which she intended doing herself and left an example which women of this country would do well to follow.

"May her soul rest in peace."- United Press.

GHAZIABAD MOURNS KAMALA NEHRU

At a meeting held under the presidency of the Town Congress Committee of Ghaziabad, a resolution was passed regretting the death of Shrimati Kamala Nehru and expressing sympathy with the bereaved family.

All schools and business houses were closed as a mark of sorrow.

AGRA SHOCKED

The news of Mrs. Kamala Nehru's death caused a great shock in the Congress circles. Several offices and shops closed and the city will observe a complete 'hartal' tomorrow. Pt. Sri Krishna Datt Paliwal interviewed, said : "I am choked with grief. We have heard of the tests of purer and greater personalities, but the Nehru family is a living embodiment of India's sacrifice. It is God alone who gives power and courage to Pandit Jawaharlal to stand his ground all along."

LAWYER'S CONDOLENCE

The Bulandshahr Bar Association has passed the following resolution :

"This meeting of the Bulandshahr Bar Association has heard with greatest pain the sad news of Mrs. Kamala Nehru's untimely death at a time when everyone had begun to hope for the best and offers its most heartfelt condolence to Pt. Jawaharlal and his distinguished family in their very sad bereavement which is already an even of a nation-wide mourning.

AT INDORE

The news of Mrs. Kamala Nehru's death was received here with grief. A largely attended condolence meeting was held this evening in Bajaj Khana Chowk under the presidentship of Seth Chhotelal. Speeches were made by several citizens on the life of Mrs. Kamala Nehru and the sacrifices made by the Nehru family in the cause of India. A condolence resolution was passed, all standing.

AT MUZAFFAR NAGAR

The news of Mrs. Kamala Nehru's death spread in the town quickly. A mourning procession started from the Arya Dharamshala and terminated at the Sanatan Dharmashala. A resolution expressing the town's condolence on the untimely death of Mrs. Jawaharlal and sympathizing with her hausband, the President-elect of the Congress, Shrimati Swaruprani and Shrimati Rajpati Kaul in their grief, was passed.

Sir Tej Bahadur Sapru's Homage

I largely attended public meeting of the citizens of Allahabad held this evening under the presidency of Sir Tej Bahadur Sapru passed a resolutiuon expressing profound sorrow at the demise of Mrs. Kamala Nehru and conveying its deep sympathy to Pandit Jawaharlal Nehru.

Sir Tej Bahadur Sapru was visibly moved when he made his speech.

Babu Purshottamdas Tandon moved the resolution which was seconded by Sir Shafat Ahmed Khan. - United News.

AMRITSAR IN MOURNING

The news of Kamala Nehru's death received here last night was proclaimed by the local Congress Committee by a beat of drum, and a hartal was announced today. The city is observing a complete hartal, cloth, grains, bullion and several other markets being closed for the day. Satta exchanges, municipal offices and schools are also closed down. Public mourning is being organised by the city Congress. Tarn Taran, an important town in Amritsar district, and its mandi is also observing complete hartal. A public meeting held under the auspices of the local Congress Committee passed a resolution expressing sorrow at the untimely death of Mrs. Kamala Nehru, which was a great national loss. The meeting also resolved to send condolence messages to the bereaved family. - A.P.I.

INDIAN MERCHANTS' CHAMBER'S SORROW

Bombay. A meeting of the Committee of the Indian Merchants' Chamber passed a resolution expressing sorrow at the death of Mrs. Kamala Nehru and conveying sincere condolences to Pandit Jawaharlal Nehru. - United Press.

BOMBAY PUBLIC MEETING

A resolution expressing deep sorrow at the untimely death of Mrs. Kamala Nehru and recalling her unique contribution to the Indian struggle for the attainment of freedom was passed at a meeting of the Bombay Provincial Congress Committee held this evening under the presidency of Mr. K.F. Nariman, Mayor of Bombay. Among those who attended the meeting were Mr. Bhulabhai Desai M.L.A., Mr. K.M. Munshi, and Mrs. Leelavati Munshi.

The meeting conveyed its deepest sympathy to Pandit Jawaharlal Nehru in his irreparable loss.

The meeting passed a similar resolution about Sir Dinshaw Wacha, the oldest Congress president, who died recently. - United Press.

LAW ASSOCIATION'S CONDOLENCE

Bareilly City. The Bareilly College Law Association expressed its heartfelt grief and sorrow at the sad demise of Mrs. Kamala Nehru and offered its respectful condolences to Pt. Jawaharlal Nehru in his bereavement. The law lectures were suspended for the day as a mark of respect.

LUCKNOW'S GRIEF

Glowing tributes were paid to the memory of Mrs. Kamala Nehru, and her manifold services and sacrifices in the cause of the Congress and the country were recalled at a public meeting of the citizens of Lucknow held this evening here to mourn her death. Mr. Chandrabhan Gupta, president of the City Congress Committee, presided.

A condolence resolution was passed at the meeting.

The city observed a complete 'hartal'. A number of educational institutions were closed as a mark of respect to the deceased.

Congress flags at Moti Nagar and other places were half masted.

A meeting of the Lucknow Municipal Board, held today, was also adjourned as a mark of respect to the memory of Mrs. Kamala Nehru. - United Press.

HARTAL IN MEERUT

The news of Mrs. Kamala Nehru's death, received here this morning plunged the city in mourning. The town Congress authorities immediately announced a 'hartal'. Business in all quarters was suspended. The Municipal schools, the Meerut College and other institutions were closed. In the College, a condolence meeting under the chairmanship of Mr. Tamma, Vice-Principal, was held in the afternoon. A silent bareheaded procession paraded the main streets. On its termination, a mass meeting was held at the Town Hall grounds under the presidentship of Nawab Amirullah Khan, Chairman, Municipal Board. Glowing tributes were paid to the memory of the deceased. A condolence resolution was passed, all standing.

LAHORE, A MOURNING CITY

A complete 'hartal' was observed in Lahore city today as a mark of respect to the memory of Mrs. Nehru. In response to the appeal issued by Maulana Zafar Ali Khan and Maulana Abdul Qadir Kasuri, prominent ex-Congress leaders of the Punjab, the majority of Muslim shopkeepers also suspended business. In the evening, a public meeting under the auspices of the Lahore District Congress Committee was held at the Lajpat Rai Hall, at which Dr. Satyapal, President of the P.P.C.C. and other leaders paid a tribute to Mrs. Nehru. A condolence resolution touching on the death of Mrs. Kamala Nehru and sympathyizing with Pandit Jawaharlal in his bereavement was adopted, all standing.

"The Servants of People society members is deeply grieved to learn about the said demise of Kamalaji. Her death deprives the nation of one of the finest specimens of Indian womenhood and an unique patriot."—A.P.I.

AT CAWNPORE

Cawnpore observed "hartal" today as a mark of respect to the memory of Mrs. Kamala Nehru. - A.P.I.

'HER DEATH IS MOURNED IN COUNTLESS HOMES' MALAVIYAJI'S TRIBUTE

Benares. Mrs. Kamala Nehru's death is mourned deeply and is regarded as a national loss. Pandit Malaviya was deeply pained to hear her passing away. Panditji said "I am deeply grieved to hear the sad and premature death of Mrs. Kamala Nehru. She was a noble soul, an ardent patriot, and a devoted wife of her beloved husband whose constant solicitude for the freedom of Motherland she fully shared by the purity of her life and by her sacrifices and sufferings in the cause of the country. She had won the affection and respect of millions of her countrymen and countrywomen. Her death is being mourned by countless homes today. It is national loss and to me a personal bereavement which was caused me deep pain. My heartfelt sympathy goes out to Pandit Jawaharlal Nehru, his revered mother, his dear daughter Indira and other members of the bereaved family.

Malaviyaji has cabled to Pandit Jawaharlal Nehru :

"Deeply grieved. Countless millions share sorrow."

Malaviyaji has wired to Mrs. Motilal Nehru :

"Deeply grieved to hear Kamalaji has passed away. Offer you and family my sincerest condolence." - A.P.I.

BENARES PUBLIC'S GRIEF

The news of the death of Mrs. Kamala Nehru reached Benares this morning and spread throughout the city. The national flags on the city Congress office, the Vidyapith, the "Aa", the Sevaupvan Sevashram and residential buildings were lowered half-must. The university was closed as a mark of respect to her memory.

General 'hartal' will be observed tomorrow when a public meeting will be held at Ahalyabai Ghat.

Mr. Shivaprasad Gupta has sent a cablegram to Pt. Jawaharlal Nehru expressing his deep grief.

A condolence meeting was held at the Hindu University under the presidentship of Pt. Madan Mohan Malaviya at which a resolution expressing heartfelt grief at Mrs. Kamala Nehru's death was adopted.—United Press.

THE RICH TRIBUTE

Delhi : The Delhi Municipality passed a resolution of condolence over the demise of Shrimati Kamala Nehru at its weekly meeting yesterday.

The Committee further resolved to send a message of sympathy to Pandit Jawaharlal Nehru and other members of the family.

Hafiz Abdul Aziz, Advocate, Presided.

Glowing tributes were paid to the memory of the deceased by Lala Hari Chand and Khan Bahadur S.M. Abdullah, mover and seconder of the resolution. They said that Mrs. Kamala Nehru was an ideal wife and a noble daughter of Delhi. Her services to the country were a pride to Delhi, the city of her birth.

Mrs. Kamala Nehru was a most dutiful wife who had cheerfully borne sufferings to be a true companion to her husband. India needed more and more noble daughters like her.

INDRAPRASTHA GIRLS' CONDOLENCE

The secretary, Inderaprastha Girls' High School, writes :

"The news of the death of Mrs. Kamala Nehru - one of the best old students of our school - was received with great shock by the staff and the students of the above school, which was closed in her honour on February 29, 1936. On the reopening of the school on Monday it was resolved to offer our heart felt sympathy and sorrow to the bereaved family."

Similar resolutions were passed by the Mushturka Board Muslim Anjuman Hal, International Aryan League, Delhi Jewellers' Association and a number of other local bodies.

MATHURA HARTAL

Resolution of Sympathy on Mrs. Nehru's Death

The citizens of Mathura observed complete 'hartal' yesterday and all business was suspended for the day as a mark of sorrow at the sad and untimely death of Mrs. Nehru. A bare headed procession started from the Gandhi Park and paraded the principal parts of the city and terminated at a public meeting. Dr. S.N. Bhargava, president city Congress Committee presided. A resolution expressing deep sympathy towards the bereaved family, was passed.

The local Arya Kumar Sabha has elected the following office-bearers for this year : President - Mr. Fateh Bahadur, Vice-President - Mr. Udaiprakashji and Secretary - Shivlal Tavanar.

AT ALIGARH VARSITY

The Aligarh Muslim University was shocked to hear the news of the sad and untimely death of Mrs. Kamala Nehru.

Sincere sympathy is expressed for Pandit Jawaharlal.

ROHTAK BAR'S CONDOLENCE

The Bar association, Rohtak, placed on record its sense of pro-found grief at the sudden and untimely demise of Mrs. Kamala Nehru and expressed its heartfelt sorrow and sympathy with Pandit Jawaharlal Nehru in his sad bereavement.

AT BAREILLY

The members of the Bareilly College Union assembled in a meeting at about 12-30 p.m. today and passed a resolution of condolence on the death of Mrs. Kamala Nehru. The College was closed for a day as a mark of respect to the memory of the departed soul.

The local Congress Committee has announced 'hartal' and a condolence meeting for tomorrow.

MEERUT DISTRICT BOARD'S CONDOLENCE

A general meeting of the Meerut District Board to elect members for the Education Committee was held here this afternoon. Captain Nawab Jamshed Ali Khan was in the chair.

At the very outset a condolence resolution on the sad demise of Shrimati Kamala Nehru was adopted and the meeting of the Board was adjourned for some time as a mark of respect to the memory of the deceased.

ANGLO-INDIAN COMMUNITY'S GRIEF

The following message of sympathy was sent by Sir Henry Gidney on behalf of the Anglo-Indian Community of Pandit Jawaharlal Nehru :

"On behalf of the Anglo-Indian Community I offer you and your bereaved family our deepest sympathy and share with you your sorrows in the lamentable death of your wife. Her untimely death is a great loss to India at a time when Indian women are struggling hard to secure their emancipation, without which India can and will never progress. Her heroic devotion to the upliftment of Indian women will ever remain an inspiration for others to emulate. May the Divine Creator endow you with that manly fortitude with which bravely to bear your irreparable loss."

BOMBAY TRIBUTE

Corporation Passes Resolution

The Bombay Municipal Corporation was adjourned without transacting any business today as a mark of respect to Mrs. Nehru. Several speakers paid tribute to Mrs. Nehru.

Mr. Nariman, the Mayor, declared that Mrs. Nehru represented the best in Indian womanhood and it was a matter of great regret that the best doctors and all that science had provided could not cure her of her illness. Sir Boman Behram then moved a condolence resolution which was passed unanimously.

On Mr. Meherali's motion, the House adjourned. - A.P.I.

AMBALA'S GRIEF

A 'hartal' was observed in Ambala yesterday to mourn the death of Mrs. Kamala Nehru.

A condolence public meeting was held in the Grain Market under the presidentship of Pandit Bhagat Ram Shukla, when speeches were delivered by various speakers, on the life of the deceased and a condolence resolution was passed.

Condolence resolutions were passed also by the Friends' Union and by the Cloth Merchants' Association, as also by some other institutions.

Thus the rich tributes paid to her by people of every walk of life show her much popularity among the common Indians. During her stay at Anand Bhawan, Allahabad for about two decades, she had made herself busy in constructive work having deep bearing on Swaraj for our sub-continent.

7

The Assessment

Krishna Huthee Singh's *We Nehrus* is a nice work giving out details about the Nehru family, its style of living in Anand Bhawan, Allahabad, its social contacts and last but not the least about Kamala Nehru, her role in the family.

Kamala Nehru always encouraged her husband in his participation in the freedom struggle. There were differences of opinion between the father and the son, but Kamala used to have the well-balanced and effective voice, not annoying any of the two. She was the disciple of Gandhiji and always showed interest and keenness in his political programme which he had launched soon after the Jallianwala Bagh Tragedy.

Undoubtedly Kamala Nehru led an austere and simple life when Jawaharlal Nehru finally decided to participate in the freedom struggle. The meals served at Anand Bhavan changed into purely Indian style; khadi replaced silken garments and indeed the entire structure of daily life in the spacious house was changed. The socio-political life made the Nehru family the symbol of the nation and the gates of the Anand Bhavan were thrown open to the common man, woman and the youth. They indeed knocked at the door with hope but mainly with an urge to receive advice and guidance from the family. The problems of the people were complex and ticklish and their solution became the responsibility of the Nehru family. In this scenario Kamala Nehru made herself very busy and much attached to the daily programme that came in her life. Though her health did not permit all this, even then she did play in appreciable role.

On the other hand, young Nehru, with radical views, could not tolerate the prevailing societal backwardness and wished to have a new picture of India where each and every Indian - in all the regions of India - should be self-sufficient. He opined thus.

I was filled with the shame and sorrow - shame at my own easy-going and comfortable life and our petty politics of the city which ignored the vast multitude of semi-naked sons and daughters of India, sorrow at the degradation and overwhelming poverty of India. A new picture of India seemed to rise before me, naked, starving, crushed, and utterly miserable.

Thus Kamala Nehru was a political companion of Jawaharlal Nehru. She always supported him and shared his feeling regarding his social and political work among the masses. When Nehru commenced his tours in Sultanpur and other areas near Allahabad, he had to cover long distances in the villages where people met him freely and apprised him of their socio-economic difficulties. In this context Kamala Nehru proved to be a good companion as she soon picked up the magnitude of problems of the villagers and peasantry, which Nehru was determined to solve. On several occasions she had to wait anxiously for Nehru when he was away among the villagers. She, in due course of time, began to have patience like a true and sincere Indian wife. She never let the Nehru family about her feelings of loneliness and by and large she faced such difficulties while occupying herself for constructive work.

I am very glad that a definite treatment has been commenced and have no doubt that you have fully satisfied yourself about its efficacy. All that remains is, I suppose, to make satisfactory arrangements for the comfortable living of you all while the treatment goes on . . . . The account you give of Kamala was quite satisfactory - only the diagnosis confirmed the presence of TB bacilli and the sputum has proved that I was wrong in thinking that she was not suffering from the disease at all and shows what value can be placed on the opinion of doctors even so eminent as of Bombay. It is, however, a great consolation that we have detected the mischief quite early and secured the best possible treatment. The discovery of the solitary bacilli does not therefore worry me much and is only a warning that the utmost care should be paid of which I have no doubt now . . . .

Motilal Nehru expressed the sense of unhappiness when he knew about the proposal for the sale of Kamala's bangles. 'I was much pained to read you letter advising sale of Kamala's gold bangles. As you say yourself, these things will not go very far and it is certainly not necessary to dispose them of for her treatment.

I was disturbed to read that part of your letter in which you wrote about your removal to a less comfortable *pension* situated on the outskirts of the city and so cheap that it would be impossible to find anything cheaper . . . . You ask me not to worry but it is you who are worrying over the unavoidable expense of a most necessary trip to Europe.

It seems as if you have undertaken the trip merely to demonstrate how cheaply it is possible for a man, wife and child to live in a European town. It was hardly necessary to go so far afield for such a practical demonstration of domestic economy. I would have appreciated your attempt if you were on a pleasure trip.

But having gone of Europe for a definite object involving an issue of life and death anything which is in the least likely to retard its achievement is not only false economy but something more serious . . . . My fear is that you are trying to be very economical and not providing yourself and Kamala with the necessary comforts and assistance from others. This will prove a very false economy, as by saving necessary expenditure you would be defeating the very object of your visit.

I see signs of this in your not providing yourself and Kamala with the necessary comforts and assistance from others. This will prove a very false economy as . . . . I see sings of this in your not providing yourself with an overcoat until after you had actually caught a chill and giving to Kamala some very inferior stuff . . . .

When Indira was hardly five years old, Jawahar, who was serving a prison sentence in the district jail, Lucknow, wrote to his father :

Kamala writes to say that Indu is becoming more and more intractable and pays no heed to any kind of study. I wish some arrangement could be made for her lessons. I am confident that

I could have managed her easily but I am in barrack No. 4. So some other arrangement must be thought of. I do not suppose that she will acquire the habit of doing lessons. The longer this is delayed the more difficult it will be for her and for others. As it is she is past the age when she should have begun her studies seriously.

The year 1920 began quietly. Gandhiji did not immediately renew his *Satyagraha* Movement and, though Father was committed to his cause, he was able to continue the practice of his profession. In one great case he earned a fee of two lakhs (200,000) of rupees. Anand Bhawan continued to function at full tilt with all the horses, dogs, servants and luxury to which we were accustomed.

The shadow on our lives was Kamala's failing health. Ever since Indira's birth she had seemed frail and easily tired; now she began running a low temperature and feeling miserable. Of course Bhai and Father go the best doctors for her but it was a long time before they diagnosed her illness. Meanwhile they ordered Kamala and my mother, who was also ill, up to Mussoorie in the hills. Bhai went with them.

It was at Mussoorie that Bhai had his first direct clash with the British. It happened that delegates from Afghanistan were there to meeting British envoys to settle a little war they had in 1919. Unfortunately they were staying at the same hotel as my family. Suddenly one evening the superintendent of police called on my brother and asked him to promise not to have an contacts with the Afghans - supposedly because such a dangerous character as Bhai might stiffen their resistance against British demands.

Bhai did not know any of the Afghans or especially desire to, but this suggestion provoked his stuborn pride. He absolutely refused.

From prison Bhai wrote the Mahatma what the latter described as "a freezing letter," and received a sorrowful reply detailing all Gandhiji's reasons for his action. And it may well be that he was right and Bhai wrong; for Gandhiji had an uncanny sensitivity for the feelings of the Indian masses. He instinctively knew just what they thought and how they would act in given circumstances, and he foresaw that in their present emotional condition Chauri Chaura was not an isolated incident but the precursor of bloody revolution which would have betrayed everything that Gandhiji believed in.

This was not the only difference of opinion between my brother and Mahatma Gandhi. Bhai, committed to the Socialist school of thought, considered Gandhiji's Rousseau-like idea of returning India to a primitive cottage-industry economy as pure fantasy. He went along with it because he recognized its value as a symbol and inspiration for the Indian people, but he firmly believe that the cure of India's economic ills was more, not less, industrialization. He knew that no large country could exist in the modern world without employing all the machinery of modern life.

In addition, Bhai had a personal foundness for modern inventions. He wrote, "I have always liked big machines and fast travel." And he delighted in modern gadgets. In 1948, when he was Prime Minister of India, someone gave him his first electric razor. He was so fascinated by it that at a dinner party in his house on York Road he sent for the razor and demonstrated it to his guests by shaving himself at the table.

Another thing that troubled Bhai was Gandhiji's deeply religious emphasis, though in the exalted mood of 1921 he was almost caught up in it. He wrote : "I came nearer to a religious frame of mind in 1921 than at any other time since my early boyhood. Even so I did not come very near."

What bothered my brother, beyond the nagging thought that religion had been used so often to exploit the masses, was that it tended to divide people. Not Gandhiji's religion, which was an idealistic bend of the truths of all religions, a true spirituality; but the fact that others in his camp used religious phrases to strengthen dogmatic ends. He wrote, "I used to be troubled sometimes at the growth of this religious element in our politics, both on the Hindu and Muslim side. I did not like it all. Much that the Moulvis and Maulanas and Swamis and the like said in their public addressed seemed to me most unfortunate . . . . The religious twist that was given to everything prevented all clear thinking. Even some of Gandhiji's phrases sometimes jarred upon me . . . ."

In short, Bhai recognized that in India religion was not a unifying but a divisive influence. He feared it as such, and he was right; for it brought about the fatal division of India and Pakistan. At the same time he realized that : "(Gandhiji) was a great and unique man, and a glorious leader, and, having put our faith in him, we gave him an almost blank check, for the time being at least."

Soon after Gandhiji stopped *Satyagraha,* Bhai was released from prison, on March 3, 1922. The British had discovered that there was no law on the books against distributing pamphlets calling for a *hartal.* Of course, Bhai immediately started working for the Movement again. As he had been doing ever since 1920 – he went out among the villagers, talking to them about the Movement and learning about their needs. Despite her slight fever, Kamala often insisted on going with him. She never took her temperature and indeed she could not take proper care of herself when she was travelling around by train and car. She was very shy at first with the crowds of people but later she started making speeches and going to the villages on her own when Bhai was in prison. She carried on and let nothing upset her.

Bhai was always tremendously moved and encouraged by his reception in those small, impoverished places, where the peasants, scratching the arid soil with wooden plows.

The following June, when we had managed a little vacation at Simla in the hills of the Punjab, a telegram came telling us that C.R. Das had died suddenly. Father was completely stricken. He sat unmoving with his head bowed in grief for a long time. Thereafter for as long as it existed Father alone led the Swaraj Party.

During all this period Bhai was working for the Congress party with no salary. Even though he and Kamala were living at Anand Bhawan and had few expenses, he was very unhappy at being dependent on Father for money. He had long discussions on the subject with Gandhiji, who advised him that if he felt that way he should take time off from public service and get a job. Father would not hear of it. He pointed out the immense importance to the country of the work Bhai was doing, and that he and Kamala spent so little on themselves - they wore simple clothes, and Bhai always travelled third class on his constant political trips - that their support was no burden on him at all.

Father still had considerable means through he had refused to take any new cases. I remember one client who came with a lakh of rupees in cash hoping that the sight of the money would tempt him. Father looked at it frostily and said to me, "Well, Beti, do you think I should take it?"

I hesitated only long enough to sense his feelings, with which my own were in full accord; then I said, "No, Father, I don't think you should."

He gave my hand a quick squeeze and said to the client, "I'm sorry, but I cannot take your case. You see even my daughter knows it would be wrong."

However, now that Non-Co-operation had been cancelled, there was no reason why Father should not practice and he began to take a few cases. But in spite of this easing of his finances, in his argument with his son Father ran into Bhai's stubborn pride, and the discussion continued until it was settled by an unhappy event.

A son had been born to Kamala and Bhai in September 1924; but instead of joy there was great sorrow, for he only lived about a week. In addition Kamala was very ill, and her trouble was diagnosed as tuberculosis. In those days that was close to being a death sentence. After over a year, in which she slowly got worse instead of better, the doctors declared that her only chance was to go to Switzerland where the air was pure and sunny, and where the leading experts on her disease might be able to help her. Father and Bhai were willing to do anything to save her so it was decided. Bhai and Kamala and Indira, who was now nine years old, sailed for Europe in March 1926, on the same ship with my sister Nan and her husband, Ranjit Pandit, who were going on a long-planned holiday.

Father badly need rest and change and he planned to sail in June to join Bhai and Kamala, taking me with him. I was tremendously excited. But in May the blow fell. The great Lakhna inheritance case - Father's first big one, began in 1894 - came up for final adjudication. It was one thing to refuse new clients, but loyalty and gratitude combined to make Father feel he must finish what he had begun thirty-two years ago. He cancelled his passage. I was plunged into despair.

However, my father was a very extraordinary person, for an Indian father, or any other for that matter. He said I could go to Europe alone, because I could be of great help to Bhai with Kamala and Indira.

The night before I was to leave was long and trying. First my mother took me to her room. Sitting there amid her divans and delicately carved furniture, the very essence of old India, she begged me not to go. Every tradition and instinct of her orthodox Hindu soul opposed the idea of a girl of nineteen going off alone and unchaperoned to lands which she undoubtedly considered Godless and probably barbaric. To tempt me she said that if I would remain only a week more in India she would arrange for me to become engaged to one of the young men whom she had in mind for me. She ticked them all off on her fingers. All of them I had known, some since childhood. I told her that I did not want to marry any of them and that I was determined to go, although in my heart I was a little frightened at the prospect. She pleaded with me for two hours using every weapon of religion, respect and love. But despite my quavers, I held firm.

As I came out of her room my father's valet was waiting to intercept me with the message that Father wanted to see me. I thought, Not again! - I can't go through any more! But I had to go.

I fairly stalked into his room and before he could say a word I burst a tirade. "Look, Father," I said, "if you're going to give me another lecture I'd rather not go at all. Mother has been talking for two hours, beggining me not to go or at least to get engaged before I do. I'm sick and tired of listening to all this. So whether you like it or not, I do not wish to have another lecture thrust on me, and I will not go abroad if I have to listen to one."

Father looked at me over his glasses with that charming quizzical smile of his, and he said, "Why do you jump to conclusions?"

"I'm so fed up," I answered.

He said, "Now, darling, sit down and don't interrupt".

So I sat on the edge of the straightest Victorian chair I could find with my back stiff with resentment and all he said to me was, "I only want you to bear one thing in mind. You have the gambling spirit. You are going to be alone on a ship that takes seventeen days to reach Italy. Do not play card abroad ship, because I am not going to pay your debts.

"And secondly, he said, "I want you to remember your duty to us, and I want you to be, as you always have been, frank and straightforward with me. Promise me that you won't do anything about which you cannot write me."

I promised him, not knowing what I was in for, because there were often times when I was away that I wanted to do things, to go out alone with young men, to gamble - he was right about me there - and to do other things he would not approve of. But I always remembered Father sitting there so generous and so liberal, making it possible for me to go, and throughout my two years abroad I don't think I ever broke my promise to him.

Bhai met me at Naples and took me to some of the Italian cities I had read about. Rome, Florence, Milan and other smaller places on the way to Geneva. With my background of Western education they were both familiar and strange, like meeting a long-standing friend of one's family with whose picture one is familiar. I was enchanted and thrilled, the more so since, with his knowledge and, above all, his enthusiasm, Bhai was the perfect guide. We really became friends on that trip, for he was no longer my awesome big brother busy with great affairs, with time only to pat me kindly on the head. He was an ideal companion, sharing his thoughts with me and delighting in my pleasure at the beauty of those ancient sunlit building of Italy. I had never been so happy.

Finally we reached Geneva. I loved Switzerland with its cool, invigorating air and snow-topped mountains, though I did not love it quite so much as Kashmir. Fine as they are, the Alps are only a reminder of the Himalayas; they never equal their overpowering, dramatic impact.

Bhai's little flat delighted me because I had never before lived in anything so small. Kamala was taking treatments in Geneva and lived at home. Bhai told me that she had not improved as much as he had hoped, and I must take care of her and the flat, and cook for them. That meant starting from scratch, for I had never cooked before except to dabble in doing some of our exotic

Indian dishes. I managed somehow. Luckly I had studied French, but how little practical use my irregular verbs were I only learned when I went to market with our maid Marguerite. It sounded like an entirely different language from that spoken by my British teachers in Allahabad.

Indira was with us, too, until the time came for her to go to the good boarding school at Bex in which her father had entered her. There she learned to speak the excellent French she has kept ever since. Her education was, to say the least, sporadic, because of all the places her father and mother lived. Naturally, she did not have an English governess as we did, but she picked up English because all of us at Anand Bhawan spoke it as much as Hindustani - even after Father joined the Movement. And she always had a good mind and that intense, unchildlike concentration that enabled her to master any subject and make the best of what each school had to offer.

As soon as I had settled in, Bhai gave me a French dictionary, a map of Geneva and some tram and bus tickets, and told me to get out on my own. I was rather nervous, but I soon became very independent, and proud of it.

I studied French with a delightful Swiss girl and then Bhai arranged for me to go to the International Summer School. That was a great experience, for I met people from all over the world. Many of the leading statesman of Europe, who came to meetings at the League of Nations, lectured there. One day Albert Einstein drifted into a lecture room so quietly that at first no one knew he was there. But that unforgettable face and lion's mane of graying hair could not long go unnoticed, and when he was discovered there was an uproar in which the poor lecturer was quite forgotten.

A little later Einstein came to my brother's flat. I was too overpowered by his towering intellect to do more than mumble, "How do you do?" but Bhai engaged him in a rapid and interesting conversation. When the great physicist shyly smiled at some quip of Bhai's I began to feel completely at ease, though I never go the courage to talk to him.

Bhai also took me with him to call on Romain Rolland in his villa at Villeneuve not far from Geneva. They had a great deal in common, for the great French author had written a biography of Mahatma Gandhi, though he had not yet met him. Once again I played the quiet mouse - not my accustomed role.

Bhai never could be still a moment. He was forever rushing off to meetings in different European capitals, and he told me that if learned typing and could act as his secretary he would take me with him. So I learned to type and after that I often went along.

It was interesting to see Bhai growing in ease and authority as his knowledge of the world and, particularly, its economic problems expanded under the influence of the liberal leaders from many nations whom he met. Ever since his return from England, in 1912, he had lived within the closed circle of Indian affairs, concentrating on the ultimate goal of our independence, thinking of little else. Though it was caused by the unhappy circumstance of dear Kamala's illness, it is not too much to say that his long stay in Europe was an essential element in his education for the great role he was to play.

Naturally Bhai was a magnet for all the Indian exiles in Europe. To me they were legendary figures whom I regarded with a certain awe. But my brother only pitied them because they had been left so far behind by onrushing events that they seemed to him figures of futility, like half-forgotten ghosts that only materialize when someone happens to remember them.

As autumn came on, it was evident that Kamala's health was not improving. On the doctor's recommendation Bhai decided to take her to a sanitarium at Montana-Vermala high in the Alps near Bex, where Indu was in school. It was a small town, hardly more than a village, and when the deep snows came we seemed cut off from the world. The strangest thing to me was the silence at night, a stillness so dense that it was like a curtain of white velvet - it is always noisy in India.

Bhai and I went in for skating and skating. He has written about how clumsy he felt flopping all over the slopes before he learned the art of it, but that was just my perfectionist brother. Because of his natural timing and the superb control of his body his Yoga exercises had given him, he learned very quickly. Soon he was skimming over the snow, a slim, graceful figure, glorying in his swift passage. I did rather well also, which was another bond between us. The next summer we went mountaineering and climbed half-way up Mong Blanc.

However, nothing but prison bars could keep Bhai in one place for long. With Kamala well cared for, we had more freedom of movement. In December he went to Berlin, at that time in its post-war decadence of hopeless poverty and the extravagant night life.

With Bhai in prison and Father busy directing the Congress campaign it was up to the women to represent the family in the active phase of the Movement. As mass arrests began this same thing was going on all over the country; for the first time, Indian women came out of their traditional seclusion to stand beside their men in the front lines of our struggle for independence.

My sister Nan and her husband had returned from Calcutta to Allahabad to take part in the Movement. She joined us, while Ranjit acted as secretary to a Congress Committee. She and I worked all days directing the volunteers, attending meetings, and picketing merchants who sold English goods. More extraordinary, my delicate little mother, who had always been cared for like a china doll, came out in the blazing sun and hundred-degree heat to match in the picket lines.

And Kamalal! Kamala, whose fatal disease had returned, was the most active of all. She became the best organizer, the most intrepid marcher and the leading spirit of the women of Allahabad, up at 5 A.M. to drill volunteers, on the picket lines at eight.

One day I found our house full of children from about ten to fifteen years old, the girls were dressed like the boys in khadi trousers and *kurtas*. They were chattering like parakeets. Indu was organizing what she named the Monkey Brigade to take part in the Movement. As she said, "I wanted to join the Congress, but they told me I'd have to wait until I was eighteen. So I got mad and said, "I'll have my own organization."

The name was an echo of the Hindus legend about the time when Rama's wife, Sita, was held prisoner by the Demon Ravana on the island of Ceylon. The Monkey God Hanumana called all the monkeys of India to the rescue. They formed a living bridge, hands grasping tails, from India to Ceylon. Sita walked over the bridge in safety to rejoin Rama in the jungle abode of his exile. Ever since then, monkeys have been honoured by the Hindus; and it is as sinful to kill one as to kill a sacred now.

Indu's Monkey Brigade grew to several thousand children. At a mass meeting she could not make her voice carry to all of them so she used "human loudspeakers." She'd shout a sentence and a boy or girl in the crowd would turn and bellow it to those further back and so on. He executive ability at the age of twelve or thirteen was remarkable. Though we laughted at her monkeys at first, they proved very useful. They took over jobs like addressing envelopes, making flags, and cooking. When they marched in processions waving flags and making a lot of noise, the police would not touch them.

This immunity made them good for carrying messages between officials of the Congress and the Volunteers, unnoticed and unsuspected because they were children. They could even get through to the outer doors of the jails and when they saw someone going in, whisper a message to be delivered to a prisoner. And they gathered intelligence. Policemen sitting outside their station houses talking about their orders and plans would take no notice of some kids playing hopscotch in the street, never thinking they were acting as tape recorders.

But do not think it was all deadly serious business. The Monkeys had great fun planning their coups. It was like a glorious but dangerous game of hide-and-seek played for high stakes. Nor was Indu overly solemn. She was now a lithe and leggy teenager dedicated like her father to freedom for India, and with his abounding vitality. Sarojini Naidu, poetess and Congress leader, who was our great friend, referred to Indira in letter to my brother as being like, "Atalanta, fleet of foot with surprise in her eyes."

My brother was thrilled by the news of our activities. He wrote from prison, "By the time I come out I expect to find the women running everything."

Oddly enough I was the first of us to be arrested. On November 11, some members of the Youth League of which I was secretary were to be tried; and with my cousin, Miss Shyama Kumari Nehru, who was a lawyer, I went to Magistrate Bomford, whom I knew well, for a permit to attend the trial.

To return to important things. Back in June, I had gone to Bombay, the stormiest city, with Father and Mother and Kamala. Father received a tremendous reception. But we also saw some terrible attacks by police on peaceful Congress processions; horses charging and the sickening crack of *lathis* on bare skulls. When we came back to Allahabad, Father was utterly exhausted. He planned to go to Mussoorie for a short rest on July 1. In the early morning of June 30, he was arrested while still in bed and taken to join Bhai in Naini Prison just across the Jumna River.

The government had suddenly declared the Congress Working Committee an illegal body, so that any or all of its members could be taken at will. As fast as they were arrested other patriots were appointed to take their places. Kamala, too, was given this great honour.

In prison Father was quartered in a small barracks with Bhai and two old friends, Narmada Prasad Singh and the Mohammedan Congress leader, Doctor Syed Mahmud. In his exhausted condition it was very difficult for him, even though we were allowed to send his food in from Anand Bhawan. The four men occupied four tiny cells in a separate barracks and, as the monsoon was on, the roof leaked in the torrents of rain. At night it was difficult to find a dry spot on the narrow verandah on which to put my Father's cot. He had frequent bouts of fever.

Bhai nursed him devotedly. Father wrote to me : "Please tell everyone that I am quite well now. [This was not true.] Hari [his valet] would do well to take a leaf out of Jawahar's book. From early morning tea to the time I retire for the night, I find everything I need in its place . . . It has never become necessary to ask for anything which had so frequently to be done at Anand Bhawan involving a fair amount of shouting . . . Mahmud lends a helping hand but the chief burden falls on Jawahar . . . . I wish there were many fathers to boast of such sons . . ."

In August, Father and Bhai were asked to go to Poona to confer with Gandhiji in Yeravda Prison, for peace talks arranged with Lord Irwin by Doctor Tej Bahadur Sapru and M.R. Jayakar. When they consented, the government provided a special train. Though its schedule was secret, the word-of-mouth telegraph alerted the people and great crowds cheered them through the stations *en route*.

At Yeravda, Colonel Martin, the superintendent, courteously asked my father what kind of food he would like. "I eat very light, simple things," Father said. He then outlined menus from morning tea to dinner.

The superintendent was aghast. As Bhai said, "Very probably at the Ritz or the Savoy it would have been considered simple."

Three days of conferences with Gandhiji, Sapru and Jayakar resulted in a statement of the conditions under which they would call off civil disobedience. These were not acceptable to the Viceroy, so nothing came of it. But Father never recovered from the strain of those meetings. When next we saw him in Naini Prison, his face was swollen and he seemed very ill although he laughed and cracked jokes in his old way. In September his condition was so bad that government doctors, as well as his own, recommended his release. Weak as he was, Father telegraphed the Viceroy that he wanted no special favours. Nevertheless, Lord Irwin, who was both humane and intelligent enough not to want a dead martyr on his hands, ordered his release.

Mother, Nan and I took Father to Mussoorie for treatment - Kamala remained in Allahabad for her work on the Congress Working Committee. The cool, high air had a wonderful effect. When Bhai, having served out his sentence, arrived with Kamala for a three-day visit, they thought Father had turned the corner.

Bhai was only out of jail eight days. During that time he started a tremendous new campaign against the government. At meetings with thousands of *kisans* (peasants) he organized a movement against paying land taxes that spread throughout India. The government could not wait to clap him back in jail again; they also took Ranjit Pandit. On the first of January, 1931, Kamala was imprisoned. Bhai wrote, "I was pleased, for she had so longed to follow many comrades to prison."

My brother had no time for mourning. The day Father died, the Indian members of the first Round Table Conference landed in Bombay. Srinivasa Sastri, Sir Tej Bahadur Sapru and M.R. Jayakar hurried directly to Allahabad for the funeral ceremonies. The next day they met with Gandhiji, Bhai and other members of the Working Committee to give an account of the Conference. From what they said it was evident thet very little had been accomplished. However, the consideration with which the British had been accomplished. However, the consideration with which the British had treated them gave them hope that a second proposed Round Table Conference would accomplish something - Sastri, Sapru, Jayakar, were incorrigible optimists.

After two days of discussion someone proposed that Gandhiji should write to Lord Irwin and ask for an interview and have a frank talk with him. Bhai opposed the proposal; but Gandhiji, who liked to meet those who disagreed with him face to face accepted the suggestion.

"Dear Friend" : he wrote to the Viceroy. "As a rule I neither wait for outward prompting nor stand on ceremony, but straightway seek personal contact with officials whenever I feel such contact is needed .... But somehow or other in the present case I have missed the guidance of the Inner voice.

"But I have received suggestions from friends whose advice I value that I should seek an interview with you. . . . I was felt that, before the Working Committee took any final decision, it might be better for me to meet you and discuss our difficulties with you. I therefore ask you, if you are willing, to send me an appointment as early as may be possible . . ."

I am,
Yours faithful friend
M. K. Gandhi

Lord Irwin's affirmative reply flashed back immediately. On February 17, Gandhiji walked five miles from Doctor Ansari's house where he was staying in Old Delhi to the Viceroy's House and that famous meeting. The fact that it took place at all made the British Tories livid. Winston Churchill expressed their feelings in his thunderous style : "The nauseating and humiliating spectacle of this one-time Inner Temple Lawyer, now seditious fakir, striding half naked up the steps of the Viceroy's palaces to parley on equal terms with the representative of the King-Emperor." That was the sort of thing Lord Irwin had to combat in his honest attempts to reach agreement with the Indian leaders.

Gandhiji did not "stride up the steps," but was ceremoniously escorted by two gorgeously uniformed troopers of the Viceroy's Guard through a side door. Lady Irwin noted that almost all the servants found some reason to be on hand for a glimpse of the Mahatma. It must have been quite crowded as there were over seven hundred of them.

Lord Irwin and Gandhiji hit it off at once. So different in background and appearance, the formally dressed Viceroy towering like a telegraph pole over the small figure in his loincloth and shawl, they each appreciated the good will and sincerity of the other. Their sense of humor was also in accord. Once Lord Irwin asked the Mahatma if he would like a cup of tea. "Thank you," Gandhiji said producing a little paper bag out of his shawl. "I will put some of this salt in it to remind us of the famous Boston Tea Party." They laughed together. When Sir Cecil Griffin, who disliked Gandhiji, asked Lord Irwin if the Mahatma had been "tiresome," the Viceroy remarked, "Some people found Our Lord very tiresome."

On January 4, 1932, Bhai's trial took place in Naini Prison. He was sentenced to two years, regorous imprisonment and a fine of 500 rupees or six months more if he did not pay it.

On that same day Gandhiji was arrested; so was the president of the Congress, Vallabhbhai Patel. The Congress and all its committees were declared illegal organisations; and thousands more were arrested, so many, that soon all the jail in India were filled up and large temporary camp-jail were built. The new Conservative British Government had decided to stamp out the Indian National Congress.

With Bhai and most of the other leaders in jail, we women took up their work though we knew that in the present mood of the government we would not last long. Dear Kamala had paid the price of her activity at her husband's side and was prostrate in Bombay, grieving that she could not take part in the movement. Nan and I and our mother went to work with all our strength and enthusiasm. We visited the nearby villages, encouraging the peasants to hold fast against paying rent, and we began picketing boycotted merchants again. In mid-January we were served with an injunction against taking part in any *hartals,* processions or meetings. Independence Day, January 26, was only two weeks off and a great meeting was planned for that day, so we laid low.

The outdoor meeting was the largest held in Allahabad up to that time. Stretching as far as we could see from the platform, white *dhotis* and Gandhi caps and rainbow clusters of saris rippled with the movement of a crowd whose attention is not yet fixed, while the noise of their chattering seemed likely to make speaking impossible. Yet when mother was introduced and stood at the tall microphones they were silent and still as though frozen.

That was one of the most extraordinary things. A tiny, fragile Hindu lady, born to the luxury and seclusion of strict orthodoxy, suddenly became a revolutionary orator. Her fiery speech swayed and roused the vast crowd to a peak of high emotion voiced in their wild, shrill shouts of "Swaraj Ki Jai! Nehru Ki Jai!"

Then the *lathi* charges began. Amid confusion and the cracking of heads, the police broke up the meeting. Many people were arrested then and there. Somehow we managed to get mother safely back to Anand Bhawan. My sister and I were a little disappointed that we had not been arrested.

We need not have worried. The next morning at 9:30 the police car arrived. While the anxious servants huddled in the hall, Nan and I were told we were under arrest. The inspector was, an usual, courteous and rather embarrassed, and gave us time to collect our things and say good-bye to mother and Bibi Amma. Then he drove us to the district jail where we found many of our women friends. They were all cheerful and excited and our mood matched theirs.

We were signed in, weighed and given a cursory physical examination. Then we were taken inside the prison. It had no special women's quarters, as female prisoners were only held there until tried. One yard was set aside for them. Our fellow prisoners, apart from our comrades, were mostly thieves, professional criminals and prostitutes with the usual diseases. We were looked up four to a call.

It was one thing to be a cheerful martyr in the high excitement of being arrested for love of your country, and quite another to spend night after night in a filthy cell full of insects crawling about the grim walls. For several nights we could not sleep, lying there imagining that some slimy thing would crawl over our bodies; nor was it all imagination - they did. Then we got sensible and cleaned the whole cell out every night before going to bed. The reassurance this gave us, and sheer exhaustion, made us sleep at last.

Every morning we were routed out early for the English superintendent to inspect us and make sure on one was missing. One day two of us were rather late for the lineup. As soon as he saw us the superintendent shouted. "Hurry up! Hurry up! I can't wait here all day; there's tennis tournament I want to see and you're holding me up in this unpleasant place."

I shouted back. "We find this filthy place even more annoying than you do. Why shouldn't you miss the gennis one day when we have to miss it every day?"

Fortunately my marriage took place during one of the lulls in India's struggle for freedom. Gandhiji had once again called off *Satyagraha,* and the British were letting people out of prison instead of putting more in. So my family was together again.

The person who was most delighted with my engagement was Kamala. She liked Raja the very first time she met him. She had always loved me dearly, more as a daughter than as a sister-in-law, and I think she had almost given up hope of my ever marrying, because I had refused so many offers; so she was thrilled that I had, at last, chosen someone whom she and all the family liked.

Though she was far from well that autumn of 1933, Kamala took enormous pains with my trousseau, and saw to all the details of the wedding. The one thing that upset her was that our family had very little money left. Nearly all her jewellry, and mother's, too, had been sold; there was not much left for me. But still she gave me part of what little jewellery she still had; and mother gave me a little of hers. It was Kamala more than anyone else who made my wedding a gay and happy occasion.

I was married at Anand Bhawan on October 20, 1933, at nine o'clock in the morning by civil registration because, since I was a Brahman and Raja a Jain, no Hindu ceremony would have been legal at that time; also, mother was still very weak and could not endure a prolonged ceremony. Kamala always hoped that we could have a religious rite later, but we never did.

I was more annoyed by the fact that I had to wear khadi, but it was not the type of khadi I had when the movement began. I wore a peach-coloured sari made of gossamer-fine, hand-spun cotton with a broad gold border, and I wore a little jewellry. I had wanted to be married in my father's bedroom, but nobody would agree to that, so the big sitting room was decorated with bright flowers and ribbons, and ashoka leaves were hung on the doorway through which I entered, because that tree is supposed to be very auspicious.

When Bhai came upstairs to take me down, he thought I did not look much like a bride, for I had no pearls in my hair, or the other jewels that are usually worn. He took a rose from a vase and stuck it in my jet-black hair and said, "Well, now you look better." Then he took me downstairs.

Raja was waiting there in his Indian clothes, a fitted sherwani over a *dhoti* with a gandhi cap. I don't like that costume at all, but I must say he looked very elegant in it. Mother was reclining on a chaise longue; the others were standing. Raja and I said the usual things that are said at a civil marriage and signed the book. It was very different from my brother's and sister's marriages; but life was very different. Nan had a hundred and one saris in her trousseau; I had thirteen. She had diamonds, emeralds and pearls in matched sets of necklaces, rings, bangles and earrings : I had the scraps that my mother and Kamala's kindness found for me. There were no sacred fire and chanting priests. But they were not needed, for as things turned out it was a good marriage.

Raja's mother was too ill to come from Ahmedabad, but his brothers, Surottam and Shanti came, and some other relatives, among them his uncle, Kasturbhai Lalbhai, a leading industrialist, who was very fond of Raja.

A strange thing happened at the wedding. We signed the documents and shook hands with the registrar. Then my brother put his arms around my husband and me. Suddenly Raja was missing. I look around and saw him bent double touching his uncle's feet. Then he tugged at my sari wanting me to do so, too. I had told him I would not, but with all his relatives' eyes on me, I gave in, and very awkwardly and abruptly touched his uncle's feet. Raja brought up his brothers and sister and I had to do it again and again. By that time I was getting mad so, though it is not our custom, I made Raja touch the feet of my entire family, beginning with my mother who was still lying on the chaise longue, and Bibi Amma. He took it for granted and did it naturally and gracefully.

Bhai told the Hutheesings that they were invited for lunch, and there would only be members of our family. Their faces were study when they found there were a hundred and fifty of us.

After lunch Raja and I went to the house Bhai had taken for the Hutheesings in Allahabad. There was more foot-touching and when it came time for our traditional return to my family home, the Hutheesings loaded me with jewels, more even than Nan had, until I looked like an overdecorated Christmas tree. I arrived at Anand Bhawan, glittering and rather elated.

After being in jail in Calcutta, where the climate plus his confinement made him lose weight and become quite ill, Bhai was sent again to Dehra Dun. On a cold and somber day Raja and I went there with Kamala to see him. Not yet recovered, he looked terribly thin and careworn. Kamala and I were much upset, but the effect on Raja was far worse. He had never been to a prison before and sight of Jawahar looking so pale and sad in his drab little cell, with a cot, a few books, and a spinning wheel in one corner, completely unnerved him. When we returned to our hotel, Raja went straight to his room and lay on his bed for hours staring at the ceiling in unseeing misery.

Soon after this visit, Kamala's disease flared up again. All through this period she had ups and downs, slight improvements that brought hope to us all, followed each time by a worse relapse. For a few days she was so ill that Bhai was temporarily released from prison to be with her. When she recovered somewhat, he was sent to Naini Prison close at hand. Then her doctors ordered her to Bhowali in the hills, and the authorities thoughtfully transferred Bhai to Almora Prison where he was allowed out occasionally to visit her in her room at the sanitarium. Indu was also in Bhowali, having left school to be with her mother.

Meanwhile, after living with Raja's family in their house in Bombay for several months, we took a little flat of our own on Warden Road. I loved it, and we were very happy there. I was expecting my first child, who was born on February 1, 1935. He was the first boy, who lived, in our immediate family since the birth of my brother forty-five years before. Naturally there were great rejoicings. My brother sent me a telegram from Almora Prison : *Cheerio get well soon and bring the howling infant here for display and criticism love Jawahar.*

Kamala wrote ecstatically from her sanitarium and added, "Bring him here for me to see."

I named him Harsha, which means "joy", and is also the name of an ancient king of Kanauj; and as soon as he was old enough to travel - my friends said it was much too soon - I took him to Bhowali to show him to Bhai and to Kamala. So he had his first glimpse of a prison at the age of six weeks, which is other early even for a Nehru.

When I brought Harsha into the room in the sanitarium where Kamala was lying in her bed, she instinctively stretched out her arms to take the baby, who was big and fat and healthy. Then suddenly she drew back. With tears in her eyes she said, "No. I don't want him to catch my disease."

This aroused such a storm of love and sorrow in my heart that I wanted to just fling him into her arms, and I said, "Oh, I couldn't care less!"

But she refused to touch him, and lay there beaming and smiling all the time in her joy for me and delight in my son.

That was the only time she ever saw him; for soon afterward the doctors ordered her to go to Badenweiler in the Black Forest in Germany. And we did not see her again.

Kamala died in Lausanne on February 28, 1936. Indira, who had accompanied her to Europe, was with her, and so was Bhai, who had been released from prison on September 4, 1935, when the government learned that Kamala was dying. Three days later my second son, Ajit, was born in Bombay; but all the joy he might have brought me was drowned in my sorrow.

Bhai was truly bereft. He blamed himself that his preoccupation with India's struggle for freedom had kept them so much apart and robbed Kamala of years of happiness they might have shared. Not that Kamala ever expressed such a thought; she was as dedicated to *Swaraj* as he. It was the price that leaders of men and those who love them must pay, and she would not have had it otherwise. But to Bhai, in his sorrow and loneliness, it seemed too high a price.

He had Kamala cremated in Europe and brought her ashes home with him. Though Indu would have been a great comfort to him, he unselfishly decided not to embroil her yet in the bitter struggle that he knew would engulf him again on his return to India, for in his absence he had been elected president of the Congress for the second time. So he took her to England, where he put her in the Badminton School in Bristol, and came home alone.

Motilal, a believer in homeopathy, even tried doctoring her himself :

I have been studying Kamala's case for some days and have come to the conclusion that it is 80 per cent hysteria and 20 per cent other minor causes which combine to give her a headache.

I spent the whole morning with her putting together the various indications of different remedies and taking a nod of her head for reply on each point . . . . Yesterday she was crying with pain but today Nan [Vijayalakshmi] and she have been cooking various things for tea.

As a necessary part of the treatment I have cancelled the order about writing short descriptive essays or letters. I am almost certain that her headache was chiefly, if not entirely, due to the constant nagging to which I subjected her by insisting on her writing something. Instead of writing she got the headache - the result of pure nervousness at her inability.

But the headaches continued and a few days later, Motilal stated thus :

Kamala, I am sorry to say, has had another severe attack of headache. I have her the remedies which were indicated by her symptoms as far as they were known to me. But it is always very difficult to get at all the symptoms of a young girl as so much depends upon things she will never tell you about . . . . And homeopathic remedies require exact and great details.

In a letter written from Naini Tal on May 24, 1918, he said :

I have decided in favour Mussoorie and wired to take Kandi Lodge immediately. I hope Kamala is now fit for the journey and that you will all start off as soon as possible. It has no doubt been a change for the better to come up here but Naini Tal has already begun to tire me. You cannot take a turn without coming upon some ICS man or other. They have collected all the good houses and all the good things - you cannot even have a decent pony for love or money. I wish you would leave Allahabad at once and settle down at Kandi Lodge. Even Government House here cannot claim the same advantages. I enclose a cheque for Rs. 1,500 which ought to cover the travelling and other preliminary expenses at both ends.

He wrote from Mussoorie on May 30; "Do you think an ordinary dandi (an open type of palanquin) will do for Kamala? If not, an ambulance can be easily arranged for. I wish you would consult other doctors about Kamala besides the Dufferin Hospital women."

'At first poor Kamala was completely confused and uncomfortable in a place so different from her home. The big dinners with crystal and china on the long table and rows of wine glasses at everyone's place, the strange food, and, most of all perhaps, the quick loud voices of our many British guests, made her feel lost and lonely.

But all the family liked her and did their best to help. Being very intelligent she soon learned how to handle things. When eventually she came to live at Anand Bhavan as a daughter-in-law she won all our hearts.

My father doted on her, and my mother was very fond of her. They had their disagreements though, because mother was quite a queen in her own domain and Kamala, for all her sweetness, was a spirited girl - as she was to show when the going got rough in our long fight for independence. My sister Nan, who was almost exactly her age, felt the usual complicated sister-in-law's feeling towards her.'

Appendix

A CHANGE

The Jallianwala Bagh tragedy on April 13, 1919 shocked and angered the entire country. If any incentive was needed to strengthen Jawaharlal's resolve to join the freedom movement, the massacre at Jallianwala provided it. The outward veneer of westernisation slipped off the Nehru family, and a totally Indian ways of life took place. For Kamala, it was like going back to her roots. She had never been comfortable in the luxurious and opulent life-style of her in-laws. She gladly abandoned expensive silks and ostentation for khadi and austerity. This change brought her and Jawaharlal closer, and the wide gap in their upbringing seemed to lessen.

Ironically, although the freedom movement created a better understanding between Kamala and Jawaharlal, it was also responsible for keeping them apart. For now began the many spells of prison life for the Nehrus both father and son. As their involvement in the national movement grew, the family faced many hardships. Money was often in short supply. Jawaharlal had no independent income of his own and although it was suggested that as one of the General Secretaries of Congress he should be paid a salary, Motilal opposed the move. He thought it was wrong to use public funds for salaries. Thus apart from a small sum that Jawaharlal received as dividend from shares, he was quite dependent in his father. If this situation was galling for Jawaharlal, it was even more so for his wife. She denied herself many things in the early years of her married life. She reduced her needs to a bare minimum, but still felt humiliated at her dependence.

Kamala worried about Indira, her education and her nature. All this and her lineliness put in added burden on her frail health, and there were days when life seemed increasingly difficult for the young Kamala.

IN SWITZERLAND

Between December 1921 and March 1923, Jawaharlal spent over 350 days in prison. In late 1924, a son was born to Kamala. He survived for two days. His birth made Kamala seriously ill. Her illness was diagnosed as tuberculosis. On the advice of doctors, she was taken to Switzerland for treatment.

Motilal had always doted on his daughter-in-law, and in spite of straitened resources, he was determined that no stone should be left unturned in nursing Kamala back to health.

Jawaharlal used his stay in Geneva to attend various conferences and to meet people where he spoke passionately of India's fight for freedom. Indira was placed in a boarding school nearby.

Kamala, unwell and often alone, still very young, found time hanging heavily on her hands. She used this period to look around her, to write to friends, to read and to teach herself, among other things, to read and write in Urdu. Her stay in Europe showed Kamala the enormous difference in the levels of progress between women there and those in India. She realised that education was the first step in creating equality between men and women.

WOMEN'S ROLE

As the wife of Jawaharlal who had, moreover, been educated in some of the best institutions in the world Kamala felt keenly the burden of one who had been denied formal education simply because she was a girl. She wanted desperately to be the equal of her husband, as well as to be financially independent. She was convinced that while the women remained uneducated the country could not move forward. She found hard to understand those Indian women who had been lucky enough to be educated but were content to marry and stay at home Kamala strongly felt that the country needed them and their contribution.

Purdah was another custom that enslaved women and kept them housebound. Kamala's letters from Europe to family friend Dr. Syed Mahmud and his wife reveal her feelings on the subject. She wrote to Dr. Mahmud asking him to educate his daughters and free them from purdah. Lack of education and purdah were keeping a whole generation of Indian women from knowing and recognizing their capabilities, and their rights. From her sickbed in Switzerland, Kamala determined to come back to India and work to improve the lot of the women in her country. She believed that she and the other women had as much to contribute to the freedom struggle as the men. She prayed fervently to God to give her strength for her work for the country. By the end of 1927, Kamala's health improved, and they sailed for home.

DEVOTION TO GANDHIJI

As soon as they reached India, Jawaharlal was instantly caught up in national politics. He was in the forefront of anti-government demonstrations, often with Kamala at his side. Kamala was deeply attached to Gandhiji, as indeed he was to her, regarding her as a daughter. Her own temperament enabled her to identify easily with Gandhiji's ideology. Quiet and reserved, she was never aggressive or loud. Yet Kamala's convictions and beliefs strongly influenced three generations of the Nehru family—Motilal, Jawaharlal and Indira.

In an article written in November 1957, Indira Gandhi recalled how a relative had brought a beautiful dress for the young Indira. Kamala returned the dress, saying the family only wore khadi then. When the visitor insisted, saying the child should be allowed to make up her own mind, Kamala called her daughter.

"Indu . . . . Aunty has brought you a foreign frock. It is very pretty and you can wear it if you like, but first think of the big fire where we burnt our foreign things. Would you like to wear this . . . . when the rest of us are wearing khadi?"

Indira returned the dress in spite of her great desire to possess it–that was her first encounter with 'conscience and duty'. Familiar words she grew up with, the true meaning of which she imbibed from the example of her parents, specially her mother.

At the Congress session in Lahore, in December 1929, Motilal handed over the presidency to his son Jawaharlal. In January 1930, with the complete approval and backing of Kamala, Jawaharlal read out his declaration for complete independence, 'Purna Swaraj', and Gandhiji called for a countrywide satyagraha. By April, the country was seething with unrest as the civil disobedience movement gathered momentum. Jawaharlal and most other Congress leaders were put behind bars.

It was at this juncture that Kamala Nehru and other women took up the cudgels for the freedom of the nation. Kamala, in spite of frail health, was constantly on the move, urging more and more women to abandon purdah and to come out of their homes and fight for independence. They picketed shops that sold foreign cloth, took out processions, organised meetings and braved lathi charges.

COURTING ARREST

Since the Congress Working Committee had been declared unlawful, its members were constantly being arrested. Soon it was recruiting women as substitute members. In the vanguard of its new members was Kamala Nehru. She travelled extensively, courted arrest, braved the weather and neglected her health and even Indira. During this period, Kamala was also President of the Allahabad District Congress and constantly toured the town and district to mobilise volunteers and support for the civil disobedience movement.

In response to Gandhiji's call to fight for freedom, a group of women in Bombay had formed the Rashtriya Stree Sabha or the National Council for Women in 1921. Kamala had been a member for many years and in this capacity, she worked hard for the cause of Harijans, and in getting temples to throw open their doors to all people, irrespective of their caste.

On January 1, 1931, Kamala was arrested for reading out the same speech her husband had made, demanding 'Purna Swaraj'. Although she worried about Indira, Kamala was content that she and her husband were in prison for a cause that was dear to them both, for following Gandhiji, and for the struggle for the freedom of the country.

Motilal Nehru died on February 6, 1931 and Kamala was released before time. The loss of Motilal affected both Jawaharlal and Kamala deeply. Once he had accepted his son's involvement in the freedom movement Motilal stood solidly behind Jawaharlal. After his death, without Motilal's constant care and with Jawaharlal often in jail, Kamala's health took a turn for the worse. Yet the work had to go on.

ILL-HEALTH

Kamala had been actively involved in what was then begun as the Allahabad Congress Hospital in Swaraj Bhawan. In April 1932, the hospital shifted to a building adjoining Swaraj Bhawan, since in January that year, the British Government had taken possession of the building and medical supplies worth thousands. Somehow the hospital struggled on. Years later, after Kamala's death, Gandhiji laid the corner stone of the Kamala Nehru Memorial Hospital in Allahabad on November 9, 1939, and fifteen months later performed the opening ceremony of the hospital. Today, the hospital is one of the best equipped hospitals in Uttar Pradesh. It is a fitting memorial to Kamala and the years of service and effort she put into it.

In the years between 1931 to 1934, Kamala's health continued to cause grave concern. She was lonely with Jawaharlal spending long periods in prison. She was also unhappy that her poor health should keep her in bed so often. Yet whenever her condition improved even slightly, she was up and about, organising and addressing meetings. She worked in spite of a fever that exhausted her. When Jawaharlal was out of prison, touring the country, she was at his side, and her husband could see how weak she had become. "It is only her enthusiasm and will that carry her on," he wrote to Gandhiji. When Jawaharlal was with her, Kamala felt better; yet when the British Government offered to release him on the condition that he gave up political activity, Kamala was the first to protest.

Apart from her political work, after Motilal's death and with Jawaharlal in prison, most of the time Kamala felt responsible for the family affairs as well. In October 1933, Jawaharlal's younger sister, Krishna, was married at Anand Bhawan, and in her role of the daughter-in-law of the family, Kamala took upon herself the organisation of the wedding.

INDIAN VALUES

During her many visits to Calcutta for party work, for treatment under the eminent physician Dr. B.C. Roy, and later when Indira was admitted to Gurudev Tagore's Santiniketan, Kamala had come into contact with the Ramakrishna Mission there, and she was instantly attracted to it. She had been born with traditional Indian values and beliefs and these had remained unchanged over the years. Her contact with Gandhiji, her years of struggle with an illness that defied treatment, only accentuated her innate simplicity and spiritualism. She had taken to wearing only khadi and had completely given up wearing jewellery of any sort. Her life was frugal and austere and after her association with the Ramakrishna Mission at Belur Math in Calcutta, she spent many hours in meditation. She had been deeply impressed by the life and teachings of Sri Ramakrishna Paramhamsa and Swami Vivekananda. She also read the *Bhagavad Gita* and wrote that it gave her 'much pleasure'.

Kamala's mother-in-law Swarup Rani was often upset at the almost ascetic life-style of her daughter-in-law. Although the Nehru family had long given up any remnants of their earlier luxurious way of life, Swarup Rani wished that Kamala would wear some jewellery—a necklace or a couple of bangles as was considered proper for a Hindu wife. But Kamala had left such ritualistic customs far behind. She moved towards her gaol of service with a single-mindedness and sincerity that was astonishing for one so young and so constantly ill. She felt it was 'criminal to walk on the streets exhibiting my jewellery while the people of my country do not have enough food to satisfy their hunger'.

On another occasion when Kamala and Swarup Rani sat without using a fan on an oppressively hot day Swami Abhayanand described the anguish of Swarup Rani. She burst into tears at the thought of her son rotting in prison without a fan. In a moment Kamala's gentle appearance assumed a severity. With great emotion she said : "Mother, you are only thinking of your own Jawahar. Have you forgotten the plight of 30 or 35,000 young men and women wasting at present in British jails?"

The Bihar earthquake in 1934 saw Kamala hurrying to the affected areas. She moved among the poor and homeless, distributed medicines and other articles. But this visit took a heavy tool of her health, and her condition steadily deteriorated. Her disease was now clearly established as tuberculosis, and as Allahabad had few facilities for treatment, early in October 1934 Kamala was moved to the Bhowali Sanatorium in the Kumaon Hills.

Kamala's stay in the Bhowali Sanatorium improved her condition for a time. The rest, treatment, and climate stabilised her ailment; from an acute stage it became a chronic one. In consideration of Kamala's state of health, the British Government shifted Jawaharlal from the prison in Naini, near Allahabad, to Almora near Bhowali. He was allowed to see his wife about once in three weeks. These visits were precious to both husband and wife; specially to Jawaharlal who was haunted by the fear that just as he was really getting to know and understand Kamala, she might be snatched away from him by death.

BRAVE SPIRIT

By March 1935, the doctors in Bhowali felt that Kamala needed to go to Europe for further treatment. Since Jawaharlal was still in prison, Kamala left for Europe with daughter Indira and a cousin, Dr. Madan Atal. In September, her condition seemed to worsen and Jawaharlal was released from Almora jail. On September 9, Jawaharlal flew to Badenweiler in Germany to be with his ailing wife. His arrival helped Kamala to survive the crisis and she seemed to get a little better. Jawaharlal stayed in a nearby guest house or pension and morning and afternoon walked over to spend what time her could with her. Kamala was still very ill and long conversations cited her. Yet her brave spirit looked to the future, and she and Jawaharlal often spoke of India, its cause and what might await them on their return.

As Kamala's improvement continued, Jawaharlal and Indira went to England on a brief visit. At Christmas, Kamala suffered another setback and although she fought back with all the strength she had, the writing was on the wall, and it was obvious that the end was near. Kamala wanted to be moved from the sanatorium in Badenweiler. One of the factors responsible for this was the sudden death of another patient in the sanatorium—a young Irish boy who had occasionally visited Kamala and who had seemed much better and stronger that Kamala. At the end of January 1936, Kamala was shifted to another sanatorium near Lausanne in Switzerland Indira's school, too, was not far away.

THE TRAGEDY

Jawaharlal, in the meantime, had been elected President of the Indian National Congress for the second time. After agonising over whether to leave Kamala and return to India briefly, or whether to decline the presidentship Jawaharlal had decided to leave by the end of February. But Kamala's brave battle with the disease that he devastated her body was about to end. Early in the morning of February 28, at the age of 37, Kamala Nehru was no more.

Her death caused widespread sorrow, not only in Allahabad where the AICC suspended work and flags were flown at half-mast, but among all those who had come in contact with her. For many months, in spite of his involvement with his political work, Jawaharlal was a shattered person. He missed Kamala's quiet but strong moral support at every turn. After her death, he felt that he had neglected her; he recalled her long periods of loneliness and isolation at such a young age, and he blamed himself for not taking adequate care of her during her illness, albeit in a cause that was important to both of them.

It is testimonial to the unique character of Kamala Nehru that, in spite of being a part of the first family of the Indian struggle for freedom, a family of political and intellectual giants, she not only held her own, but was directly responsible for influencing them at crucial moments. This was due to her innate strength of character, and what Dr. B.C. Roy called 'the sterling qualities of head and heart'. Gandhiji said of her—"I have not known a truer, braver and more God-fearing woman."

In spite of her tragically brief life span and poor health, Kamala Nehru made lasting contributions to the Indian national movement. She was the traditional Indian woman, yet a great fighter for women's rights. She was the picture of the strong Indian woman who formed the backbone of the family, stoically and courageously accepting her ill-health and other reverses in her life. A person of great pride, self-respect and a deep-rooted confidence, she had few needs. She lived in a turbulent age, that brought to the fore many great men and women. Yet, it will be a long time before India can forget Kamala Nehru, and it may be years before another such is born.

"I thought of the early years of our marriage when, with all my tremendous liking for Kamala, I almost forgot her and denied her, in so many ways, that comradeship which was her due . . . And yet I was very far from forgetting her, and I came back to her again and again as to a sure when. . . . I had taken from her what she gave me.

What had I given to her in exchange during these early years? I had failed evidently and, possibly, she carried the deep impress of those days upon her. With her inordinate pride and sensitiveness she did not want to come to me to ask for help, although I could have given her that help more than anyone else. She wanted to pay her own part in the national struggle and not be merely a hanger on and a shadow of her husband . . . . Like Chitra in Tagore's play, she seemed to say to me : 'I am Chitra. No goddess to be worshipped, nor of the object of common pity to be brushed aside like a moth with indifference. If you deign to keep me by your side in the path of danger and daring, if you allow me share the great duties of your life, then you will know my true self.'

But she did not say this to me in words and it was only gradually that I read the message of her eyes."

Jawaharlal Nehru

Bibliography

UNPUBISHED AND PUBLISHED SOURCES

A.I.C.C. Papers, 1920-22.

The Collected Works of Mahatma Gandhi, relevant volumes.

Young India, relevant volumes.

Selected Works of Jawaharlal Nehru, relevant volumes (edt.) S. Gopal.

Selected Works of Motilal Nehru, NMML.

PRIVATE PAPERS

Gandhi Papers

Jawaharlal Nehru Papers

Motilal Nehru Papers

ORAL HISTORY INTERVIEWS AVAILABLE IN NEHRU MEMORIAL MUSEUM AND LIBRARY, NEW DELHI

Smt. Vijay Lakshmi Pandit

NEWSPAPERS

The Hindustan Times

Times of India

Amrita Bazar Patrika

The Leader

The Tribune

The Searchlight

SECONDARY WORKS

Abbot, G.F., *Turkey in Transition,* London, 1909.

Afzal Iqbal (ed)., *Select Writings and Speeches of Maulana Muhammad Ali,* Lahore, 1944.

Aga Khan, *India in Transition,* London, 1918.

Agarwal, Amar Narain, *Gandhism : A Socialistic Approach,* Allahabad, 1944.

Agarwala, M.M., *The Hindu-Muslim Riots : Their Causes and Cures,* Lucknow, 1944.

Aiyar, R.P. & Bhandare, L.S., *The Congress Caravan : The History of the Indian National Congress and of India's Struggle for Swaraj, 1885-1945,* Bombay, 1945.

Alexander, Horace, *Social and Political Ideas of Mahatma Gandhi,* Delhi, 1949.

Ali, Ameer Syed, *The Spirit of Islam,* London, 1935.

Ali Brothers, *For India and Islam,* Calcutta, 1922.

Ali Muhammad, *Freedom of Faith and its Price,* London, 1919.

———, *My Life - A Fragment,* Lahore, 1946.

Amery, L.S., *India and Freedom,* London, 1942.

Andrews, C.F., *How India Can Be Free,* Madras, 1921.

———, *The Indian Problems,* Madras, 1921.

———, *The Meaning of Non-Cooperation,* Madras, 1923.

———, *Mahatma Gandhi at Work,* New York, 1931.

———, *Mahatma Gandhi's Ideas,* London, 1949.

Anjaria, J.J., *Essays on Gandhian Economics,* Bombay, 1945.

Appadorai, A., *Dyarchy in Practice,* London, 1937.

Arberry, J. and Landau Rom, *Kslam Today,* London, 1942.

Argov Daniel, *Moderates and Extremists in the Indian Nationalist Movement, 1883-1920,* Bombay, 1961.

Arnold, Thomas W., *The Caliphate,* Oxford, 1924.

Asaf Ali, M., *Constructive Non-Cooperation,* Madras, 1921.

Asquith, *Memories and Recollections, Vols., I and II,* Boston, 1928.

Athlye, D.V., *The Life of Mahatma Gandhi,* Poona, 1923.

Ayengar, A.S., *All Through the Gandhian Era, Indian, 1915-50,* Bombay, 1950.

Azad, Maulana Abul Kalam, *India Wins Freedom,* Delhi, 1959.

Aziz, K.K., *Britain and Muslim India,* London, 1963.

Baksh, S. Khuda, *Caliphate,* Lahore, 1954.

Bakshi, S.R., *Simon Commission and Indian Nationalism,* Delhi, 1977.

———, *Gandhi and Salt Satyagraha,* Delhi, 1981.

———, *Jallianwalala Bagh Tragedy,* Delhi, 1982.

Bamford, P.C., *Histories of the Non-Cooperation and Khilafat Movement,* Delhi, 1974.

Bandyopadhyaya, J., *Social and Political Thought of Gandhi,* Calcutta, 1969.

Banerji, Nripendra Chandra, *Gandhism in Theory and Practice,* Madras, 1923.

Benerji, R.C., *The Story of the Khilafat,* Jessore, 1922.

Banerjea, S.N., *A Nation in Making : Being the Reminiscences of Fifty Years of Public Life,* London, 1925.

Barkatullah, Mohammed, *The Khilafat,* London, 1924.

Barns, Margarite, *India : Today and Tomorrow,* London, 1937.

Basu, Aparna, *The Growth of Education and Political Development in India, 1898-1920,* Delhi, 1974.

Bayly, C.A., *The Local Roots of Indian Politics, Allahabad, 1880-1920,* Oxford, 1975.

Besant, Annie, *How India Wrought for Freedom,* Madras, 1915 .

———, *The Birth of New India,* Madras, 1917.

———, *Gandhian Non-Cooperation or Shall India Commit Suicide?,* Madras, 1920.

———, *Shall India Live or Die?,* Madras, 1925.

———, *India : A Nation,* Madras, 1930.

———, *India : Today and Tomorrow,* London, 1937.

———, *India : Bond or Free,* Adyar, 1939.

———, *Speeches and Writings,* Madras, n.d.

Besterman, Theodore, *Mrs. Annie Besant : A Modern Prophet,* London, 1934.

Bevan, Edywn, *Indian Nationalism : An Independent Estimate in India,* Delhi, 1966.

Bhagwan Das, *The Meaning of Swaraj or Self-Government,* Banaras, 1921.

———, *The Philosophy of Non-Cooperation,* Madras, 1922.

Bipan Chandra, *Rise and Growth of Economic Nationalism in India,* Delhi, 1966.

———, *Nationalism and Colonialism in Modern India,* Delhi, 1979

Birla, G.D., *In the Shadow of the Mahatma : Personal Memoirs,* Bombay, 1968.

Bisheshwar Prasad, *Bandage and Freedom : A History of Modern India, 1707-1947, Vol. II, Freedom, 1858-1947,* Delhi, 1979.

Bolitho, Hector, *Jinnah : Creator of Pakistan,* London, 1954.

Bondurant, Joan V., *Conquest of Violence : The Gandhian Philosophy of Conflict,* London, 1959.

Bose, Nirmal Kumar, *Studies in Gandhism,* Calcutta, 1962.

Bose, Nirmal Kumar and Patwardhan, P.H., *Gandhi in Indian Politics,* Bombay, 1967.

Bose, Subhas Chandra, *The Indian Struggle, 1920-42,* New York, 1964.

Brailsford, Henry Noel, *Rebel India,* New York, 1931.

———, *Subject India,* New York, 1943.

Brecher, Michael, *Nehru : A Political Biography,* London, 1959.

Bright, J.S., *The Himalayan Blunders of Mahatma Gandhi,* Lahore, 1946.

Brockway, A. Fenner, *Non-Cooperation in Other Lands,* Madras, 1921

———, *The Indian Crisis,* London, 1930.

Brown, Judith M., *Gandhi's Rise to Power : Indian Politics, 1915-1922,* London, 1972.

Bryant, John Forbes, *Gandhi and Indianisation of the Empire,* London, 1924.

Buch, M.A., *Rise and Growth of Indian Liberalism,* Baroda, 1938.

———, *Rise and Growth of Indian Militant Nationalism,* Bombay, 1940.

Caveeshar, Sardul Singh, *India's Fight for Freedom,* Lahore, 1936.

Chakravarty, Amiya, *Mahatma Gandhi and Modern World,* Calcutta, 1945.

Chatterjee, B.C., *Gandhi and Aurobindo,* Calcutta, 1967.

Chatterjee Dilip Kumar, *C.R. Das and Indian National Movement,* Calcutta, 1956.

Chatterjee, Jogesh, *The Search of Freedom,* Calcutta, 1967.

Chatterjee, Nandlal, *India's Freedom Struggle,* Allahabad, 1958.

Chesney, George, *Indian Policy : The System of Administration,* Delhi, 1976.

Chintamani, C.Y., *Indian Politics Since the Mutiny,* Allahabad, 1947.

Chirol, Valentine, *Pan-Islamism,* London, 1906.

———, *India : Old and New,* London, 1921.

———, *India,* London, 1926.

———, Cole, F. Seymour, *India Should Know Turkey,* Bombay, 1943.

———, Coupland, R., *The Indian Problem, 1833-1935,* London, 1942.

———, *The Gaol of British Rule in India,* London, 1948.

Craddock, Reginald Henry, *The Dilemma in India,* London, 1920.

Crozir, Frank Percy, *A World to Gandhi : The Lesson of Ireland,* London, 1931.

Curtis, L., *Dyarchy,* Oxford, 1920.

Das, C.R., *India for Indians,* Madras, 1921.

Das, M.N., *The Political Philosophy of Jawaharlal Nehru,* London, 1961.

———, *India Under Morley and Minto,* London, 1964.

———, *Indian National Congress Vs. The British, 1885-1918*, Delhi, 1978.

Datta, K.K., *History of the Freedom Movement in Bihar, Vol. I, 1857-1928,* Patna, 1957.

Desai, A.R., *Social Background of Indian Nationalism,* Bombay, 1959.

Desai, Mahadev, *The Story of Bardoli,* Ahmedabad, 1957.

Dhawan, Gopinath, *The Political Philosophy of Mahatma Gandhi,* Ahmedabad, 1946.

Digby William, *Prosperous British India,* London, 1901.

Diwakar, R.R., *Satyagraha : Its Technique and History,* Bombay, 1946

———, *Satyagraha in Action,* Calcutta, 1949.

———, *Satyagraha : The Power of Truth* Illinois, 1948.

Doke, Joseph, *M.K. Gandhi : An Indian Patriot in South Africa,* Madras, 1919.

Duncan, Ronald, *Select Writings of Mahatma Gandhi,* London, n.d.

Dutt, K. Iswara, *Congress Cyclopaedia, Vol. I,* Delhi, n.d.

Dutt, K.N., *Landmarks of the Freedom Struggle in Assam,* Gauhati 1958.

Dutt, R. Palme, *India Today,* Bombay, 1949.

Dutt, Ramesh Chandra, *The Economic History of India in the Victorian Age, Vol. II.*

Dwarkadas, Kanji, *India's Fight for Freedom, 1913-1937,* Bombay, 1966.

Edib, Halide, *Conflict of East and West in Turkey,* Delhi, 1935.

Elwin, Harry Verrier Holman, *Mahatma Gandhi,* London, 1932.

Fischer, Louis, *The Life of Mahatma Gandhi,* New York, 1950.

———, *The Essential Gandhi,* London, 1963.

Fraser, Andrew, *Among Indian Rajahs and Ryots,* London, 1911.

Fuller, Bampfylde, *The Empire of India,* London, 1913.

Fuller, J.F.C., *Indian in Revolt,* London, 1931.

Gallagher, J., Johnson, G. and Seal, A. (ed.), *Locality, Province and National : Essays on Indian Politics, 1870-1940,* Cambridge, 1973.

Gandhi, M.K., *An Autobiography or the Story of My Experiments with Truth,* Ahmedabad, 1958.

———, *Hind Swaraj,* Madras, 1921.

———, *Swaraj in One Year,* Madras, 1921.

———, *Communal Unity,* Ahmedabad, 1948.

———, *Non-Violence in Peace and War,* Ahmedabad, 1942.

———, *Economics of Khadi,* Ahmedabad, 1941.

———, *Constructive Programme : Its Meaning and Place,* Ahmedabad, 1948.

Ghose, P.C., *Mahatma Gandhi As I Saw Him,* Delhi, 1968.

Ghose, Shankar, *Political Ideas and Movements in India,* Calcutta, 1975.

Gokhale, G.K., *Speeches,* Madras, 1916.

Gopal, Ram, *Indian Muslims : A Political History, 1858-1947,* Bombay, 1959.

—, *How India Struggled for Freedom,* Bombay, 1967.

Gopal, S., *British Policy in India, 1858-1905,* London, 1975.

———, *Jawaharlal Nehru : A Biography, Vol. I,* London, 1975.

Gordon, Leonard, A., *Bengal : The Nationalist Movement, 1879-1940,* Delhi, 1974.

Gour, H.S., *The British Impact on India,* London, 1965.

Gregg, Richard B., *Psychology and Strategy of Gandhi's Non-violent Resistance,* Madras, 1929.

—, *Economics of Khaddar,* Ahmedabad, 1946.

Griffths, P.J., *The British Impact on India,* London, 1965.

Gupta, Nagendranath, *Indian Nationalism,* Bombay, 1946.

—, *Gandhi and Gandhism,* Bombay, 1948.

Gwyer, Maurice and Appadorai, A., *Speeches and Documents on the*

Indian Constitution, 1921-47, Vol. I, London, 1957.

Hamper, D.A., *John Morley, Liberal Intellectual in Politics,* London, 1968.

Hasan, Mushirul, *Nationalism and Communal Politics in Indian, 1916-28,* Delhi, 1974.

Holmes, John Haynes, *Gandhi before Pilate : A Sermon on the Indian Revolution,* New York, 1930.

Horne, E.A., *The Political System of British India,* Oxford, 1922.

Horniman, B.G., *Amritsar and Our Duty to India,* London, 1920.

Houghton, Bernard, *The Issue in India,* Madras, 1922.

———, *Realities of Today,* Madras, 1923.

Hoyland, John S., *The Case for India,* London, 1929.

———, *Indian Crisis : The Background,* London, 1943.

Hull, William Issac, *India's Political Crisis,* Baltimore, 1930.

Hunter, W.W., *The Indian Musalmans,* London, 1972.

Husain, Azam, *Fazl-i-Husain : A Political Biography,* Bombay, 1946.

Hyde, H. Montgomery, *Lord Reading,* London, 1967.

Hyndman, H.M., *The Awakening of Asia,* London, 1919.

Iyenger, C.S. Ranga, *India in the Crucible,* London, 1927.

—, *How to Lose India,* Lahore, 1935.

Jayakar, M.R., *The Story of My Life, 1873-1922, Vol. I,* Bombay 1958.

Jha, Shiva Nand, *A critical Study of Gandhian Economic Thought,* Agra, 1961.

Iyer, Raghavan N., *The Moral and Political Thought of Mahatma Gandhi,* London, 1978.

Kabir, Humayun, *Muslim Politics, 1906-42,* Calcutta, 1943.

Kamath, M.S. *The Home Rule League,* Madras, 1927.

Karmarkar, D.D., *Bal Gangadhar Tilak : A Study,* Bombay, 1956.

Karve, D.G. and Ambedkar, D.V. (ed.), *Speeches and Writings of Gopal Krishna Gokhale, Vol. II,* Bombay, 1966.

Kaura, Uma, *Muslim and Indian Nationalism : The Emergence of the Demand for India's Partition, 1928-40,* Delhi, 1977.

Kaushik, P.D., *The Congress Ideology and Programme, 1920-47,* Delhi, *1964.*

Keer Dhananjay, *Lokamanya Tilak : Father of Our Freedom Struggle* Bombay, 1958.

———, *Mahatma Gandhi : Political Saint and Unarmed Prophet;* Bombay,, 1973.

Keith, A.B. (ed.) *Speeches and Documents on Indian Policy, Vol. II,* London, 1922.

Kenworthy, J.W., *India : A Warning,* London, 1931.

Kidwai, Shaikh Mushir Hasan, *Pan-Islamism,* London, 1908.

Kohli, M.S., *Mahatma Gandhi's Confessions,* Lahore, 1943.

Kohn, Hans, *A History of Nationalism in the East,* New York, 1929.

Koss, Stephen E., *John Morley at the India Office, 1905-1910,* Yale University Press, 1969.

Kripalani, J.B., *The Gandhian Way,* Bombay, 1946.

———, *Gandhi : His Life and Thought,* Delhi, 1970.

Krishnamurti, Y.G., *Gandhi Era in World Politics,* Bombay, 1943.

Kumarappa, J.C., *Gandhian Economic Thought,* Bomabay, 1931.

Kurup, T.C.K., *Gospel of Gandhi,* Madras, 1921.

Lajpat Rai, *The Political Future of India,* New York, 1919.

———, *India's Will To Freedom : Writings and Speeches On the Present Situation,* Madas, 1921.

———, *Ideals of Non-Cooepration and Other Eassay,* Madras, 1924.

Lal Bahadur, *The Muslim League : Its History, Activities and Achievements,* Agra, 1954.

Lawton, Lancerton, *Empire of the East, Part II,* London, 1912.

Lovett, Verney, *A History of the Indian Naitonal Movement,* London, 1920.

Lucas, Charles, *The Empire at War,* London, 1921.

Mackenzie, Brown, *Indian Political Thought from Ranade to Bhave,* Berkeley, 1961.

MacDonald, J. Ramsay, *The Government of India,* London, n.d.

Macnicol, Nicol, *The Making of Modern India,* London, 1924.

Mahmud Ahmad; *Non-Cooperation and Islam,* Lahore, 1921.

———, *Indian Problem and its Solution,* London, 1926.

Mahmud, Syed, *The Khilafat and England,* Patna, 1922.

Majumdar, R.C., *Three Phases of India's Struggle for Freedom,* Bombay, 1961.

———, *History of Freedom Movement in India, Vol. III,* Calcutta, 1963.

Many, Countess of Minto, *India, Minto and Morley, 1906-10,* London, 1934.

Masani, R.P., *Dadabhai Naoroji : The Grand Old Man of India,* London, 1939.

Mathur, J.S., *Essays on Gandhian Economics,* Allahabad, 1960.

Mazumdar, H.T., *Gandhi : The Apostle,* Chicago, 1923.

———, *Mahatma Gandhi : Peaceful Revolutionary,* New York, 1952.

Mehrotra, S.R., *India and the Commonweath, 1885-1929,* London, 1965.

———, *Towards Indian Freedom and Partition,* Delhi, 1979.

Menon, P.K.K., *The History of Freedom Movement in Kerala, 1885-1938, Vol. II,* Trivandrum, 1972.

Meston, Lord, *India and the Empire,* London, 1924.

Mishra, D.P. (ed.), *The History of Freedom Movement in Madhya Pradesh,* Nagpur, 1956.

Mitra, S.M., *Indian Problems,* London, 1908.

Mody, H.P., *The Political Future of India,* London, 1908.

Montagu, E.S., *An Indian Diary,* London, 1930.

Moon, P., *Gandhi and Modern India,* London, 1968.

Moore, R.J., *The Crisis of Indian Unity,* Oxford, 1964.

Moraes, Frank, *Jawaharlal Nehru : A Biography,* New York, 1956.

Mukerjee, H., *India Struggles for Freedom,* Bombay, 1946.

———, *Gandhiji : A Study,* Calcutta, 1958.

Naik, V.N., *Indian Liberalism,* Bombay, 1945.

Nair, C. Sankaran, *Gandhi and Anarchy,* Madras, 1922.

Namboodiripad, E.M.S., *The Mahatma and the Ism,* Delhi, 1958.

Naoroji, Dadabhai, *Poverty and Un-British Rule in India,* Delhi, 1962.

———, *Speeeches and Writings of Dadabhai, Naoroji,* Madras, n.d.

Narayan, Shriman, *The Gandhian Plan of Economic Development of India,* Bombay, 1944.

Nariman, K.F., *Whither Congress*, Bombay, 1933.

Nehru, Jawaharlal, *An Autobiography,* London,1936.

———, *Glimpses of World History,* Bombay, 1945.

———, *The Discovery of India,* Calcutta, 1946.

———, *A Bunch of Old Letters,* Bombay, 1960.

Nevinson, Henry W., *The New Spirit in India,* Delhi, 1975.

Nomon, Mohammed, *Rise and Growth of All India Muslim League,* Allahabad, 1941.

———, *Muslim India,* Allahabad, 1942.

Nandy, Alfred, *Indian Unrest, 1919-20,* Dehradun, 1921.

O'Dwyer, Michael, *India As I Knew it, 1885-1925,* London, 1925.

Pal, B.C., *The Spirit of Indian Nationalism,* London, 1910.

———, *Nationality and Empire,* Calcutta, 1920.

———, *The Gaol and Way*, Madras, 1921.

———, *Swadeshi and Swaraj,* Calcutta, 1954.

Pande, B.N., *Nehru,* Delhi, 1977.

Panikkar, K.M., *The New Empire,* London, 1934.

Pardaman Singh, *Lord Minto and Indian Nationalism, 1905-1910,* Allahabad, 1976.

Parmanand, Bhai, *The Story of My Life,* Lahore, 1934.

Pavate, T.V., *Bal Gangadhar Tilak,* Ahmedabad, 1958.

Patil, V.T., *Nehru and the Freedom Movement,* Delhi, 1977.

Paul, K.T., *The British Connection with India,* London, 1927.

Payne, Robert, *The Life and Death of Mahatma Gandhi,* London, 1969.

Polak, H.S., and others, *Mahatma Gandhi,* London, 1949.

Pole, D. Graham, *I Refer to India,* London, 1929.

———, *India in Transition,* London, 1932.

Prabodh Chandra, *Sixty Years of Congress,* Lahore, 1946.

Pradhan, R.G., *India's Struggle for Swaraj,* Madras, 1930.

Prasad, Rajendra, *Satyagraha in Champaran,* Ahmedabad, 1949.

———, *Autobiography,* Bombay, 1957.

———, *At the Feet of Mahatma Gandhi,* Bombay, 1961.

Price, Clair, *The Rebirth of Turkey,* New York, 1923.

Pylee, M.V., *Constitutional Government in India,* Bombay, 1965.

Raju, J.B., *A Critical Study of the Non-Cooperation Movement,* Nagpur, 1920.

Ram Rattan, *Gandhi's Concept of Political Obligation,* Calcutta, 1972.

Ramachandran G., *Promotion of Gandhian Philosophy,* Mysore, 1966.

Rao, C.V.H., *Civil Disobedience Movement in India or The Indian Struggle for Freedom,* Lahore, 1946.

Ray, Prithwis Chandra, *Life and Times of C.R. Das,* Calcutta, 1927.

Readings, Marquess of, Rufus Issacs, *First Marquess of Reading, Vols. I and II,* London, 1945.

Reynolds, Reginald, *The White Sahibs in India,* London, 1937.

Rivelt, Kenneth, *Economic Thought of Mahatma Gandhi,* Delhi, 1959.

Ronaldshay, Earl of, *The Life of Lord Curzon,* London, 1928.

Roy, M.N., *One Year of Non-Cooperation from Ahmedabad to Gaya,* Calcutta, 1923.

———, *The Future of Indian Politics,* London, 1928.

Rutherford, V.H., *Modern India : Its Problems and Their Solution,* London, 1927.

Ruthnaswamy, M., *The Political Philosophy of Mr. Gandhi,* Madras, 1922.

Santhanam, K., *Gospel of Gandhi,* Bombay, 1967.

Sarkar, Sumit, *The Swadeshi Movement in Bengal, 1903-1908,* Delhi, 1973.

Shakir, Moin, *Khilafat to Pakistan,* Delhi, 1970.

Sharma, Bishan Swarup, *Gandhi As a Political Thinker,* Allahabad, 1956.

Sharp, Gene, *Gandhi Wields the Weapon of Moral Power,* Ahmedabad, 1956.

———, *The Politics of Non-Violent Action,* Boston, 1972.

Shridharni, K., *War Without Violence : A Study of Gandhi's Method and its Accomplishments,* New York, 1939.

Singh, Hira Lal, *Problems and Politics of the British in India,* Bombay, 1963.

Singh, Sita Ram, *Nationalism and Social Reform in India,* Delhi 1968.

Sitaramayya, B. Pattabhi, *History of the Indian National Congress 1885-1935, Vol. I,* Delhi, 1969.

Smith, W.C., *Modern Islam in India,* Lahore, 1947.

Smith W.R., *Nationalism and Reform in India,* London, 1973.

Speeches and Writings of Bal Gangadhar Tilak, Madras, n.d.

Sprat, P., *Gandhism : An Analysis,* Madras, 1932.

Street, C.J.C., *Lord Reading,* London, 1926.

Swinson, Arthur, *Six Minutes to Sunset,* London, 1964.

Sykes, Frederick, *From Many Angles : An Autobiography,* London, 1942.

Tara chand, *History of freedom Movement in India, Vol. III,* Delhi, 1972.

Tendulkar, D.G., *Mahatma : Life of Mohandas Karamchand Gandhi, Vols. II and III,* Delhi, 1961.

Thomson, Edward, *The Reconstruction of India,* London, 1930.

Vaswani, T.L., *Non-Coperation and National Idealism,* Calcutta, 1921.

———, *India in Chains,* Madras, 1922.

Wasti, Syed Razi, *Lord Minto and the Indian Nationalist Movement, 1905 to 1910,* Oxford University Press, 1964.

Wint, Guy, *The British in Asia,* New York, 1954.

Wolpert, Stanley A., *Tilak and Gokhale,* California, 1962.

Woodruff, Philip, *The men Who Ruled India,* London, 1974.

Woolacot, J.E., *Britain's Record in India,* London, 1927.

———, *India on trial,* London, 1929.

———, *India The Truth,* London, 1930.

Yajnik, Indulal K., *Gandhi As I Knew Him,* Delhi, 1943.

Zakaria, Rafiq, *Rise of Muslims in Indian Politics,* Bombay, 1970.

Index